Colonialism, Slavery, Rep and Trade

Colonialism, Slavery, Reparations and Trade: Remedying the 'Past'? addresses how reparations might be obtained for the legacy of the trans Atlantic slave trade. This collection lends weight to the argument that liability is not extinguished on the death of the plaintiffs or perpetrators. Arguing that the impact of the slave trade is continuing and therefore contemporary, it maintains that this trans-generational debt remains, and must be addressed. Bringing together leading scholars, practitioners, diplomats, and activists, *Colonialism, Slavery, Reparations and Trade* provides a powerful and challenging exploration of the variety of available – legal, relief-type, economic-based and multi-level – strategies, and apparent barriers, to achieving reparations for slavery.

Fernne Brennan is a Senior Lecturer in the School of Law at the University of Essex. Her research focuses on reparations, discrimination law, human rights and criminal law. Her previous publications in the field include 'Race, Rights Reparations: Exploring a Reparations Framework for Addressing Trade Inequality' in *Hamline Journal of Public Law and Policy* (2008), and *Time for a Change in Capitalism and Human Rights* (Edward Elgar Publishing Limited, 2006).

John Packer is Professor in the School of Law and Director of the Human Rights Centre. Prior to this, he was Coordinator of the global Initiative on Quiet Diplomacy and served as a consultant to several international organisations, governments and NGOs. He has been a Director of the Office of the OSCE High Commissioner on National Minorities, where he was previously Senior Legal Adviser, and he was a Human Rights Officer at the United Nations where he investigated serious violations. He is a member of a number of editorial boards of scholarly journals, and is an internationally recognised expert in the field of minority rights and conflict prevention.

Colonialism, Slavery, Reparations and Trade

Remedying the Past?

Edited by Fernne Brennan and John Packer

Routledge
Taylor & Francis Group

a GlassHouse book

First published 2012
by Routledge
2 Park Square, Milton Park, Abingdon, Oxon OX14 4RN

Simultaneously published in the USA and Canada
by Routledge
711 Third Avenue, New York, NY 10017

A GlassHouse Book

Routledge is an imprint of the Taylor & Francis Group, an informa business

First issued in paperback 2013

British Library Cataloguing in Publication Data
A catalogue record for this book is available from the British Library

Library of Congress Cataloging in Publication Data
Colonialism, slavery, reparations and trade: remedying the past?
edited by Fernne Brennan and John Packer.
p. cm.
'Simultaneously published in the USA and Canada.'
ISBN 978-0-415-61915-8 (hbk)
ISBN 978-0-203-35729-3 (ebk)
1. Slavery--Law and legislation. 2. Reparations for historical injustices.
I. Brennan, Fernne. II. Packer, John.
K3267.C645 2011
342.08'7--dc23
2011017820

ISBN 978-0-415-61915-8 (hbk)
ISBN 978-0-415-83317-2 (pbk)
ISBN 978-0-203-35729-3 (ebk)

Typeset in Times
by TW Typesetting, Plymouth, Devon

Contents

List of contributors

Katherine Bracegirdle is a Solicitor, a Lecturer School of Law, University of Sheffield and a member of the Institute of Commercial Law Studies Research Cluster. She has expertise in restitution law.

Fernne Brennan is a Senior Lecturer in the School of Law, University of Essex and a member of the Human Rights Centre. Her current research interests focuses on institutional racism and the law. She provides race equality law consultancy and training to Westminster Briefing, the Home Office and has worked with the National Centre for Social Research on Immigration decision-making in the light of the amended Race Relations Act 1976. Her work includes a joint paper with Sociolinguists at Kings College regarding interviewing and the Race Equality Duty. She is also project leader for major work concerning Slave Trade Reparations (www.essex.ac.uk/reparations) in that light she has appeared on television, American radio and has been a consultant on a new play concerning reparations. She has written several papers on the question of reparations for trading in slavery and its contemporary relevance, and worked on issues concerning racial and religious hate crimes and EU Race Equality law. She is an Honorary member of the National Commission for Reparations, Jamaica, and a member of the Gender Working Group of the Euro-Med Human Rights Network.

Chris Burnett has worked in a number of Human Rights and Development NGOs on issues of freedom of expression and transparency. He recently completed an LL.M. in International Human Rights Law.

Sheila Dziobon Dr Dziobon is a Senior Lecturer in Law, School of Law & Social Science, at the University of Plymouth. Her interest in this area was raised during 2007 at a museum exhibition in Plymouth to mark the 200th anniversary of the Abolition of the Slave Trade Act 1807. She has a long standing research interest in autonomy and self-determination and this enquiry builds on previous research and reading.

Lord Anthony Gifford is a Barrister at Law in the UK and an Advocate in Jamaica. He was one of the first people to raise the question of reparations for the slave trade at the British House of Lords in the 1990's. His recent publication, *The Passionate Advocate* was published in 2007, Arawak Publication. Two of the chapters are dedicated to reparations. He is also a member of the National Commission on Reparations – Jamaica, which is a major initiative from the Jamaican Government to find out what reparations should look like from the Jamaican point of view.

Marcus Goffe is an LLM candidate at Queen Mary, University of London. He is a Jamaican Attorney-at-Law. He worked for seven years at the Jamaican Civil and Criminal Bar and as In-house Counsel to a multimedia company in Jamaica. He is specialising in comparative and international intellectual property law with a particular interest in indigenous and traditional people's cultural rights.

Rohan Kariyawasam, is a Professor in Commercial Law, Cardiff Law School. Prior to joining Cardiff he was a lecturer at the University of Essex and a member of the Human Rights Centre and Director of their Program in Information Technology, Media and E-Commerce Law, and a Fulbright Scholar at Harvard Law School. He qualified as a solicitor with Denton Wilde Sapte and has worked as a consultant with several global law firms specialising in commercial and WTO law. His recent book, *International Economic Law and the Digital Divide: A New Silk Road?* looks at the application of WTO law to addressing the technological divide between the developed and developing worlds. Currently, he is engaged in a three year AHRC project on fair trade networks, looking specifically at trust in fair trade, the use and regulation of technology in fair trade, and free v. fair trade. He is a Fellow of the Royal Society of Arts and the founding trustee to the Rahula Trust, which provides sponsorship to poor, academically gifted children in the developing world.

His Excellency Ambassador Kwesi Quartey, Ghana's Ambassador to Ethiopia and Permanent Representative to the African Union. Former Deputy Permanent Representative of Ghana to the United Nations and Ghana's Representative on the International Law Committee of the UN General Assembly. Former Minister/Counsellor, Political and Economic Affairs, Ghana Embassy in Brussels, negotiations between ACP and EU. Barrister and Solicitor of the Supreme Court of Ghana.

Clemens Nathan, Joint Chairman, Consultative Council of Jewish Organisations (CCJO); member of the Board of the Conference on Jewish Material Claims Against Germany & Austria. He has worked with

victims problems from the Holocaust for many years, both in negotiating and working on restitution problems worldwide. The Clemens
Nathan Research Centre was named after him both for his work at the
Claims Conference and at the United Nations Human Rights Commission where he is Chairman of an NGO accredited there. The main work
has been dealing with the problems of victims and helping in the draft
of the UN Resolution for the General Assembly in creating the basic
principles and guidelines on the right to indemnity and reparation for
the victims of gross violations of international human rights law which
was passed by the third Committee unanimously in 2005.

John Packer is Professor and Director of the Human Rights Centre at the
University of Essex in the UK. He is also Senior Adviser for the global
Initiative on Conflict Prevention through Quiet Diplomacy and is a
member of the Expert Advisory Panel on Dialogue, Diversity and Social
Cohesion of the Club de Madrid. Until February 2004, Professor Packer
was Director of the Office of the OSCE High Commissioner on National
Minorities, where he previously served as Senior Legal Advisor. From
1991 to 1995, he was a Human Rights Officer at the United Nations,
where he investigated serious violations of human rights.

Steve Peers received a B.A. (Hons.) in History from McMaster University
(Canada) in 1988, an LL.B. from the University of Western Ontario
(Canada) in 1991, an LL.M. in EC Law from the London School of
Economics in 1993, and a Ph.D from the University of Essex in 2001.
His research interests include EU Justice and Home Affairs, External
Relations, Human Rights, Internal Market and Social Law. He has
written over fifty articles on many aspects of EU law in journals
including the *Common Market Law Review*, *European Law Review*,
International and Comparative Law Quarterly, *Yearbook of European
Law* and the *Cambridge Yearbook of European Legal Studies*, as well
as many chapters in books. He has worked as a consultant for the
European Parliament, the European Commission, the Foreign and
Commonwealth Office, the House of Lords Select Committee on the
European Union and the Council of Europe, and contributed to the
work of NGOs such as Amnesty International, Justice, Statewatch and
the Immigration Law Practitioners' Association.

Dinah L. Shelton, Manatt/Ahn Professor of International Law. Professor
Shelton joined the George Washington University Law School faculty in
2004. Before her appointment, she was Professor of International Law
and director of the doctoral program in international human rights law
at the University of Notre Dame Law School from 1996–2004. She has
lectured at many other universities and is a member of the Board of
Editors of the American Journal of International Law. She is the author

of numerous works including the prize-winning *Remedies in International Human Rights Law*.

Marika Sherwood is a founder member of the Black & Asian Studies Association and edited the BASA Newsletter until 2007. The author of numerous books and articles on the history of black peoples in the UK, as well as on education, she is Honorary Senior Research Fellow at the Institute of Commonwealth Studies, University of London.

Nora Wittmann is a PhD candidate at CEJI Institut des Hautes Etudes Internationales Université Panthéon Assas Paris II.

Preface

In November 2008 a conference took place at the Brunei Gallery in London to discuss the issue of slave trade and reparations. Several diplomats, academics, non-governmental organisations, students and civil society were present. These participants represented and discussed their expertise in the various fields of slave trade reparations including: the call for legislation; the numerous discussions about the historical crucible within which the seeds of the chattel slavery were born, and its lasting affects; and the issue of reparations – in its widest sense as adopted and proclaimed by the General Assembly Resolution 60/147 of 16 December 2005 (see www2.ohchr.org/english/law/remedy.htm)

From the conference it emerged that slave trade reparation issues require, powerful and critical friends in order to place it on the most powerful of agendas. Some might say that this agenda had already been produced following the World Conference against Racism, Racial Discrimination, Xenophobia and Related Intolerance in 2001. Out of that conference evolved the Declaration and Programme of Action. This document specifies many aspects about racism and it is clearly targeted towards the 192 member states of the UN.

Paragraph 13 states *that we acknowledge that slavery and the slave trade, including the transatlantic slave trade, were appalling tragedies in the history of humanity not only because of their abhorrent barbarism but also in terms of their magnitude, organized nature and especially their negation of the essence of the victims, and further acknowledge that slavery and the slave trade are a crime against humanity and should always have been so, especially the transatlantic slave trade, and are among the major sources and manifestations of racism, racial discrimination, xenophobia and related intolerance, and that Africans and people of African descent, Asians and people of Asian descent and indigenous peoples were victims of these acts and continue to be victims of their consequences.*

Importantly the Declaration recognises that the past manifests itself in the present and states have a role in dealing with the consequences. This book is situated within that context.

Acknowledgements

The conference organisers gratefully acknowledge the sponsorship received.

Participating Sponsors
   Human Rights Centre, University of Essex
   School of Oriental and African Studies
   School of Law, University of Essex
   School of Law, Queen Mary University of London
   Centre for Commercial Law Studies, Queen Mary University of London

Contributing Sponsors
   Tetley GB Ltd
   The Vice-Chancellor of the University of Essex
   Professor Janet Dine
   Taylor & Francis Group, Routledge
   Birkbeck School of Law

Material Sponsors
   Marika Footring, conference assistant
   Kadialy Kouyate, musical entertainment
   Tony Brennan, photographer
   The student helpers:Gabriela Echeverria, Joanna Frew, Laila Fathi, Shahab Uddin, Eleanor French, Alex Klein
   Keith Brooke, web site design
   Alex O'Neill and Guy Footring, web support
   The rapporteurs: Nolita Werrett and Andrea Carotti, and from the *Essex Human Rights Review* Jo Somerville and Brett Dodge
   ... and numerous others

Introduction

Fernne Brennan and John Packer

How to obtain reparation for the legacy of the transatlantic slave trade is the main theme of this book. This question has been asked, but not effectively answered, on a number of occasions. There is still room for manoeuvre. It is in this context that the chapters are situated following an international conference at the Brunei Gallery on 10 November 2008. As with the conference, we managed to bring academic scholarship, the views of non-governmental actors, and the views of diplomats and PhD students together to consider the question of slave trade reparations. The book is organised into three parts: *Economic-Based Reparations: History and Future*; *Reparations as a Legal Strategy*; and *Pluralism: Strategies for Reparations*. The various chapters give more credence to the argument that reparations are indeed due, and predict the arguments against this happening. There is an underlying assumption throughout that the liability to make reparations is not extinguished on the death of direct victims or slavers, rather that the trans-generational obligation remains to provide a remedy for the contemporary and current legacy of that transatlantic slave trade and slavery.

The chapters in Part I examine historical as well as contemporary issues. Wittmann's contribution (Chapter 1) places the slave trade and slavery within the context of international law and argues that under it slavery was **not legal** at the time. Europeans' power to enslave Africans was based on a false premise that slavery was legal; moreover Wittmann contends that the door to reparation claims is shut via the use of tools such as non-retroactivity that effectively protect states from taking the stand as the respondents/defendants to potential reparations claims. She argues that 'by whose standards would it have been legal'. This contention of legality by Wittmann is based on the colonial laws that European enslaver states passed after they had already been active in transatlantic slavery for more than a century.

However, transatlantic slavery was not legal under the laws of affected Africans, nor was it compliable with the 'international' law standards of the time, and the political entities of Europe and Africa were also subject to international law. Chapter 2 looks at contemporary claims about the legacy of the transatlantic slave trade that need to be understood within the historical paradigm. This may provide information on how this trade in human beings came about as well as show that legislation to abolish the trade was circumvented by those who had built their wealth on the trade, argues Sherwood. There was, she also contends, much evidence of circumvention – i.e. blockages – which is a matter that Wittmann refers to in Chapter 1 in the context of non-retroactivity. Jobs, plantation produce and the use of slaves meant that there was too much to gain from the slave trade and 'to take action could have been seen (in economic terms) as impoverishing Britain' suggests Sherwood. There was a great deal of legislation around the slave trade but it was ineffective because too many of the elite had their 'snouts in the trough'. Trade, according to Sherwood, was the nemesis for legislation that was aimed at abolishing it. Slavery and slave trading were to be a continuing phenomenon even after their abolition and Sherwood's argument fits in with Gifford's (Chapter 5) who points out that there is a legitimate legal claim based on the gross violation of human rights.

Thinking about how to deal with these issues can of course also lead us to consider legislation and to look to the courts for remedies, but Kariyawasam (Chapter 4) brings some fresh answers to the question of reparations. He argues that the use of a Universal Periodic Review, by which states are asked to account for certain actions under the jurisdiction of the UN, could also link these accounts to the Right to Development (RTD). In the context of reparations, Kariyawasam argues for RTD Tax Relief as a form of reparation for slavery. The 'historical transgressors [would have] to invest in technical skills, technology, research and development, education, health and services'. This could all be achieved through a 'beneficial technology transfer'. Rather than only look at the constructed barriers raised by Wittmann and Sherwood, Kariyawasam offers us a way out through what he calls 'a means of operationalising the RTD and specifically with regard to beneficial technology transfer as a means of reparations to countries impacted by the abuses of slavery'.

Our contemporaries remind us that we do not have to look only towards the past with respect to slavery since human trafficking is in the midst of us and the European Union is committed to doing something about it. They would also go on to argue that despite legislation the trade in humans as slaves still exists in the form of human trafficking. However, the approach adopted for abolishing modern day trafficking has been covered to some extent by the 'Council of Europe Convention on the issue (CETS 197)' which came into force on 1 February 2008. Kariyawasam's description of human trafficking is fairly close to that of chattel slavery which was supposed to have been abolished in 1833: 'The Convention defines trafficking in persons as 'the recruitment, transportation, transfer, harbouring or receipt of persons, by means of the threat or use of force or other forms of coercion'. In a similar vein to Sherwood's point regarding the ineffectiveness of legislation to remove the slave trade, in Chapter 3 Peers argues that CETS 197 aims to criminalise traffickers and that states which use the Convention should ensure the punishment is effective. All this remains to be seen, as for instance, not all states have signed up to or ratified this Convention. Peers makes the interesting point that victims of trafficking should not have criminal penalties imposed on them for the commission of crimes which they were forced to commit (see Chapter IV of CETS). The anti-reparations lobby would argue that Africans were collaborators and as such do they not owe reparations? Should they not be seen as collaborators? Perhaps a few were indeed collaborators but many were not 'willing' participants in this and as such should not be used as yet another reason to argue against reparations. And even if collaborators were 'willing', in Part II of the book Lord Gifford argues that they should not be viewed through the same lens as the one used for slavers.

In Chapter 5 Lord Gifford contends that chattel slavery was 'infinitely worse than indigenous African practices of enslaving'. More importantly Africans did not build up an institution that perceived them as inferior or subhuman (a point picked up by Brennan in Chapter 10 when she discusses the legacy of the slave trade, namely institutional racism). Lord Gifford puts the matter this way: 'As international law experts have written, acts which are so reprehensible as to offend the conscience of mankind, directed against civilian populations, are crimes in international law and always have been'. Like Wittmann, he argues that, 'the criterion is the conscience of decent human beings (who in Britain were indeed outraged by the slave trade), and not the standards of those who perpetrated the crimes'.

In Chapter 6 Shelton examines another problem that has the potential to jeopardise reparations claims: 'the difference between widespread historical violations and individual claims'. In the USA the individual is central to the litigation model and there appears to be no room for group claims based on historical wrongs. Further barriers here include the Statute of Limitations and the non-retroactivity of law.

We will have already seen in Wittmann's chapter that the latter can be swept away and as for the former it has previously been argued that reparations for the slave trade should not be subject to the Statute of Limitations (see B. Sundhu at www.billsundhu.ca/essays/colonialism) because tort-based claims are subject to limitation periods and it can be argued that the reparations claim is too far back to use as a basis to bring a case before the courts. However, in Shelton's view it is important not to raise obstacles to gross violations of human rights and the aspect that links past and present wrongs is precisely the fact that human rights have been grossly violated. It is vital not to ignore the fact that 'states, communities, businesses and individuals profited from many of the abuses, garnering wealth at the expense of the victim'. And such economic disparities have also continued over generations, says Shelton. This point has empathy with that of Sherwood and others who, at least impliedly, would consider the slave trade affair to be one of unjust enrichment with the theft of any surplus value created by those enslaved.

Shelton argues that solutions are difficult nonetheless – rather than do nothing one could provide for a 'full welfare or insurance system or public and private compensation system or other assistance'. Reparations should be about restorative justice and so the 'legislatures may be better suited to determine reparations', especially since 'they are not bound by precedent and legal doctrine'.

Making similar arguments to those put forward by Shelton and Gifford, His Excellency Kwesi Quartey suggests in Chapter 7 that there is a juridical basis for reparations – particularly as chattel slavery was 'underpinned by violence, rape, fraud and murder'. And in the context of Britain the country shifted from 'poacher in chief ... to the gamekeeper in chief'. The consequence of this is that the European states should be the major focus when asking for reparations. A similar argument is made by Bracegirdle in Chapter 8, who suggests that a claim could be based on the grounds of restitution. Arguably it is important not to create a loophole so courts do not become embroiled in reparations claims. But why is this necessary? Dziobon argues in Chapter 9 that contrary to 'popular' opinion some judges have been troubled by the issues raised by slavery. She contends that 'Lord Mansfield . . . accepted and endorsed the widely assumed mercantile importance of the slave trade, yet he doubted the validity of the theoretical justification of slavery', which goes to show that we should not assume that **all** judges believed slavery and its trade were morally sound. And it is worth noting that if judges are uncomfortable about the ownership of human beings during the slave trade era there may be a case for taking the matter to the European Courts.

The third part of the book looks pluralistically at the strategies for reparations. Brennan focuses in Chapter 10 on the use of reparations as proposed by Van Boven and Bassiouni as a way through the quagmire of arguments for and against reparations. She also looks at the issue of institutional racism and considers that this phenomenon, in Britain and the Caribbean at least, is a current hangover from the transatlantic slave trade. In Chapter 11 Nathan brings to the argument his direct experience as an NGO dealing with the Holocaust, as a way of helping us to think through some of the problems inherent with the post-acceptance of liability. Goffe argues (in Chapter 13) that there is a case for reparations under the umbrella of special measures.

Reparations claims for the transatlantic slave trade and its legacy have opened up a strong debate: the question is how to mould matters. These chapters deal with some of the issues and try to provide solutions but this is only the beginning of a long road that must deal with a legacy that is based on over four hundred years of enslavement. This book will take the issue further along that road.

F. Brennan

J. Packer

Part I

Economic-based reparations

History and future

Chapter I

International legal responsibility and reparations for transatlantic slavery

Nora Wittmann

Introduction

No other group has ever been subjected to attacks as serious to their physical and mental integrity over a comparable period of time as the Africans deported to the Americas and their descendants (Plumelle-Uribe 2004: 194), yet still no reparation whatsoever has ever been made. The prevalent opinion in international law seems to categorically shut the door on any such reparation claims by resorting to the principle of *non-retroactivity* and to the allegation (presented as a fact) that transatlantic slavery[1] would have been 'legal' in its time.

The principle of *non-retroactivity*, a tenet of contemporary international law, stipulates that the legal responsibility of a state can only be established if that state committed an act which was 'internationally wrongful' at the time it occurred, and this is articulated in Art. 13 of the International Law Commission (ILC)'s Draft Articles on Responsibility of States for Internationally Wrongful Acts (hereafter called 'Articles'): 'An act of a State does not constitute a breach of an international obligation unless the State is bound by the obligation in question at the time the act occurs'. According to Art. 2, an act (action or omission) of a State is internationally wrongful and engages its international responsibility if a) the act is by international law attributable to that State, and if b) it constitutes a violation of an obligation that the state owes under international law. A qualification as internationally wrongful is not affected by differing legal qualifications in internal law (Art. 3). *Non-retroactivity* has also been long featured as a general principle of international customary law.

Thus, against the background of the alleged international 'legality' at that time, *non-retroactivity* is invoked to block off all claims to reparations for transatlantic slavery on an international law level.

Yet there are serious problems with this position. If it is contended that slavery was legal, one needs to ask by whose standards it would have been legal. The contention of legality is based on the colonial laws that European enslaver states passed after they had already been active in transatlantic slavery for more than a century. However, transatlantic slavery was not legal by the laws of affected Africans, nor was it compliable with 'international law' standards of the time. It is more than questionable if it was even legal by the laws of European enslaver states, most of whom had come to pass legislation abolishing or at least severely restricting slavery in a development leading up to the sixteenth century. The genuine law(s) in force at that time need(s) to be researched in order to enable a thorough legal appraisal of reparation claims, all the while remaining respectful of international law principles such as *non-retroactivity* and their legal ratio. The historically-documented legal facts indicate that transatlantic slavery was illicit.

Contrary to what we are often led to believe, African political entities in that time were as much subjects of 'international law' as their European counterparts were if the elements of its definition are applied in an unbiased manner. In order to sustain the belief that transatlantic slavery would have been 'legal', it is usually expressed or implied that Africans' political organisation would have been 'primitive' and incapable of maintaining international legal relations and thus they would have been excluded from participating in the moulding of international law. Yet before transatlantic slavery, many parts of Africa were active participators in international relations and were also politically and socially organised as states that had a high respect for the law in both their internal and external dealings. Their legal stands on slavery must be included in an assessment of its international legal status. In the seventeenth and eighteenth centuries, when European nations started to legislate on transatlantic slavery, international law was no *tabula rasa*. Europeans, having always been a global minority (and before transatlantic slavery not a particularly powerful one), could not unilaterally decide on what international law was.

Evolution of international law before transatlentic slavery

When did 'international law' come into existence? Who participated in its genesis and development? Even if, from a definitional perspective, it can be argued that classic 'international law' was born only in the seventeenth century, it cannot be denied that regimes covering the legal regulation of international (inter-polity) contact can be traced back for much longer. *Ubi societas ibi ius* indicates that international (inter-polity) law had existed for quite some time before the late fifteenth century (when the first Africans were subjected to transatlantic slavery), because an 'international' society that maintained peaceful contacts, mostly via commerce, did exist then (Scelle 1934b: 61). It has been argued by both sociologists and international law scholars that every *de facto* society is at the same time a society *de jure*, for there can be no enduring social practice without the emission of rules regulating interactions (Scelle 1934a: 4).

Roots

If international law is perceived as the set of written and non-written rules applicable to subjects and situations that do not exclusively pertain to internal law, it can be affirmed that this has always existed (Carreau 2007: 30). It is generally agreed that international (inter-polity) law has its origins in international commerce (Hummer et al. 1997: 14ff.). Historical records leave no doubt that Africans were involved in international trade at least as much as Europeans prior to the late fifteenth century. The trade in gold, ivory, silk and spices between Africa, Persia, India, China and Europe had taken place for centuries (Hess 2000: 5).

Provisions for international law can be traced back to the Bible, the practice of Ancient Greece's city-states or the Roman Empire. These roots were to leave a footprint that is still present in contemporary international law (Carreau 2007: 30ff). Numerous passages in the Bible make reference to Africa, and both Ancient Greece and the Roman Empire maintained relations with African societies (James 1993).

The famous peace and alliance treaty concluded in 1279 BC between Ramses II of Egypt and Hattusili II of the Hittites involved an African party (Nussbaum 1954: 4ff). According to Carreau, once concluded such ancient legal agreements had to be strictly respected: thus we find here that one of the most basic premises of international law, the principle of *pacta sunt servanda*. Ambassadors had to be well treated and their person was inviolable, with every breach of this principle constituting a wrongful act that could justify a resort to war (Carreau 2007: 31). The historical evidence indicates that these rules of international contact were known and respected by African states in their dealings with European officials and traders both before and at the beginning of transatlantic slavery. Tragically, this conformity with international law was often not reciprocated by the European counterparts who disrespected agreements, ignored the sovereignty of African states and violently disposed of those rulers who were unwilling to collaborate with them in transatlantic slavery (Clarke 1998: 16).

Law scholars attest that the fundaments of international law existed not only in Europe, but also for example in the Middle East, India and Ancient China. In spite of cultural and social differences, identical legal solutions to certain problems were provisioned in these regions, such as the immunity guaranteed to emissaries (Hummer et al. 1997: 14) that was also observed by African states at that time. Within these ancient lines of international (inter-polity) law, the duty to make reparation for wrongdoings was also recognised: 'The principles of Mosaic, Islamic, and even English common

law are all rooted in *compensation for injury* caused by another ...'
(Winbush 2003: 150). Ramses II and Hattusilis III regarded the consensual
obligations of their states, stipulated in the above mentioned treaty, as
legally binding and accepted that any breach involved a duty to make
reparation (Schwarzenberger 1976: 102). In African legal traditions making
reparation was a well-established legal concept. African legal systems
placed greater emphasis on limiting the damage for the victim than on
retaliating against the aggressor. Thus, reparation and reconciliation were
accorded a high importance (Kiné Camara 2004).

Before focusing on the pertinent legal provisions of African and
European states regarding slavery, a reflection on the characteristics of
affected African societies shall show clearly that they were subject to
international law and their legal perspectives must be considered.

African states and societies before and during the slave trade

It could be interjected at this point that it would be just another analytically
biased pitfall to appraise the international legal personality of African
societies through definitional standards enunciated by Western international jurisprudence and practice. Yet it seems very likely that these
elements of definition have essentially remained the same since the
emergence of international (inter-polity) law, because they refer to the
factual capacity of territorial entities to maintain stable contacts on an
international level.

In European law doctrine, the first explicit denomination of sovereignty
as one of the essential criteria of the state was made by Jean Bodin in 1576
(Carreau 2007: 305). Thus at the time of the arrival of the first European
slave expeditions in Africa at the end of the fifteenth century, even the
European powers were not defined as 'sovereign states' because they did
not yet know about the concept. This leads to the argument that African
states were not sovereign and therefore, contrary to Europeans, not subjects
of international law *ad absurdum*. Building on Bodin, European scholars
identified the elements of the state (territory, people, sovereignty) that
remain valid up until today.

The criterion of territory refers to the geographical limits within which
the authority of a state is exclusively exercised. Legal practice recognises
this criterion as fulfilled even if a state exercises effective power only in a
core territory while the exact frontiers are not yet defined (Hummer et al.
1997, 142).

Concerning the criterion of people, jurisprudence pronounced that
'whilst size was irrelevant, in order to constitute a people the group of
persons in question must form a cohesive vibrant community ... The state,
as an amalgamation of many individuals, complements the family, which

consists of only a few members, and has the duty to promote communal life … It must be aimed at the maintenance of an essentially permanent form of communal life in the sense of sharing a common destiny' (*Duchy of Sealand* 1978: 687). International legal practice and doctrine generally define a people as a community with a common history and solidarity ties in the present and into the future, features that have always been important in African societies.

Finally, sovereignty rests on the monopoly of public administration, the capacity to edict a rule, and the ability to have it respected. It is reflected, for example, in the maintenance of a unified army. There were African regents, like Queen Nzinga, who fought the enslavers in their territory over a long time with organised armies and disposed of very well-administered kingdoms (Hess 2000: 43). In the *Greenland* affair, the PCIJ recalled that 'legislation is one of the most obvious forms of the exercise of sovereign power' (*Legal Status of Eastern Greenland* 1933: 28). The complex legislation of African states is evidenced, for example, in the records of European traders who complained about taxation laws (Chinweizu 1987: 36). In the *Lotus* affair the PCIJ insisted that in case of doubt, the limitations of sovereignty must be construed restrictively (Carreau 2007: 352).

Once the various criteria are met a state exists: 'the form of internal political organisation and the constitutional provisions are mere facts … The existence or disappearance of the state is a question of fact … the effects of recognition by other states are purely declaratory' (*Peace Conference on the former Yugoslavia* 1991: 182). Recognition has some legal significance in that it confirms the existence of statehood. In international law recognition is not subjected to formal constraint and can be given tacitly, for example through the establishment of diplomatic relations. Europeans recognised African states not only on the continent through the conclusion of treaties and the establishment of diplomatic contacts, but also on the other side of the Atlantic. In 1678 the governor of Pernambouc, as a representant of the king of Portugal, concluded a peace treaty with the Republic of Palmares, thus recognising it as a quasi-nation. In 1685, the king of Portugal, Pedro II, himself sent a communication to the leader of the Palmares Maroons, Zumbi (Police 2003: 96).

Grotius argued in the seventeenth century that extra-European territories 'now have and always have had their own kings, their own government, their own laws, and their own legal systems … The Portuguese … do not go there as sovereigns but as foreigners. Indeed they only reside there on sufferance' (Grotius 2000: 14).

Historical evidence clearly shows that European officials initially recognised African states and sovereigns as equals (Davidson 1961: 26), but why they subsequently abandoned this attitude and started to regard treaties with African states as non-binding cannot be answered here. It needs to be emphasised however that this disregard of facts cannot make criminal and genocidal behaviour legally acceptable. Alleging that people who by all standards were sovereign and equal were not so and could therefore not contribute to the development and content of international law does not turn this allegation into a reality. Concluding from such a contention that mass murder and enslaving were legal in international law would render the concept of law meaningless.

Notwithstanding the fact that many of the African entities affected were indeed states by the standards of international law others were decentralised societies, lacking a sovereign administrating force and therefore not states in the strict sense. Yet these societies knew and practised law, including conceptions of human rights. In comparative studies on historic human rights conceptions in decentralised and state societies in Africa, it has been shown that both of these knew and protected such rights. Both the Akamba of East Africa, exemplary of less rigidly organised societies, and the Akan of West Africa, a state society, recognised that as an inherently valuable being the individual was naturally endowed with certain basic rights (Wiredu 1990: 252).

African and European practice and legal conceptions of servile labour and slavery

The assessment that African states were subject to international law does not yet determine the legal status of transatlantic slavery in its time. A thorough investigation of the historical laws and legal concepts of both African and European states is needed here. It is often alleged by reparation detractors that Africans would have practised 'slavery' from time immemorial, and that they would have actively participated in transatlantic enslavement. Both contentions are of great legal significance and must therefore be confronted.

African servile labour

One must keep in mind that the use of the same semantic term to describe disparate social realities changes nothing of these realities and neither should it influence an eventual legal appraisal. The people so eagerly qualified as inter-African 'slaves' were not submitted to the dehumanisation that was integral to transatlantic slavery (Asare 2002: 20). African 'slaves' did not have their ears cut off; the name of their master was not iron-branded on their breasts; their babies were not killed when bothering the sleep of the mistress (Hess 2000: 130); they were not cruelly tortured for minor 'infractions' or roasted alive over a couple of days; and dogs were not trained to drink their blood and nourish off their flesh (Plumelle-Uribe

2001: 74). The European colonial slave codes defined the status of slaves as movables and provided for all these atrocities. This dehumanisation, both factual and legal, was unknown in African societies. The concept and reality of African 'slavery' instead coincided with the meanings of the terms 'servile labour' or 'serfdom', terms that European scholars regrettably prefer to reserve for those situations when Europeans subjugated other Europeans.

Probably the most pertinent disquisition on African systems of servile labour and slavery has been presented by Inikori. In his seminal (2001) article 'Slaves or serfs?', he applied to African evidence the formula employed by historians to distinguish slaves from serfs in pre-capitalist Europe, and concluded that 'it is ... clear that the chattel slavery experienced by Africans in the Americas was something new for them ... The claim that the pre-existence of chattel slavery in the coastal societies of western Africa facilitated the growth and development of the trans-Atlantic slave trade is not borne out of evidence ... For the few who were already in bondage before capture and forced transportation to the Americas, their socio-economic conditions in Africa were much closer (in many cases even superior) to those of serfs in medieval Europe than to those of chattel slaves' (Inikori 2001: 68).

In the Banamba society in Mali, 'slaves' had the right to free time and a plot of land. An incident is documented where a master requested millet that went beyond his rightful share. After consultation, the 'slaves' responded through their elder spokesman: 'Mahmady, I salute you; all who are here are your captives. They salute you. You have asked us for millet but you know that the millet which is in our granaries is ours, because we planted it. If we do not want to sell, it is because we want to conserve it. We will not sell it today. We have given you the part that belongs to you, because you are our master. But you shall not get more until the next harvest. Mahmady, do not count on our millet, because we will keep it for the winter' (Péroz 1889: 381). Now imagine a slave on a plantation in the Americas saying that to the master. This took place in a society that was described as having a slave system that was 'clearly among the harshest in West Africa' (Ibid.: 379), and one that had furthermore experienced centuries of enslavement by Arabs. It should not be denied that physical punishment did exist, yet young 'slaves', even if they were working for a different master, still lived with their parents. The 'slave' family was a respected institution (Ibid.: 381).

Similar records exist concerning the region of contemporary Nigeria. The land that the 'slaves' possessed for their own use was inheritable, though it could not be sold. People were paid for any additional work, such as thatching, that was done for the master (Hill 1976: 418). Hausa tradition and customary law imposed severe limitations on masters' possibilities to sell servile individuals living in a household (Inikori 2001: 60). Yet despite such facts, European scholars called these people 'slaves' and their settlements 'slave-villages' (Smith 1954).

One European explorer, a certain Monseigneur Cuvelie, wrote that the institution of 'slavery' in Kongo (the first region devastated by massive enslavement by the Portuguese) appeared tolerable, and that an honest slave could even become deputy chief. Servile labourers had civic and property rights, and there were multiple procedures for manumission, several of which could be taken on the sole initiative of the 'slave' (Ki-Zerbo 1978: 210).

Even in 'pre-European' Dahomey, whose elite were later actively involved in transatlantic slavery, individual masters did not have the right of life and death over their slaves (Avajon 2005: 38ff). Similarly with the Ashanti, before their elite had become corrupted by the European slave demand and the slave-gun cycle a quasi-unescapable reality in the region, masters did not have the right to kill a 'slave' on Ashanti territory. Anyone who killed a human, free or 'slave', without royal permission, was prosecuted for murder. Mutilating 'slaves' without permission was also forbidden, because the servile labourer was considered a human and not chattel (Testart 2001: 50f). Davidson reports a contemporary British witness as stating 'a slave might marry; own property; himself own a slave; swear an oath; be a competent witness; and ultimately become heir to his master. Such briefly were the rights of an Ashanti slave. They seemed in many cases practically the ordinary privileges of an Ashanti free man' (Davidson 1961: 38f).

In the Bamoun kingdom (Cameroun) masters also did not have the right of life and death or even of inflicting harsh physical punishment over their 'slaves'. Every act of mistreatment on a servile labourer was severely dealt with and could lead to the imposition of a death sentence for a master in cases where a servile labourer had died (Ajavon 2005: 40f). The same goes for the Senegambia region (Barry 1998: 115). Among the Diola (southern Senegal, Gambia, Guinea-Bissau) for example, slaves enjoyed a considerable amount of protection against violence or physical abuse (Baum 2010: 45ff).

In many 'pre-European' African societies, 'slaves' or their descendants gradually became members of the lineage as young people eventually became elders. The tasks of these 'slaves' may have been more menial, but they were still often granted various responsibilities in trade, craft production, and other occupations, and were treated very much as members of the household (Lovejoy 2000: 14f). The role of such 'slavery' in assimilating outsiders into the host society in Africa has been stressed by anthropologists such as Igor Kopytoff and Suzanne Miers.

In Ewe society in Ghana, '. . . before [the] intensified pursuits of the Atlantic slave trade, domestic slaves were usually criminals or debtors sold into slavery. Domestic slavery played the role prisons serve in industrialised societies ... there is now ample evidence that domestic slavery was a marginal economic and social force before Atlantic slavery took off in the fifteenth and sixteenth centuries. In fact, domestic slavery became a significant phenomenon in Africa only by the nineteenth century when it was influenced by global forces and demand' (Bailey 2007: 11). In this society and many others, one effect of transatlantic slavery was the corruption of indigenous legal institutions (Ibid.: 50). Comprehensive reparations, comprised of monetary and non-monetary measures, should also address this aspect that is at the root of many of the problems in African society today. Multiple scholars have discovered that the phenomenon of servile institutions approximating chattel slavery were new in tropical Africa, and that their development was linked strongly to growth in the export demand for captives, first across the Sahara and later across the Atlantic (Inikori 1992: 38). A UNESCO report assessed that 'the traditionally organised authorities, for example in Jolof, Cayor, Balol, Songhay, Congo and Zimbabwe, were in various ways and at various times, confronted with the pressure of European and Muslim demand for slaves ... Such upsets were accompanied by an increase of social tensions, a worsening of servitude, especially quantitatively and by a transformation of the former processes of social integration that the various forms of personal dependence provided in African society prior to the fifteenth century ... none of the experts present disputed the idea that the slave trade was responsible for the economic backwardness of Black Africa' (Inikori 1982: 58f).

When reconstructing the African legal perspectives on chattel slavery, enslaved Africans in the Americas must also be considered. The famous Republic of Palmares in Brazil maintained their armed resistance against the Portuguese for over a century. It is sometimes contended that the Palmares Maroons would have enslaved other Africans. Yet the historical evidence indicates that forced labour in the Palmares started only after the Portuguese heightened their military attacks on the Maroons. Defence and agriculture were both essential to the survival of the community. With intensified assaults by the Portuguese, all forces were needed for an immediate defence, which made it necessary to oblige newcomers to do agricultural work. Newly arrived ones first had to liberate another slave, thereby proving their loyalty, before they were given their full liberty in the Palmares and could participate in the defence of the community. This made sense because treason was always a high risk factor for all Maroon communities. Thus even if such forced labour existed in the Palmares, this reveals nothing about how the 'unfree' people were treated. There is no historical evidence about individual ownership over these labourers. Their unfree status was not fixed indefinitely, rather it depended to a large degree on the actions of an individual who could gain his full freedom by showing his loyalty to the community (Peret 1999: 92ff).

It is also vital to point out that 'slavery' in African societies was not racialised as it was in the Americas (Palmer 1998: 8). In transatlantic slavery the mere fact of being of African descent was presumptive of a slave status and that status was forever. A law in Maryland declared that 'All Negroes or other slaves within the province, all Negroes to be hereafter imported, shall serve *durante vita*: but their children were to serve likewise . . .'. A Black person in Mississippi could also be sold as a slave unless he was able to prove himself a free man (Davidson 1961: 38f).

There was no law that protected the Africans from any cruelty their white masters could conceive: 'For looking a white man in the eye the enslaved person could have his or her eyes blinded with hot irons. For speaking up in defence of a wife or woman a man could have his right hand severed . . . The enslaved person could be roasted over a slow-burning fire, left to die after having both legs and arms broken, oiled and greased and then set afire while hanging from a tree's limb, or being killed slowly as the slave owner cut the enslaved person's phallus or breasts' (Asante 2003: 7f).

Terminological confusion does not level the disparate social realities of African indigenous systems of servile labour and transatlantic chattel slavery and it must neither influence a legal apprehension of the latter.

It is a well known fact, often emphasised by European reparation opponents, that the transsahara/Arab enslavement of Africans antedated transatlantic slavery. Due to a lack of space it is not possible to develop this aspect here. Yet it should be pointed out that it seems that much of this enslavement was also illegal. Initially under Islam slaves were prisoners taken in holy wars and only those who were not Muslims were legally enslavable. This rule, however, was broken more often than not when enslaving Africans (Lovejoy 2000: 15f). This illegality of the enslavement of Africans was subject to legal debate at that time and resulted in a fatwa condemning its practice (Baba Kaké 1998: 26).

Soundjata, founder of the Mali Empire, fought against the institution of slavery in this Islamised part of Africa. Upon his instalment as Emperor in 1213, he proclaimed the Manden Charter in which slavery was explicitly outlawed. He also organised armed brigades that made certain the enforcement of this law. The Charter contained an explicit recognition of the human right to life: 'Every human life is a life. One life is not superior to another. Every wrong done to a life demands reparation' (Plumelle-Uribe 2008: 52).

African collaboration and resistance

Regarding the contention of African collaboration, it is necessary to keep in mind that throughout transatlantic slavery African sovereigns and people never ceased their fight to stop this genocide.

When Portuguese slaving activities first began in Kongo, they were based on a mutual agreement with the Kongo king, and were conforming to the customary act of one monarch turning over to another, his ally, a quantity of captives. This custom was common in both Africa and Europe. However, the Portuguese did not honour the agreement. It was under these circumstances that in 1526 King Afonso I of Kongo sent a letter to his Portuguese homologue John III, stating that 'We cannot reckon how great the damage is, since the above-mentioned merchants daily seize our subjects, sons of the land and sons of our noblemen and vassals and our relatives. Thieves and men of evil conscience take them . . . They grab them and cause them to be sold: and so great, Sir, is their corruption and licentiousness that our country is utterly depopulated. The King of Portugal should not countenance such practices . . . we ask of Your Highness to . . . assist us in this matter, commanding your factors that they should send here neither merchants nor wares, because it is our will that in these kingdoms [of Kongo] there should not be any trade in slaves nor market for slaves' (Davidson 1961: 158f).The addressee ignored this note of protestation.

In 1540 the Portuguese tried to assassinate the resisting King, and after his death a few years later, a dozen of his family members were intercepted during a voyage destined to Portugal and enslaved to Brazil (Ajavon 2005: 77). Yet Kongolese resistance to enslavement continued, so in 1556 the ruler of Ndongo, one of the provinces of the Kongo empire, was counselled by Portuguese slavers to resign his submission to the Kongo king. In the ensuing war Ndongo, armed and aided by the Portuguese, was victorious, further deminishing Kongo's power to put a stop to slaving. The lesson for future kings of Kongo was that they needed to comply with Portuguese interests if they wanted to maintain their position (Plumelle-Uribe 2008: 63f). Yet the resistance was not completely crushed. In 1704, the young woman Kimpa Vita called on the population to fight to regain Kongolese sovereignty. Captured in 1706, she was burned alive together with her baby by the Portuguese at the age of 22.

In Angola Queen Nzinga Mbandi federated the region into the United Provinces and allied them to resistance rebels in Kongo. She maintained the rebellion against Portuguese enslavers for approximately thirty years (Ajavon 2005: 114).

In Benin, the reigning king from 1504 to 1550, thus at the beginning of Portuguese slaving activities in the region, was actively opposed to transatlantic slavery. Capable of raising armies of 10–20,000 men, he seized all slavers and any of their ships that intruded on his territory (Ibid.: 115).

In 1720, Tamba, king in the Rio Nunez region (Guinea), organised his people against European and African slavers. He obstructed their trade and executed any captured middlemen. However, due to the might of European firearms, he was caught and enslaved but still organised a revolt among the captives on the ship. This was brutally put down, Tamba was killed and his liver was fed to his supporters – who were subsequently executed (Rashid 2003: 137).

The available evidence suggests that, especially in the first decades and centuries, rulers and leaders actively resisted transatlantic slavery, whereas with the advance of time collaborators gained the upper hand, helped by access to European firearms. It also appears from the historical records that the majority of African people always resisted transatlantic slavery and adopted various strategies to oppose it from the fifteenth to the nineteenth century (Adu-Boahen 1985: 3).

African slaves were not available in abundance, only waiting to be purchased by Europeans as has been often suggested. Portuguese ship captains engaged in kidnapping people in Senegal and Gambia, sometimes being met by boats full of Africans who were armed with bows and poisoned arrows (Klein 2010: 19). Early Portuguese enslavers were able to kidnap only children because of the strength of the resistance to enslavement (eZurara 1994 [1453]: 186f).

African people opposed transatlantic slavery to the extent that Europeans gave instructions that as soon as they approached their ships 'the crew is ordered to take up arms, the cannons are aimed, and the fuses are lighted. One must, without any hesitation, shoot at them and not spare them. The loss of the vessel and the life of the crew are at stake' (Durand 1807: 191).

It is also documented that from the early sixteenth century ships belonging to an African fraternity patrolled in the Golf of Guinea, armed with spears and shields, and attacked slave vessels (Lara 1997: 169). Until the mid-eighteenth century the entire countryside from Sierra Leone to Cape Mount was rife with rebellions. Not a single year passed without groups of Africans attacking some slave vessel. People succeeded in establishing free zones on the coast and attracting runaway slaves from all over the area (Barry 1998: 122).

On the other side of the Atlantic, African resistance began with the first ship that landed and never ceased. Countless revolts throughout the Americas were recorded (Palmer 1998: 15ff).

Most contributors to the UNESCO *General History of Africa* editions agree that the deprivation of sovereignty through transatlantic slavery was a crime that was perpetrated against Africa very much contrary to the expressed will of the masses of African people and their rulers throughout the continent and in the diaspora (Adu-Boahen 1985: 3). This documented resistance by numerous African rulers and the African people against enslavement bears witness to the fact that they recognised transatlantic slavery as illegal.

Tragically, by some means or other, European slavers could always find individual Africans who would collaborate with them in supplying captives: 'It only required a few greedy or opportunistic persons, who felt they should enrich themselves rather than resist the inexorable pressures of supply and demand, to keep the slave trade alive. Those suppliers, in turn, rapidly became wealthy enough to become a focus of power to whom others had to accommodate' (Manning 1990: 34).

This scheme resulted in a situation where the choice for most Africans was either to be enslaved or to enslave others (Ibid.: 47). This is legally significant when contemplating the question of African collaboration and responsibility. It was stated by the Nuremberg Tribunal that 'necessity is a defence when it is shown that the act charged was done to avoid an evil both serious and irreparable; that there was no other adequate means of escape; and that the remedy was not disproportionate to the evil' (Lumb 1968: 78). In the Farben Trial, the tribunal specified that the plea of necessity has to be evaluated in light of whether a moral choice was possible. The majority of the defendants were acquitted on this ground (Ibid.). In all regions affected by transatlantic slavery the acquisition of firearms became a necessity for self-defence as slave raiding by others, who had been armed by Europeans, increased. Guns could only be acquired from European slave traders in exchange for slaves (Inikori 1982: 136ff). For many African communities and states, the only way to resist enslavement was to become slavers themselves (Rashid 2003: 141). Thus, a 'moral choice' in many instances was not possible. Historical evidence gives accounts of Europeans who also armed African groups with the explicit intent to procure slaves, such as happened during the Sagbadre War (Bailey 2007: 169).

If such manipulation failed, records show that Europeans did not hesitate to get rid of those African rulers who did not comply with them by shipping them off (Diouf 2003: 87f).

In addition we cannot be sure if African collaborators, in the majority, knew about or could even imagine the unimaginable horrors that existed on the slave ships and the American plantations, since nothing comparable existed in 'pre-European' Africa.

The legal situation in Europe

Chattel slavery, such as was practised in the transatlantic system, was not legal under the national laws of the European slaver nations. Though slavery had a long tradition in Iberian societies who had initiated transatlantic slavery, it had become legally regulated in the body of laws known as the *Siete Partidas*. The *Siete Partidas* protected slaves from abuse by their masters, permitted marriages, allowed the slaves ownership of property within certain limits, and provided for manumission under a variety of circumstances. Fundamentally, the *Siete Partidas* departed from the premise that freedom was the essential right of every human being (Palmer 1998: 11). That the provisions of the *Siete Partidas* were not enforced in the Spanish and Portuguese colonies does not change the fact that they were the formally valid and relevant legal basis in the matter.

Slavery had also been outlawed in England by the time when its people became active in the transatlantic system (Davidson 1961: 61). As stated by the court in the famous *Somerset* case, English law only recognised 'slavish servitude' (Van Cleeve 2006). In 1596, in a case involving a slave brought from Russia, it was ruled that chattel slavery was incompatible with English law (Mtubani 1983: 71). In 1667 however, motivated by the enormous economic gains expected from transatlantic slavery, a Crown legal position was issued that declared Africans as goods. Yet such an Act of legislation could not, and therefore did not, change the fact that Africans were humans. This must therefore be considered futile and void, whereas the English laws prohibiting chattel slavery remained in force.

Royal proclamations however in 1517 and 1607 declared that France permitted no slaves: 'All persons are free in this kingdom: as soon as a slave has reached those frontiers, and become baptised, he is free' (Davidson 1961: 62).

In European legal law doctrine of the time of transatlantic slavery, slavery was a much discussed subject. The majority rejected it or recognised the serious boundaries imposed by natural law. Thus, according to Suarez, slavery was admissible merely as part of positive penal law, whereas he recognised liberty positively as a part of natural law (Lumb 1968: 59). Francisco de Vitoria (1480–1564), often considered as the forefather of 'classic' international law, wrote in his *Reflectiones de Indis* that according to divine and natural law all men and all people were equal partners and that the sovereignty of indigenous rulers had to be respected in the same manner as that of Europeans (Hummer et al. 1997: 20).

In 1474 the trial against Peter von Hagenbach took place, commonly considered as one of the first international war crime trials. The Duke Charles of Burgundy got possessions on Upper Rhine from the Archduke of Austria as a pledge in 1469, and nominated Peter von Hagenbach as governor. Hagenbach installed a 'regime of arbitrariness and terror, extended to murder, rape, illegal taxation and wanton confiscation of private property' (Schwarzenberger 1968: 46f) until this was stopped by an alliance of Austria, Berne, France et al. He was accused of having 'trampled under foot the laws of God and man' and 'was charged with murder, rape, perjury and other *malefacta*' (Ibid.: 47ff). While the defendant and his attorney invoked the defence of superior orders, the *ad-hoc* tribunal, consisting of 28 judges from the allies, refused this request on the grounds that to accept it would be contrary to the laws of God. Hagenbach was found guilty and condemned to death. Since the condemned acts had been committed before the outbreak of open war they were not war crimes in a strict legal sense, rather these were subsumed under the category of *crime against humanity* (Ibid.: 50f). This trial bears witness that the notions of *war crime* and *crime against humanity* existed in international law at the time of transatlantic slavery, and that principles of natural law and humanity were considered as positive law and were actually relied upon in international judicial decisions.

Summarising the African and European evidence leads to the conclusion that transatlantic slavery was illegal from its inception. A violently illegal crime cannot be rendered legal by its perpetrators by simply extending it over a long period of four hundred years and then declaring that it would have been licit from the start.

Responsibility

Without the European demand for African slaves, there would have been no transatlantic slavery. The main aspects of this *crime against humanity* were planned in Europe where everything from an investor's potential profit to the insurance premiums on slaves was calculated (Bailey, 2007: 117f). Little was left to chance in this because for Europe it was economically a highly profitable 'enterprise'. Conditions on the slave ships were truly hellish and closely linked to the existing European knowledge about slave mortality and technological advances in the European shipping industry (Ibid.: 130).

European states profited from the granting of trade company charters as well as from a direct investment in enslavement. Transatlantic slavery was started as a royal enterprise based on a state monopoly (Andrade 1995: 76). Though this direct state involvement was to decrease, it was still dominated by state-chartered European companies throughout the seventeenth and eighteenth centuries: Portugal, Spain, England, France, Sweden, Denmark, The United Provinces, Brandenburg and Scotland were all involved in this way. European state officials were also appointed to reside on the African coast to ensure the smooth running of transatlantic slavery and ships sailed under European national flags (Bailey 2007: 115). All the European countries who joined in with the transatlantic slavery system, either directly or through chartered companies, captured significant tax revenues (Outterson 2003: 137).

Last but not least, European sovereigns promulgated the law codes that aimed to legitimise the extreme brutalisation and denial of humanity of Africans, such as the *Code Noir* enacted by Louis XIV in 1685 or the Spanish *Codigo Negro* of 1784 (Somé 1998: 531). It was also in and through these legal documents that the genocidal character of transatlantic slavery was manifested, since they denied the humanity of Africans. The legal definition of genocide implies the intent to destroy the victim group. The legislated denial of the humanity of Africans in these codices clearly encompassed such an intent and this is one of the exclusivities of transatlantic slavery that has no precedent in history (Plumelle-Uribe 2008: 115f). The legislation and practice of transatlantic slavery also testify to *dolus eventualis* on the part of the Europeans. Even if the prime motivation may not have been to destroy African people as an end in itself, their destruction was approved in the name of economic profits. The underlying principle was that African slave labour had to be obtained by any means and at the lowest cost possible, irrelevant of the consequences of the destruction of Africans, both individually and as peoples. The living conditions imposed on enslaved Africans in the Americas were also so exhausting that they sometimes were not able to reproduce. On the Fontezuela plantation in Brazil, owned by the Betlemitas Order, only eight babies were born over a period of fifty years, six of whom died before their first birthday (Ibid.: 97).

Conclusion

In view of the argument presented here it needs to be acknowledged that the prohibition of slavery is today clearly recognised as a part of *jus cogens* – that is, the category of international law norms considered so fundamental to the existence of the international community that they cannot be derogated by states. International law doctrine accredits that the core of this public order always exists while its precise content evolves with the level of organisation of international society (Carreau 2007: 93). Given this utilitarian character of *jus cogens*, it would be hard to think of anything more important to the superior interests of 'international society' than the interdiction of genocide and transatlantic slavery clearly was a genocide. The Nuremberg Tribunal, which was first to make the legal concept of genocide explicit, stated that its prohibition was not new law, but based in confirmed international law concepts that had found acceptance over the previous centuries (Gifford: 5.9.2010).

It is also necessary to keep in mind that international jurisprudence has relied extensively on principles of justice and humanity. Thus, in *Cayugas Indians* the tribunal invoked 'general and universally recognised principles of justice and fair dealing' and sustained that 'the claim of the Canadian Cayugas . . . is founded in the elementary principle of justice that requires us to look at the substance and to not stick in the bark of the legal form' (Reports of International Arbitral Awards 1926). The ICJ in the *Corfu Channel* case based its decision on 'certain general and well recognised principles, namely: elementary considerations of humanity' (*Corfu Channel case* 1949). In the *Continental Shelf* affair the court made it clear that 'Equity as a legal concept is a direct emanation of the idea of justice. The Court whose task is by definition to administer justice is bound to apply it . . . [In] international law . . . the legal concept of equity is a general principle directly applicable as law. Moreover, when applying positive international law, a court may choose among several possible interpretations of the law the one which appears, in the light of the circumstances of the case, to be closest to the requirements of justice' (*Continental Shelf* 1982).

The disastrous legacy of transatlantic slavery continues to weigh heavily on the lives of millions of people. The enslavement of Africans undermined not only the life chances of its direct victims, but also destroyed many potentialities for their posterity on both sides of the Atlantic (Asante 2003: 10). Reparations are not about making the current generations of slave owner/nation descendants personally guilty for the actions of their ancestors, but about the responsibility for perpetuating and profiting from the structures that were set in place through this crime against humanity.

If the international law community continues to ignore the legitimacy of reparations claims, then international law can certainly not be comprehended as a legal system whose *raison d'être* is to promote international justice.

Note

1 I use the term 'transatlantic slavery' instead of the more common 'transatlantic slave trade', because the latter suggests that the African victims would have been slaves awaiting sale in Africa, which is contradicted by historical facts. Most had been free people on the African Continent. Their violent seizure did not entail any transaction, and many affected African communities were not involved in business deals.

Bibliography

Adu-Boahen, A. (1985) *General History of Africa, Vol. VII: Africa Under Colonial Domination 1880–1935*. California: Heinemann & UNESCO.

Andrade, E.S. (1995) 'Le Cap-Vert dans l'expansion européenne', in E.M'Bokolo (ed.), *L'Afrique entre l'Europe et l'Amerique. Le rôle de l'Afrique dans la rencontre de deux mondes 1492–1992*. Paris : UNESCO, 69–79.

Asante, M.K. (2003) 'The African American Warrant for Reparations', in R.A.Winbush (ed.), *Should America Pay? Slavery and the Raging Debate on Reparations*. New York: Amistad, 3–13.

Asare, W.K. (2002) *Slavery Reparations in Perspective*. Victoria: Trafford.

Avajon, L.P. (2005) *Traite et Escalvage des Noirs: Quelle responsablité Africaine?*. Paris : Editions MENAIBUC.

Baba Kaké, I. (1998) 'La vulgarisation de l'histoire de la traite négrière', in D. Diène (ed.), *La chaine et le lien: Une vision de la traite négrière*. Paris: UNESCO, 25–29.

Bailey, A. C. (2007) *African Voices of the Atlantic Slave Trade*. Kingston/Miami: Ian Randle.

Barry, B. (1998) *Senegambia and the Atlantic Slave Trade*. Cambridge: Cambridge University Press.

Baum, R. (2010) 'Slaves without Rulers: Domestic Slavery among the Diola of Senegambia', in J. Spaulding and S. Beswick (eds), *African Systems of Slavery*. Trenton: Africa World Press, 45–66.

Carreau, D. (2007) *Droit International*. Paris: Editions Pedone.

Chinweizu (1987) *The West and the Rest of Us*. Lagos: Pero.

Clarke, J.H. (1998) *Christopher Columbus and the Afrikan Holocaust: Slavery and the Rise of European Capitalism*. New York: A&B Publisher Group.

Davidson, B. (1961) *The African Slave Trade*. Boston/New York: Back Bay Books.

Diouf, S.A. (2003) 'The Last Resort. Redeeming Family and Friends', in S.A. Diouf (ed.), *Fighting the Slave Trade: West African Strategies*. Athens: Ohio University Press, 81–100.

Durand, J.B. (1807) *Voyage au u Sénégal fait dans les années 1785 et 1786*. Paris: Dentu.

eZurara, G.E. (1994 [1453]). *Chronique de Guinée*. Paris: Editions Chandeigne.

Grotius (2000) *The Freedom of the Sea*. Ontario: Batoche Books.

Hess, P. (2000) *Overturning the Culture of Violence*. St Petersburg: Burning Spear Uhuru.

Hill, P. (1976) 'From Slavery to Freedom: The Case of Farm-Slavery in Nigerian Hausaland', *Comparative Studies in Society and History*. 18(3): 395–426.

Hummer, W., Neuhold, H. and Schreuer, C. (1997) Österreichisches Handbuch des Völkerrechts, Vol. 1. Wien: Manz.

Inikori, J.E. (1982) *Forced Migration: The Impact of the Export Slave Trade on African Societies*. New York: Africana.

Inikori, J.E. (1992) *The Chaining of a Continent: Export Demand for Captives and the History of Africa South of the Sahara, 1450–1870*. Kingston: UWI, Institute of Social and Economic Research.

Inikori, J.E. (2001) 'Slaves or Serfs? A Comparative Study of Slavery and Serfdom in Europe and Africa' in I. Okpewho, B.C. Davies and A.A. Mazrui (eds), *The African Diaspora: African Origins and New World Identities*. Bloomington: Indiana University Press, 49–75.

James, G. (1993) *Stolen Legacy*. New York: Africa World Press.

Kiné Camara, F. (2004) *Pouvoir et justice dans la tradition des peuples noirs*. Paris: L'Harmattan.

Ki-Zerbo, J. (1978) *Histoire de l'Afrique Noire*. Paris: Hatier.

Klein, M.A. (2010) 'Slavery in the Western Sudan', in J.Spaulding and S.Beswick (eds), *African Systems of Slavery*. Trenton: Africa World Press, 11–43.

Lara, O.D. (1997) 'Résistances et luttes', in *Diogène*, No. 179, 167–185.

Lovejoy, P. (2000) *Transformations in Slavery: A History of Slavery in Africa*. Cambridge: Cambridge University Press.

Lumb, D. (1968) 'Legality and Legitimacy: The Limits of the Duty of Obedience to the State', in C. Alexandrowicz (ed.), *Studies in the History of the Laws of Nations*. The Hague: Grotian Press Society, 52–82.

Manning, P. (1990) *Slavery and African Life: Occidental, Oriental and African Slave Trades*, Melksham: Redwood Press.

Mtubani, C.D. Victor (1983) 'African Slaves and English Law', *PULA Botswana Journal of African Studies*, 3(2): 71–75.

Nussbaum, A. (1954) *A Concise History of the Law of Nations*. New York: Macmillan.

Outterson, K. (2003) 'Slave Taxes', in R.A. Winbush (ed.), *Should America Pay? Slavery and the Raging Debate on Reparations*. New York: Amistad, 135–149.

Palmer, C.A. (1998) 'Introduction', in C.A. Palmer (ed.), *The Worlds of Unfree Labour: From Indentured Servitude to Slavery*. New York: Ashgate, 1–11, 8.

Peret, B. (1999) *La Commune des Palmares*. Paris: Editions Syllepse.

Péroz, E. (1889) 'Au Soudan Francais: Souvenirs de Guerre et de Mission', cited in R. Roberts and M. Klein (1980) 'The Banamba Slave Exodus of 1905', *Journal of African History*, 21(3): 375–394.

Plumelle-Uribe, R.A. (2004) 'Les crimes contre l'humanité et le devoir de réparation', in L. de Chazournes et al. (eds), *Crimes de l'histoire et réparations: les réponses du droit et de la justice*, Brussels: Editions Bruylant, 187–202.

Plumelle-Uribe, R.A. (2008) *Traite des Blancs, Traite des Noirs: Aspects méconnus et conséquences actuelles*. Paris: L'Harmattan.

Police, G. (2003) *Quilombos dos Palmares: Lecture sur un marronnage Bresilien*. Guyane: Ibis Rouge Editions.

Rashid, I. (2003) 'A Devotion to the Idea of Liberty at any Price: Rebellion and Anti-Slavery in the Upper Guinea Coast in the Eighteenth and Nineteenth Centuries', in S. Diouf (ed.), *Fighting the Slave Trade: West African Strategies*. Athens: Ohio University Press, 132–151.

Rodney, W. (1970) *A History of the Upper Guinea Coast 1545–1800*. New York: Monthly Review Press.

Scelle, G. (1934a) *Précis de Droit des Gens, Vol. 1*. Paris: Librairie du Recueil Sirey.

Scelle, G. (1934b) *Précis de Droit des Gens, Vol. 2*. Paris: Librairie du Recueil Sirey.

Schwarzenberger, G. (1968) 'Breisach Revisited: The Hagenbach Trial of 1474', in C. Alexandrowicz (ed.), *Studies in the History of the Laws of Nations*. The Hague: Grotian Press Society, 46–51.

Schwarzenberger, G. (1976) 'Towards a Comparative History of International Law', in M.K. Nawaz (ed.) *Essays on International Law: In Honour of Krishne Rao*. Leiden: Sijthoff, 92–106.

Smith, M. (1954) *Baba of Karo: A Woman of the Muslim Hausa*. London: Faber and Faber.

Somé, R. (1998) 'Esclavage, génocide ou holocauste ?', in D. Diène (ed.), *La chaine et le lien: Une vision de la traite négrière*. Paris: UNESCO, 527–542.

Testart, A. (2001) *L'esclave la dette et le pouvoir*. Paris: Errance.

Van Cleeve, G. (2006) 'Somerset's Case Revisited: Somerset's Case and its Antecedents in Imperial Perspective', *Law and History Review*, 24(3).

Winbush, O.I. (2003) 'Reflections on Homer Plessy and Reparations', in R.A. Winbush (ed.), *Should America Pay? Slavery and the Raging Debate on Reparations*. New York: Amistad, 150–162.

Wiredu, K. (1990) 'An Akan Perspective on Human Rights', in A. An-Na'im and F. Deng (eds), *Human Rights in Africa: Cross-Cultural Perspectives*. Washington, DC: Brookings Institution, 243–260.

Judicial decisions and opinions

Continental Shelf (Tunisia vs. Libya), Judgement of 24 February 1982, ICJ Reports 1982.
Corfu Channel case, ICJ Reports 1949.
Duchy of Sealand (Administrative Court of Cologne), Judgement of 3 May 1978, ILR 1989.
Legal Status of Eastern Greenland (Denmark vs. Norway), Judgement of 5 April 1933, PCIJ, Ser. A./B., No. 53.
Peace Conference on the former Yugoslavia (Arbitration Commission), opinion n° 1 of 29 November 1991, cited in A. Pellet (1992) 'The Opinions of the Badinter Arbitration Committee: A Second Breath for the Self-Determination of Peoples', *European Journal of International Law*, 3(1): 178–185.

Online sources

Gifford, A. *The legal basis of the claim for Reparations*. Available at <http://www.arm.arc.co.uk/legalBasis.html> (accessed 5.9.2010).
Reports of International Arbitral Awards (1926) *Cayuga Indians (Great Britain) v. United States*, 22 January 1926, Vol. VI, 173–190. Available at <http://untreaty.un.org/cod/riaa/cases/vol_VI/173–190_Cayuga.pdf> (accessed 16.8.2010).

Chapter 2

The trade in enslaved Africans and slavery after 1807

Marika Sherwood

Attempts to abolish the trade

After many years of campaigning, the British Parliament finally passed an Act in 1807 making it illegal to trade in enslaved Africans. Though this British Act is the one that usually grabs the headlines, in fact Denmark had abolished participation in the trade four years earlier. Within a few years the USA and most other European countries agreed to cease the trade in human beings. In 1820 Spain also agreed to cease trading if Britain paid a 'compensation'; however this had no effect, so in 1830 Britain gave Spain and Portugal £1.45 million as a further inducement. This proved equally ineffective and more treaties were signed. But the trade was not drastically reduced until the abolition of slavery itself in the colonies and countries that had imported the greatest number: the Spanish colony of Puerto Rico in 1878; Portuguese colonies in 1878; Cuba, a Spanish colony till 1870, in 1880; and Brazil in 1888 (Sherwood 2007a: Appendix 1).

The numbers involved

According to figures available on the website www.slavevoyages.org/tast/assessment/estimates.faces (1 December 2010), a total of just over twelve and a half million enslaved African men, women and children were shipped across the Atlantic to the Americas from 1501 till 1866. That is c.34,200 per annum, over three hundred and sixty-five years. But in the fifty-five years from 1811 till 1866, over three million were transported – c.54,500 annually. This indicates that what had come to be known as the 'nefarious trade' increased once it had become illegal. It must be noted here that not all shipping records have been preserved, and so these figures are an underestimate. From the same website we learn that only 86 per cent of the enslaved survived the horrors of the trans-Atlantic journey. How many died in what was called the 'seasoning' process once they had arrived and been sold is not known. Some would have died of disease, many of ill-treatment and undoubtedly many more from sorrow and depression. The question this website cannot even begin to address is this: how many were killed in the process of enslavement, in the long, enchained march to the 'barrocoons' on the coast, and how many more died in those badly ventilated, unsanitary overcrowded prisons while awaiting shipment? On top of this there were the thousands who died in the process of being captured by the slaver. So are we perhaps talking about Africa losing perhaps twenty million or more of its most able-bodied men, women and children to the trans-Atlantic slave trade?

The circumvention of Acts of Parliament and Congress

There is much evidence of circumvention of the Act by Britons. For example, on 5 March 1811 Mr Brougham MP said in the House of Commons that the 'provisions of the Act [of 1807] had been found insufficient for putting a stop to [the trade in enslaved Africans ... [H]e was in possession of various documents and sufficient evidence to prove that those laws had been violated'. Brougham and others abolitionists were to repeat these accusations many times. As a result Parliament passed more and more Acts that were intended to close the 'gaps' in previous ones. So many were passed that these even had to be 'consolidated' twice, in 1824 and again in 1842. This meant that purchasing, shipping, financing, insuring, fitting out slaving vessels or serving on them, and shipping goods to be used in the slave trade were all illegal. The 1811 Act also declared participation to be an act of felony, punishable by transportation. And yet as far as I have been able to discover, not a single person was ever transported for this crime (Sherwood 2007a: 172).

Slave trading was declared a piracy, punishable by death. However no such prosecutions were ever made, according to the historian Hugh Thomas (1997: 590). More Acts were passed – and subsequently not enforced. Why these were not enforced is open to debate. I would speculate that those making their fortunes from the trade were also in positions of power and authority, for example, as Members of Parliament, as local councillors, and certainly as owners of (or on the boards of) the companies that were profiting from the trade. These companies profited both from the sale of enslaved Africans and from the importation and local sales of the produce of the enslaved, such as sugar, coffee and cotton. Some of these products were exported, as was woven cotton cloth. In the mid-nineteenth century over half a million people were *directly* employed in the cotton business; how many more made the looms/machines, mined the coal, built and worked on the ships used in the trade? By the 1850s, textiles were 60 per cent of Britain's total exports, and in 1861, 11.53 per cent of Britain's national income was derived from cotton (Sherwood 2007b: 77–8). With so much money coming into the country from the profits made not only from the trade in enslaved Africans but also from their produce on the plantations, as well as the jobs these provided for much of the British population, to take action against this could have been seen as impoverishing Britain.

The USA never agreed to have its trading vessels searched by the British naval squadron that had been established to enforce the 1807 Act, which made ignoring Congressional mandates regarding the trade much easier. Reports of the ongoing US involvement appeared in some sections of the press, especially in the Northern states of the USA and were reported to the government and Congress. These were ignored. This eventually resulted in the American flag replacing those of Spain and Portugal on slaving vessels.[1] 'Two thirds of the slavers which reach Brazil or Cuba, maybe said to owe their safety to the US flag', it was reported in 1851 (Horne 2007: 34). According to one British researcher, the trade in human beings to the plantations in Cuba was 'financed by American capital, carried in American ships, manned by American seamen and protected by the American flag. Yet the government of the United States had declared the trade to be illegal' (Lloyd 1949: 163).

It seems that there was even less enforcement in the USA than in Britain: as Du Bois pointed out over a hundred years ago, 'much oratory and poetry were expended in celebration [of the 1807 Act] [but] there was no especial set of machinery provided for the enforcement of this Act ... and the law was probably enforced as the people who made it wished it enforced' (Du Bois 1970: 108–9).[2] This lack of 'wish' was not by any means confined to Southerners. For example, the fast sailing vessels used in this illegal trade, as it had been reported for years, were built in New York, Baltimore and Philadelphia: according to Du Bois (1970: 179), in just eighteen months from 1859 to 1860 18 slavers were fitted out in New York alone. In 1852 Joseph Story similarly reported that

> American citizens are steeped up to their very mouths in this stream of iniquity ... throng the coasts of Africa under the stained flags of Spain and Portugal, sometimes selling abroad their 'cargoes of despair', and sometimes bringing them into some of our Southern ports.
>
> (Story 1852: 122–147)

All the Acts of Parliament by different nations and all the international treaties were ineffective. Why was this so?

- At one level, as noted above, because too much money could be made.
- At another, because 'machinery' would have to be put in place to enforce the Acts and then the enforcement had to be monitored and

punishments meted out to those breaking the rules. This would cost a lot of money and might thus prove unpopular!

- And would any nation really accuse some of its well-known and very wealthy men of breaking the law?
- Many might have supported the passage of Acts which looked good, or would result in positive international publicity.
- Efforts at implementation might have come up against those who had not supported these, or had supported them almost on the understanding that there would be no enforcement – or had known that their power and influence were sufficient to prevent this. (Indeed could we see this as a forerunner of the non-implementation of Acts today? Did Parliament learn that it was enough to hold investigative Royal Commissions and to appear to be tackling an issue?)

In fact, certain measures led to an increase in the trade: one of these was the British government's decision to equalise the import duty of slave-grown and free-grown cotton, and to extend this to sugar in 1846. There had been 'rejoicings in Havanna, when the Act of 1846 was proclaimed there – it was a jubilee, there were illuminations . . . Lord Howden, writing from Rio de Janeiro: "I have estimated . . . that 60,000 have been imported as slaves into the Brazils during 1847"' (McNeile 1848: 14).[3]

It was probably at least partially Britain's complicated relationship with Brazil after its (partial) independence in 1822 as well as the free-trade arguments in Britain that resulted in the equalising of the import duty on free and slave-grown sugar (Bethell 1966; Platt 1972; Sherwood 2007a). *The Times* of London explained the situation thus on 25 July 1846, just before the parliamentary debate began:

> The wants and the commerce of the country are now requiring a great increase and cheapening of the supply. The only way to accomplish this effectually and permanently is to seek a free commercial interchange with the largest possible area of production, and certainly our best customers. The prohibition of slave-grown sugar . . . has driven us to an indirect, troublesome, and expensive mode of conducting trade. It is involving us in quarrels and endangering animosities dangerous to the peace, the power and even to the honour of this country . . . Nay, we are guilty of the gross absurdity of making that a virtue in sugar which we show to be a matter of indifference in every other article . . .

It is interesting to note that *The Times* mentions that there had been no campaign against the importation of other slave-grown produce such as tobacco or cotton.

Captain Tomlinson of HMS *Mosquito* wrote to William Wilberforce on

25 February 1815, describing the capture of a slaving vessel, the *Emannella*. It carried Spanish colours (i.e. flags) but on examination of its papers was found to be Portuguese. The vessel was 'British built and insured in London'. The horrific death toll aboard was not unusual: 120 died during the voyage to Freetown from where the slaver had been captured (Tomlinson 1816). In 1816 Captain Curran of HMS *Tyne* reported seizing the *Franklin*, an American slaver from Havannah, which was carrying Spanish papers (Curran 1817).

On 12 December 1840 Captain Denman of the Anti-Slave Trade Squadron reported to Parliament that 'on the River Gallinas legitimate trade has withered . . . at length totally annihilated by the establishment of a permanent slave factory in-shore by Pedro Blanco about fifteen years ago. Since then the slave trade has been the only pursuit' (Denman 1842).

Attempts at enforcement

The British government's only measure of enforcement for the 1807 Act was to set up an Anti-Slave Trade Squadron to monitor the West African coastline. However, to begin with only a very few old, small and slow vessels were sent – and then only intermittently. The minuscule effect of this was reported at the Annual General Meeting of the African Institution in London in 1818: a letter from Sierra Leone dated 21 July 1817, stated that 'the Slave Trade is raging dreadfully on the coast . . . There has been no man-of-war [warship] on the coast since March'. Another letter dated 8 November 1817, from Port Louis in Senegal, asserted that 'personal liberty is again at an end, the Natives are armed against one another and the great demand for slaves has renewed wars in the interior . . . Slave traders in the settlement provide them with arms and ammunition for this purpose. Slave ships are now armed and do battle with the Royal Navy. Many [are] American vessels, which are very fast, so most escape' (African Association 1818).

Even more was revealed at this annual meeting of the Association about the techniques used by slavers: the captured American slaver *Rose* was found by the Royal Navy to be 'the property of an English passenger on board . . . an old slave trader from Mesurado'. Captain Tuckey reported that 'a brig under Spanish colours arrived (on the Congo River) . . . Her nominal mate, but real captain, and a number of their crew, being English and Irish, tho' pretended Americans, left no doubt of her being either English or American property' (African Association 1818). And to give just one more example: in 1816 the British Squadron captured the *Dorset* of Baltimore; it was also known as the Spanish *Triumvirate*; it had an American 'supercargo', a Spanish captain, and an American, French, Spanish and English crew (Du Bois 1970: 112).

These reports, and many others bearing similar information, revealed the methods used by the slavers to circumvent whatever international agreements were then current, and avoid persecution and prosecution: they used multiple identities, forged ships' documentation and provided the most convenient names for the crews. That the slave trade caused wars was now also explained to the public quite explicitly, as was the ever-increasing trade in guns and ammunition, which also provided a vast income for British and American manufacturers of armaments.

What also has to be acknowledged here is that in order to encourage Britons to serve on the dreaded, malaria-infested African coast, an inducement had to be offered to those in the Anti-Slave Trade Squadron: in this case prize money was offered. For example, those on board HMS *Mosquito* which had captured three vessels claimed £4,945 in 1818. The three captured and condemned vessels had carried 290 slaves. How many of the Africans had died before the 'cargo' was freed is not known. Nor do we know about the fee charged by the 'prize agents' who normally submitted such claims to governments. When the captured vessel was sold, half went to the Crown and the rest to its captors. Thus the exercise could become quite lucrative, even if one was serving on the Slave Coast (Lloyd 1949: 80).

Fearful of the increasing competition from slave-grown produce arriving from Spanish, Portuguese and French colonies, the British at last sent some vessels to intercept the traders and actually also increased their numbers and quality in the 1840s. The other signatories to the various agreements and treaties did not bother. The USA's squadron, according to Gerald Horne's *The Deepest South*, 'never consisted of more than seven ships and the average was less than five [and it] was based on the relatively more healthy Cape Verde Islands, which were almost 3000 miles and at least a month's sail from the southern slave trading areas' (Horne 2007: 10).

By 1836 Britain also had a viable squadron along the American coasts and waters, but these vessels had too large an area to cover and their duties were not exclusively to suppress the trade in humans. Very few slavers were captured and even fewer were condemned. As explained by the historian of the squadron, Christopher Lloyd, 'the North American station . . . covered the most important trade routes in the world. Its ships had, therefore, many other duties to perform besides suppressing the Slave Trade' (Lloyd 1949: 164–165).[4]

When Britain set up the Mixed Commission Courts in Freetown, Sierra Leone, to adjudicate on captured slaving vessels, the treaty signatories were supposed to send a judicial representative, but they did not do so. For some years there was no qualified judge in charge (Bethell 1966; Sherwood 2007a: 15; 114–115). And, as reported in the pamphlet *Present State of the Foreign Slave Trade* (1831), 'at Sierra Leone the condemned vessels are re-purchased for the slave-trade . . . Many of the negroes whom we had liberated there are fraudulently carried from that settlement and resold into slavery' (Anonymous 1831: 4).

Eventually such courts were established in Cape of Good Hope, Loanda, Rio de Janeiro and Havana, but they were singularly inactive and unsuccessful in condemning the slavers brought before them. And somewhat similarly to the Freetown Court, the court in Havana permitted the crews of the few vessels who were condemned to re-enter the slave trade (Anonymous 1831: 4). Most courts only survived very briefly due to lack of cases to deal with (Bethell 1966; Sherwood 2007a: 114–115).

What of those human beings in the captured ships' holds? They had to remain there – but at least on the voyage to the courts the chains were removed. Once anchored their confinement continued, because if the ship was not condemned it could resume its voyage to the Americas and sell its cargo as usual. In those pestilential holds, this resulted in more deaths. If the men, women and children were freed they were landed in Sierra Leone, a British colony, and 'apprenticed' to the residents there (Goddard 1925: 31–32).

The residents, or 'settlers' as they became known, were mainly freed slaves from the Caribbean and the British colonies in North America, Nova Scotia and the Caribbean who had emigrated there voluntarily.[5] They saw themselves as superior to the native peoples and attempted to 'apprentice' some of them to grow food for them. This notion of 'apprenticeship' was British: the Emancipation Act of 1833 had decreed a long 'apprenticeship' period during which the 'freed' slaves would have to continue working without pay in order to learn the skills they had been practising for years! Revolts in the Caribbean resulted in freedom in 1838 (see for example Hart 1985). Liberated Africans were shipped into 'apprenticeships' in Trinidad, used in the same way as in Sierra Leone, and also recruited into what was called the West India Regiment in Sierra Leone (Goddard 1925: 34; Blackburn 1988: 419–472).

Once freed, these former slaves could attempt to return home or find ways of surviving in Sierra Leone. The indigenous peoples however had no conception of *selling* land: their practice was for chiefs to own and distribute land according to need. Thus this new practice and the settling of thousands of people (called 'Liberated Africans') were to cause ongoing problems. About 65,000 were set free by the court in Sierra Leone.[6]

The British tried to minimise this by exporting 'apprentices' from the slaving vessels condemned in Africa and the Americas to the Caribbean plantations. Having freed the enslaved, cheap new labour was wanted in order to remain in competition with other colonies. Naturally this led to much opposition from competitors, as explained by Eric Williams:

> African immigration was contemplated, principally from Sierra Leone. One important source of African recruits was the slaves captured by

British men of war from . . . slave ships which persisted in carrying on the slave trade in contravention of the declaration of the European powers against the slave trade at the Congress of Vienna in 1815. For some thirty years Britain's relations with Spain, France and the USA were bedevilled and jeopardised by Britain's insistence on . . . their transportation of the captured slaves to British colonies, particularly Trinidad. It was hardly to be expected that Britain's rivals would see in Britain's policy anything more than a hypocritical attempt by Britain, under the guise of the suppression of the slave trade, to supply Negro labour to its under-developed colonies like Trinidad, without exposing itself to the charge that it was engaged in the slave trade.

(Williams 1962: 98–99)[7]

Britain abolished slavery?

When the ending of slavery was mooted and debated in Parliament, its proposers, presumably to obtain support, promised £20 million (c. £16,782 million in 2008) as compensation to the owners of slaves in the Caribbean. The Act emancipating slaves in the Caribbean 'possessions', Ceylon, Canada and Cape Town was passed in 1833. India (then still under the aegis of the East India Company) was specifically excluded and other colonies were not even mentioned. It was proposed that those 'freed' should serve forty years' apprenticeship (in order to learn to do what they had already been doing); this was then reduced, and altogether abandoned when there were too many uprisings. By 1838 however there were no slaves in the British-'owned' islands in the Caribbean.

Those who had been set free were offered nothing by the British, except the lowest possible wages for continuing to labour on the plantations. On some islands, for example Barbados, all the land was owned by Whites. This led to emigration to islands with unclaimed land as well as to the mainland.

Slavery was not abolished in India when it came under the direct control of Britain in 1858. It was estimated in 1883 that there were about 9 million slaves in British India and another 16 million in the free states on the continent. Some estimates are much higher. The emigration of 'indentured' labourers to other colonies, to make up for the loss of enslaved labour, was much encouraged by the British government. India was, of course, a large captive market for British goods while British importers made huge profits from cheaply produced agricultural goods and other items (Frere 1883: 355).[8]

As indicated previously, because of the demand for African produce, new forms of domestic slavery were introduced in West Africa. For some time this was not even raised in Parliament. When it was, the governors along the coast introduced local ordinances forbidding this, but again these were not enforced. The slave trade within the area increased as a result. It was not until slavery became an international issue under the aegis of the League of Nations after WWI that attempts were made to enforce the prohibition. Final ordinances abolishing slavery in some of the British colonies in Africa were passed in Egypt in 1895; Nigeria in 1901; Sierra Leone in 1928; and Ghana in 1935 (Sherwood 2007a: 120–136).

'Slavery' was often replaced in legal terminology by 'forced' or 'compulsory' labour. For example, in the Gold Coast colony (Ghana since independence in 1957) a British official investigating labour issues in 1932 reported that 'Africans were unaccustomed to wage-earning, and that colonial governments lacked money to pay labourers. As a result, 'coercion was resorted to freely by almost all the various [colonial] administrations' to recruit labour. Consequently, forced or compulsory labour was fundamental to the implementation of colonial economic ventures such as mining, building of roads and railways, plantation agriculture and head-porterage.' There is also some evidence that some of the African troops used by Britain in WWI were 'recruited' by a 'variety of methods of compulsion ranging from exhortation laced with insult and threat to direct orders' (Akurang-Parry 2000: 1, 125).

The *Anti-Slavery Reporter* published a 'Letter from Brazil', which confirmed that the importation of slaves had stopped 'but internal trade continues . . . I could say a great deal – how largely English Capital is engaged in supporting the system of slavery' (*Anti-Slavery Reporter* 1853: 58). As late as 1879 the US Consul in Rio reported to Washington that 'English capital, English goods, English subsidised steamship lines and English influence' were very much in evidence (Horne 2007: 246).

Some still well-known names were indirectly involved in slavery or the trade in slaves. Barings, for example, an international banking firm until it was bankrupted in 1995, financed the slave-states of Louisiana, Mississippi, Alabama and Virginia; the company also dealt in slave-grown cotton from the Southern states, slave-grown sugar from Cuba, and slave-grown coffee from Brazil. In addition it financed some slave traders as well (Sherwood 2007a: 79).

In 1853 the *Anti-Slavery Reporter* recorded that Julian de Zulueta, a famous (or infamous) Cuban slave trader and slave owner, had had his latest vessel, the *Lady Suffolk*, built in Baltimore. Julian's cousin Pedro, who was a British citizen, lived in London. Pedro was not only a trader in slaves and in slave-grown goods, but was also a shareholder and founder director of the P&O shipping company. When taken to court for trading in slaves, he was found innocent on 'technical' grounds (*Anti-Slavery Reporter* 1853: 9). Among the many who spoke up in court to support Zulueta's innocence was the banker Lionel de Rothschild. The Rothschilds' bank financed Brazil and was involved in trading in slave-grown goods from both North and South America (Sherwood 2007a: 68, 76, 80–81,

105). Another British bank which started its life in the slaving business is Barclays. According to an anonymous pamphlet, *Cotton Importers* (Anonymous 1830) Barclays were major importers of slave-grown cotton and tobacco from New Orleans.

The city of Manchester and many of the surrounding towns in the county of Lancashire were built on the cotton-trade. Almost all its cotton was slave-grown. The city of Liverpool, which was expected to collapse after the 1807 Act, in fact grew. This was partly based on building and equipping ships for the trade in slaves (and for the Confederates, which was also illegal[9]) and on the trade in slave-grown produce and goods manufactured from these (Sherwood 2007b: 16–22).

As was argued by the anonymous author of the pamphlet *Reasons for Withdrawing from our Trading Connection with the American Slaveholder*, published in Manchester in 1846:

> If we purchase American cotton we become aiders and abettors of the American slaveholder and participators with him in the criminality of the system of American Slavery – not only the merchant, the spinner and the manufacturer . . . but our whole manufacturing community . . . and the nation itself.

Some twenty-two years previously, in *Immediate not gradual Abolition*, yet another unnamed author had pointed out that by purchasing slave-grown sugar:

> Are we, <u>ourselves</u> sincere or hypocritical? . . . We are all guilty of supporting and perpetuating slavery . . . We furnish the stimulant to all this injustice, rapacity and cruelty by PURCHASING ITS PRODUCE . . . Abstinence from West Indian sugar alone would sign the death warrant of West Indian slavery.
>
> (Anonymous 1824)

It is interesting to note that not only did these authors choose to write anonymously, but also that their efforts were completely ignored.

Eventually more Acts were passed by the British Parliament, making it illegal for Britons to own slaves. But this could also be circumvented, or simply ignored. For example, the Select Committee on the Slave Trade was informed in 1850 that 'there was British capital employed in mining quite ostensibly. The great mines of Brazil, called Congo Socco belong to an English company.' These mines were worked by enslaved Africans (Sherwood and Sherwood 2007: 40).

The booming economy of Brazil, and undoubtedly the profits to be derived from the use of unpaid labour, attracted much British interest. As always, the British & Foreign Anti-Slavery Society collected and publicised the information it received regarding Britons who were ignoring Parliamentary strictures. For example, in 1855 the Society informed the Foreign Secretary, Lord Clarendon, that it had been advised that the British Consul in Pará, Brazil, had just bought three slaves from another Briton living there, Alexander Dickson. Dickson was probably from the firm of G.F. Dickson & Co., London merchants who were trading with South America, mainly in gunpowder, which was then one of the main exports to Africa used to purchase slaves. In the same year the *Reporter* also advised its readers of British slave-holders in the Dutch colony of Surinam, adjacent to the British colony of Guiana (today's Guyana) (*Anti-Slavery Reporter* 1855: 138, 207).

Britons also owned slaves in Africa and purchased produce grown by enslaved Africans there. There had been no 'plantation economy' prior to the arrival of the Europeans. The British traders involved in Africa, now having to avoid the Anti-Slave Trade Squadron and perhaps wary of transgressing slave-trading laws, realised they could continue to exploit the continent by purchasing African products such as palm oil. They turned a blind eye to the 'serfs/slaves' producing these trade goods. What was going on was reported to Parliament by some of the more assiduous squadron captains, such as Captain Colomb:

> What is the painful, yet undoubted fact about the West Coast, now that the export trade is suppressed? It is that the articles exported are slave-produced, that a raging slave trade sweeps over the interior, and that furious wars everywhere surround the British settlements . . . Take Gambia in 1865 . . . the cultivation of ground nuts by slaves for exports . . . wars constantly taking place between the natives, and prisoners are made slaves, and were either returned to work for their masters, or are sold to other parts of the country for the same purpose . . . It is the same on the Gold Coast . . . in Lagos . . .
>
> (Colomb 1873: 45–46)

Consequences

While the importation of Africans totally transformed the islands of the Caribbean and introduced new peoples to the American mainland, the most devastating effects were – and still are – on Africa. The continent lost millions of its most productive inhabitants. As summarised by the historian Benedict Der, writing on Northern Ghana (to take just one example), 'the main effects of the slave trade were depopulation, devastation, insecurity and loss of life and property. Agriculture and the local arts were disrupted while people lived in constant fear for their lives . . . The long term effect . . . was that it retarded development in the area' (1998: 31).

And as historian Gerald Horne reported:

> US nationals – and some from Europe and Brazil, 'acting alone or in conjunction with the bandits, intervened in the affairs of these [African] chiefdoms to provoke conflicts that generated export captives. The Igbo example clearly shows that slavery and the slave trade were the primary cause of violence in the West African sub-region for over three centuries . . . [S]lavers forment brawls among Chiefs' . . .
>
> (Horne 2007: 3)

G.N. Uzoigwe explains this further:

> The economic, social and political consequences of this drainage of human resources were bound to be disastrous for future African history and development . . . The slave trade undoubtedly helped certain states to enlarge their political authority . . . it caused others to decrease theirs.
>
> (Uzoigwe 1973: 208–209)

After the cessation of this export trade, Africa became subject to Europe's hunger for its mineral and agricultural products. This led to the division of Africa by Europeans among themselves in 1885 – in order to not waste time, effort and funds in fighting each other for possession.[10] Depleted, war-torn Africa could not resist. It was divided up, without any recognition of its language, cultural or historical boundaries. The consequences remain with us today.[11]

Reparations? Where to begin? Had it not been for this European onslaught Africa would have progressed in the same manner as Europe, or India, or China, or the Americas, from early kingdoms, dukedoms, less hierarchical societies to the modern world. But in Africa's history, *Africa's natural development was brutally stopped for about three hundred years.* One possible beginning here would be a rethink by the IMF, the World Bank (e.g., to cancel all debts), and those 'aid' givers who pay high salaries to endless numbers of 'advisors' who then recommend the purchase of what are not the best materials or expertise, but what is available from their own countries. (And thus they are benefiting their own economies.) Similarly, the export of goods to Africa which prevents the development of local agriculture and manufacturing should be halted.

Notes

1 See, for example, the pioneering report by W.E.B. Du Bois, originally published in 1896 (Du Bois 1970).
2 See Du Bois 1970: Appendix B for US and international legislation.

3 On import duties, see Schuyler 1918: 77–92; Curtin 1954: 157–164; Eltis 1982: 195–213.
4 See also Bethell 1970: Chapter 5; Conrad 1969: 618–638.
5 On these 'residents', see for example Walker 1976; Sherwood 1998: 219–236).
6 On the early history of Sierra Leone, see for example (Goddard 1925; Fyfe 1962).
7 Williams, who started life as a historian, became the first Prime Minister of an independent Trinidad and Tobago in 1962.
8 On the export of Indian labourers, see Tinker 1993. The net profits of the East India Company were roughly £760,000 and £800,000 annually between 1793 and 1828 (Mui and Mui 1984: 152). India became the source of the opium exported to China which led to the Opium Wars, i.e., the British attempts to conquer China, beginning in 1839 (see for example Inglis 1976; Hanes and Sanello 2002).
9 Though Britain had declared its neutrality, the Confederates received much – illegal – support. (see for example Bulloch 2001 [1884]; Hollett 1993; Sherwood 1999: 174–200).
10 The classic study on underdevelopment is Rodney (1973). On the Berlin Conference, see for example Wesseling (1996).
11 It is not only in African that national unity can be difficult to achieve: for example, look at the (dis)United Kingdom today, or the struggles of the relatively newly independent states of the former USSR.

Bibliography

African Association (1818) in *African Association, 12th Report and Annual General Meeting 9 April 1818*, London.

Akurang-Parry, K.O. (2000) 'Colonial forced labour policies, 1900–1940', *African Economic History*, 28: 1–25.

Anonymous (1824) *Immediate not gradual Abolition*, pamphlet by unknown author, England.

Anonymous (1830) *Cotton Importers*, pamphlet by unknown author, London.

Anonymous (1831) *Present State of the Foreign Slave Trade*, pamphlet by unknown author, London.

Anonymous (1846) *Reasons for Withdrawing from our Trading Connection with the American Slaveholder*, pamphlet by unknown author, Manchester.

Bethell, L. (1966) 'The mixed-commissions for the suppression of the transatlantic slave trade in the 19th century', *Journal of African History* 7/1: 79–93.

Bethell, L. (1970) *The Abolition of the Brazilian Slave Trade*. Cambridge: Cambridge University Press.

Blackburn, R. (1988) *The Overthrow of Colonial Slavery, 1776–1848*. London: Verso.

Bulloch, J.D. (2001 [1884]) *The Secret Service of the Confederate States in Europe*. New York: Modern Library.

Capt. Colomb (1968 [1873]) *Slave Catching in the Indian Ocean*. London: Dawsons of Pall Mall.

Capt. Curran (1817) in *African Association, 11th Report and Annual General Meeting 26 March 1817*, London.

Capt. Denman (1842) in *Reports from the Committees – the West Coast of Africa*, Parliamentary Papers, volume 12. London: Hansard.

Capt. Tomlinson (1816) in *African Association, 10th Report and Annual General Meeting 27 March 1816*, London.

Conrad, R. (1969) 'The contraband slave trade to Brazil 1831–1845', *Hispanic American Historical Review*, 49: 618–638.

Curtin, P.D. (1954) 'The British sugar duties and West Indian prosperity', *Journal of Economic History*, 14/2: 157–164.

Der, B.G. (1998) *The Slave Trade in Northern Ghana*. Accra: Woeli.

Du Bois, W.E.B. (1970) *The Suppression of the African Slave-Trade to the United States of America, 1638–1870*. New York: Dover.

Eltis, D. (1982) 'Abolitionist perceptions of society after slavery', in James Walvin (ed.), *Slavery and British Society 1776–1846*. London: Macmillan.

Frere, H.B.E. (1883) in *Fortnightly Review*. London.

Fyfe, C. (1962) *A History of Sierra Leone*. Oxford: Oxford University Press.

Goddard, T.N. (1925) *The Handbook of Sierra Leone*. London: Richards.

Hanes, W.T. and Sanello, F. (2002) *The Opium Wars: The Addiction of One Empire and the Corruption of Another*. Naperville: Sourcebooks.

Hart, R. (1985) *Slaves Who Abolished Slavery*. Jamaica: ISER, University of the West Indies.

Hollett, D. (1993) *The Alabama Affair*. Wilmslow: Sigma.

Horne, G. (2007) *The Deepest South: the United States, Brazil and the African Slave Trade*. New York: New York University Press.

Inglis, B. (1976) *The Opium War*. London: Hodder and Stoughton.

Lloyd, C. (1949) *The Navy and the Slave Trade*. London: Longmans Green.

Mui, H.-C. and Mui, L.H. (1984) *The Management of Monopoly*. Vancouver: University of British Columbia Press.

Revd. Dr McNeile (1848), *Slave Labour versus Free Labour: speech at public meeting in Liverpool, 13 June 1848*, London.

Platt, D.C.M. (1972) *Latin America and British Trade 1806–1914*. London: Adam & Charles Black.

Rodney, W. (1973) *How Europe Underdeveloped Africa*. London: Bogle L'Ouverture.

Schuyler, R.L. (1918) 'The abolition of British imperial preference 1846–1860', *Political Science Quarterly*, 33/1: 77–92.

Sherwood, M. (1998) 'Jamaicans and Barbadians in the Province of Freedom: Sierra Leone 1802–1841', *Caribbean Studies*, 13/2–3: 219–236.

Sherwood, M. (1999) 'Perfidious Albion: Britain, the USA and slavery in the 1840s and 1860s', *Contributions to Black Studies*, 13/14: 174–200.

Sherwood, M. (2007a) *After Abolition: Britain and the Slave Trade Since 1807*. London: I B Tauris.

Sherwood, M. (2007b) 'Manchester, Liverpool and Slavery', *North West Labour History Journal*, 32: 16–22.

Sherwood, M. and Sherwood, K. (2007) *Britain, the Slave Trade and Slavery, from 1562 to the 1880s*. Kent: Savannah.

Story, J. (1852) 'Piracy and the slave trade', in William W. Story (ed.), *The Miscellaneous Writings of Joseph Story*. Boston, MA: Little, Brown.

Thomas, H. (1997) *The Slave Trade*. London: Picador.

Thomas, R. (DATE) 'Military recruitment in the Gold Coast during the First World War', *Cahiers d'Etudes Africaines*, 15/57: 57–83.

Thomas, R.G. (1973) 'Forced labour in British West Africa', *Journal of African History*, 14/1: 79–103.

Tinker, H. (1993) *A New System of Slavery*. London: Hansib.

Uzoigwe, G.N. (1973) 'The slave trade and African societies', *Transactions of the Historical Society of Ghana*, 14/2: 208–9.

Walker, J.W.StG. (1976) *The Black Loyalists*. London: Longman.

Wesseling, H.L. (1996) *Divide and Rule: the Partition of Africa 1880–1914*. Westport, CT: Praeger.

Williams, E. (1962) *History of the People of Trinidad and Tobago*. Port-of-Spain: PNM Publishing Co.

Chapter 3

Learning lessons from history?

The international legal framework for combating modern slavery

Steve Peers

Introduction

While slavery in the traditional sense was abolished by international treaties and national laws in the nineteenth and twentieth centuries, a type of slavery still exists in the twenty-first century, in the form of trafficking in human beings. The acts designed to abolish the transatlantic slave trade were fraught with problems. To what extent does the current international legal framework, which has developed quickly in recent years, effectively address this problem?

This chapter examines that issue by examining in turn the legal framework established by the Council of Europe, the United Nations and the European Union as regards trafficking in persons.[1]

Council of Europe

Council of Europe Convention

The most comprehensive international instrument on trafficking in persons is the Council of Europe Convention on the issue (CETS 197), which was opened for signature by the 47 Council of Europe Member States, several non-European States and the European Community (as it was then) in May 2005 and which came into force on 1 February 2008. At the time of writing the Convention has 33 parties and ten further signatories.[2]

The Convention defines trafficking in persons as 'the recruitment, transportation, transfer, harbouring or receipt of persons, by means of the threat or use of force or other forms of coercion, of abduction, of fraud, of deception, of the abuse of power or of a position of vulnerability or of the giving or receiving of payments or benefits to achieve the consent of a person having control over another person, for the purpose of exploitation'. In turn, the concept of 'exploitation' must 'include, at a minimum, the exploitation of the prostitution of others or other forms of sexual exploitation, forced labour or services, slavery or practices similar to slavery, servitude or the removal of organs'.[3] The apparent consent of a victim to this exploitation is 'irrelevant' if any of the means described in the Convention have been used,[4] and the recruitment, etc. of a child 'for the purpose of exploitation' is considered to be trafficking 'even if this does not involve any of [those] means'.[5] A 'child' is any person under eighteen,[6] and a 'victim' is 'any natural person who is subject to trafficking in human beings as defined' in the Convention.[7]

A key part of the Convention is Chapter VI, which addresses substantive criminal law issues. Parties are required to criminalise the conduct of trafficking, if committed intentionally.[8] The Convention also requires parties to criminalise related actions concerning the forgery of travel and identity documents, and states that parties shall 'consider' criminalising the use of services of a victim, 'with the knowledge that the person is a victim of trafficking in human beings'.[9] The parties must also criminalise attempts and aiding and abetting any of these offences.[10] Legal persons must also be subject to liability, which need not necessarily be criminal in nature.[11]

As for penalties for the offences, they must be 'effective, proportionate and dissuasive'.[12] Legal persons must be subject to sanctions, which need not be criminal.[13] State Parties must provide that it is an 'aggravating circumstance' if: the core offence has 'deliberately or by gross negligence endangered the life of the victim'; 'the offence was committed against a child'; 'the offence was committed by a public official in the performance of her/his duties'; or 'the offence was committed within the framework of a criminal organisation'.[14] They must also provide for the confiscation of instrumentalities and proceeds of trafficking offences,[15] and shut down establishments where the offence was committed or deprive a person of the exercise of an activity in the course of which the offence was committed.[16]

Parties are obliged to adopt legislation to take into account previous convictions for trafficking handed down in other States when determining a sentence.[17] Finally, Chapter IV of the Convention provides that Parties must provide for the possibility of not imposing penalties on trafficking victims for the commission of crimes which they were forced to commit.[18]

Chapter V of the Convention contains a number of provisions relevant to criminal procedure. As for jurisdiction, Parties are obliged to take jurisdiction where the offence took place in its territory, in a ship flying its flag, in an aircraft registered there, by one of its citizens or a stateless person habitually resident there (subject to further conditions) or against one its citizens.[19] However, Parties can enter a reservation not to apply one or both of the final two requirements.[20] Parties must establish jurisdiction over an offender if they refuse to extradite him or her on grounds of nationality.[21] In the event that an offence falls within the jurisdiction of more than one party, parties shall 'consult with a view to determining the most appropriate jurisdiction for prosecution'.[22]

This Chapter also provides that the prosecution of an offence must not be made dependent on a complaint by the victim, at least where the act took place in whole or part on its territory.[23] If the offence took place in a State where the victim does not reside, there is a procedure to transmit the complaint from the State of residence to another State.[24] Relevant NGOs must be able to assist the victim.[25] State Parties must protect victims, witnesses and other collaborators from retaliation.[26] There should be specialists and coordination bodies in place as regards trafficking offences, as well as the training of officials and possibly national rapporteurs.[27] As regards court proceedings, State Parties must protect victims' private life, identity and safety.[28]

The Convention also contains rules on: the prevention of trafficking and measures to discourage demand;[29] border measures;[30] the security, control, legitimacy and validity of documents;[31] victims' rights (as regards identification, protection of private life, assistance to victims, a recovery and reflection period, a residence permit, compensation, and repatriation and return);[32] international cooperation and cooperation with civil society;[33] a monitoring mechanism;[34] and final provisions.[35]

European Convention on Human Rights (ECHR)

All 47 Council of Europe members have ratified the ECHR. As regards trafficking in persons, Article 4(1) ECHR prohibits holding people in slavery or servitude,[36] and Article 4(2) proscribes any requirement to perform forced or compulsory labour.[37] According to the European Court of Human Rights, Article 4 creates positive obligations for States to criminalise actions by private persons; 'forced or compulsory labour' covers cases where an underage migrant who had not been authorised to reside feared police arrest and expulsion and was induced by promises of a regularised status; 'slavery' means a case of actual ownership of a person; and 'servitude' is 'an obligation to provide one's services that is imposed by the use of coercion'.[38] Moreover, trafficking in persons, as defined *inter alia* in the Council of Europe Convention, falls within the scope of Article 4, and there is a positive obligation on States to take operational measures to protect persons from trafficking if their authorities 'were aware, or ought to have been aware, of circumstances giving rise to a credible suspicion that an identified individual had been, or was at a real and immediate risk of being, trafficked'.[39]

United Nations

The main United Nations' measure in this area is a Protocol to the UN Covnention on transnational organised crime (the 'UN Protocol'), which was signed in 2000 and entered into force on 25 December 2003.[40] It now has 143 parties. This Protocol defines 'trafficking in persons' in the same way as the Council of Europe Convention,[41] although it only applies where the offence is transnational.[42] State Parties must criminalise the offence concerned.[43]

Chapter II of the Protocol concerns the protection of victims, and contains rules on assistance to and the protection of victims, the immigration status of victims and the repatriation of victims.[44] Chapter III concerns the prevention of trafficking, information exchange, border measures, security and the control of documents, and the legitimacy and validity of documents.[45] There is a 'savings clause' for international human rights and refugee law, along with non-discrimination principles.[46]

EU measures

The EU has adopted not only criminal law measures dealing with trafficking in persons (section 4.1), but also a Directive on the immigration status of trafficking victims who assist in prosecutions (section 4.2),[47] as well as a number of soft law measures.[48] The EU has also concluded the relevant Protocol to the UN Convention on organised crime.[49]

Criminal law framework

The first EU measure to address the issue of trafficking in persons, which also reflects obligations pursuant to international human rights law to combat slavery and forced labour,[50] was a Joint Action adopted in 1997, which also addressed the issue of pornography and prostitution.[51] This was replaced in 2002 by a Framework Decision, which Member States had to implement by 1 August 2004.[52] That measure will in turn be replaced in 2011 by a Directive proposed by the Commission in March 2010,[53] which was agreed by the Council in June 2010,[54] and then between the Council and the EP in December 2010.[55] It should be noted at the outset that neither the 2002 Framework Decision nor the 2010 proposal limit themselves to the issue of persons trafficked for the purposes of prostitution.

The EU's Framework Decision applies to all 27 Member States, of which 20 have ratified the Council of Europe's Convention and 26 have ratified the UN Protocol at time of writing.[56] Moreover, the Framework Decision had to be applied before the Council of Europe Convention was even signed.[57] The Framework Decision is in principle subject to the jurisdiction of the EU's Court of Justice, either by means of a reference from the national courts of the 19 Member States which have opted into the Court's jurisdiction over EU criminal law measures adopted before the entry into force of the Treaty of Lisbon,[58] or by means of a request to settle a dispute about the application of the Framework Decision between Member States.[59] However, the replacement EU Directive will only apply to 25 Member States, since the legal framework allows the UK to opt-out and requires Denmark to do so.[60] But the existing Framework Decision will remain in force as regards the UK and Denmark, and also as regards other EU Member States and those countries.[61] Also, the judicial framework as regards EU criminal law has changed following the Treaty of Lisbon: the Directive will be subject to references to the EU's Court of Justice from any of the national courts in any of the Member States which will be bound by the Directive, and the EU Commission will have the power to bring infringement proceedings against Member States to ensure that the Directive is applied on time and transposed correctly.

The Framework Decision requires Member States to adopt criminal sanctions to combat trafficking in human beings, a concept with a three-part definition which closely matches the definition in the earlier UN Protocol and the later Council of Europe Convention on this issue. The only differences are that there is no reference to the removal of organs in the Framework Decision, whereas the Framework Decision (but not the Council of Europe Convention or the UN Protocol) makes an additional reference to trafficking for the purposes of pornography.[62] As with the Council of Europe Convention and the UN Protocol, where the specified types of force are applied, the consent of the victim is irrelevant,[63] and where a child is involved, there is no requirement that force was used.[64] There is no requirement of a cross-border element to the offence, or that the victim must be the national of another State. However, it is notable that the Framework Decision, unlike the Convention and Protocol, does not require the acts to be intentional in order for them to be criminalised. Moreover, the Framework Decision does not require Member States to provide for offences as regards the forgery of documents relating to trafficking, or to consider criminalising the use of services of a victim.

As noted above, at the end of 2010, the Council and European Parliament agreed on a new Directive on trafficking in persons, which will, after adoption, replace the existing Framework Decision on this issue.[65] The agreed Directive will amend the definition of 'exploitation' to include the exploitation of 'begging' or of criminal activities, or the removal of organs.[66] The acts will also have to be intentional.[67] Also, the Directive, like the Convention, will require Member States to consider criminalising the use of services of a victim, if there is knowledge that the person concerned was the victim of trafficking.[68] On this point, it should also be noted that a subsequent Directive requires Member States to criminalise employers who use 'work or services exacted from an illegally staying third-country national with the knowledge that he or she is a victim of trafficking in human beings', where the employer has not been charged or convicted of an offence pursuant to the Framework Decision on trafficking in persons.[69]

In light of this, the trafficking Directive will only be relevant on this point where a person who is *not* an employer uses the services of trafficking victims – for example a prostitute's client.[70]

The Framework Decision (and in future the Directive) also require Member States to criminalise aiding and abetting trafficking offences, as well as attempts to commit such offences or to instigate them.[71]

There is a basic obligation under the Framework Decision to impose 'effective, proportionate and dissuasive' criminal penalties for commission of the relevant offences.[72] The Directive will oblige Member States instead to provide for a possible maximum sentence of at least five years in duration for trafficking offences.[73]

Furthermore, Member States must ensure that a maximum sentence of at least eight years for trafficking in persons is possible,[74] in four particularly serious circumstances: endangering the life of the victim deliberately or by gross negligence;[75] committing the offence against a 'particularly vulnerable' victim, including at least children below the age of sexual majority trafficked for the purpose of sexual exploitation;[76] using serious violence in order to commit the offence or causing 'particularly serious harm to the victim';[77] or committing the crime within the framework of a 'criminal organisation' as defined by an EU measure on organised crime, but without the threshold for criminal liability set out in that measure.[78] In the future Directive, the maximum possible sentence in these cases will be raised to ten years from eight, and the definition of a 'particularly vulnerable' victim will now include *all* child victims.[79] The Directive will also require Member States to treat cases where a public official committed the offence in the performance of his or her duties as an aggravated circumstance, although it will not specify a minimum increased penalty in this case.[80] There are also standard provisions on the liability of legal persons.[81]

As for previous convictions for trafficking,[82] the EU has more general legislation on this issue, which requires all prior convictions handed down by other Member States to be taken into account as regards all aspects of criminal procedure in a Member State.[83] The Directive will include a rule, based on the Convention, which requires Member States to confiscate the proceeds and instrumentalities related to trafficking offences.[84]

It should be noted that there is a separate Framework Decision on the confiscation of criminal proceeds, which requires Member States to take measures against the proceeds of this crime in certain circumstances.[85] Moreover, the EU's mutual recognition measures have generally required Member States to relinquish the dual criminality principle as regards the crime of trafficking in human beings,[86] meaning that proceedings for this crime involving two Member States should in principle be simplified.

Next, the Directive will provide, like the Council of Europe Convention, that Member States shall provide that national authorities are entitled not to prosecute or impose penalties on the victims of trafficking offences, where they were compelled to commit criminal activities as a direct consequence of being victims of trafficking.[87]

As for jurisdiction over trafficking offences, the Framework Decision requires Member States to take jurisdiction where an act is carried out on its territory, by one of its nationals or for the benefit of a legal person established in its territory.[88] Member States can derogate from the second and third jurisdictional rules if they inform the Council.[89] In any event, each Member State must either prosecute or extradite when the relevant conduct has been committed by its own nationals outside its territory.[90] There is no requirement to consult in the event of competing jurisdiction,[91] but then a later Framework Decision addresses this issue in more detail as regards all crimes.[92] It should also be noted that EU law includes rules preventing prosecution in multiple Member States for the same acts, once a trial has been disposed of finally in a first Member State; these rules are undoubtedly applicable to trafficking offences.[93] Under the agreed Directive on trafficking in persons, jurisdiction over human trafficking offences will be extended also to any offences committed by nationals of a Member State, without any possibility of derogation by Member States.[94] As regards offences committed by their citizens outside their territory, Member States will not be allowed to make prosecution dependent upon the act being an offence in the territory where it was committed, upon a report by the victim or upon a denunciation by the State where the act was committed.[95]

The Framework Decision, like the Council of Europe Convention, requires Member States to permit investigations or prosecutions to begin in the absence of a complaint by a victim, at least in cases where the acts took place on national territory.[96] The future Directive will go further, by removing the territorial limitation on this point, and by requiring Member States to ensure that 'criminal proceedings may continue even if the victim has withdrawn his or her statement.'[97] The Directive will also provide for Member States to permit prosecutions for trafficking for 'a sufficient period of time after the victim has reached the age of majority', and will require that Member States ensure that the relevant persons receive training and that there must be 'effective investigative tools' available to investigators and prosecutors.[98]

Member States are obliged to protect the child victims of trafficking by reference to the EU's Framework Decision on crime victims' rights;[99] the latter measure also (*inter alia*) sets out a procedure to transfer a victim's complaint between Member States.[100] The future Directive will include further detailed new rules on protection and assistance for victims,[101] in particular child victims.

As for the prevention of trafficking, the Directive includes some general provisions.[102] Finally, the Directive requires Member States to establish national rapporteurs on trafficking, and sets out the details of their role;[103] it also requires the EU to set up an anti-trafficking coordinator.[104]

According to the Commission's report on the national application of the Framework Decision,[105] most Member States implemented the definition of trafficking sufficiently in national law, including as regards inchoate offences. Equally Member States had applied the rules on penalties, although there was a wide variation in penalties in practice. The large majority of Member States applied the rules concerning extra-territorial jurisdiction,[106] but it was difficult for the Commission to assess whether the specific provisions on victims were complied with.

Further information on the practical application of the Framework Decision is set out in the Commission's 2008 communication on the issue of trafficking in persons,[107] which states that there has been a steady increase in the number of prosecutions for trafficking related to sexual exploitation to 1,500 a year by 2006, although this fell short of estimates of 500,000 persons trafficked each year into the EU.[108] Most countries offered police protection and compensation to very few victims in practice.

Immigration status of trafficking victims

Due to public concern about the fate of victims of trafficking in persons and the apparent difficulties in prosecuting the perpetrators of trafficking crimes, since the victims who could testify against them were usually irregular migrants subject in principle to expulsion, the Council considered it necessary to adopt Directive 2004/81 in April 2004, addressing the issue of the immigration status of these victims.[109] Member States had to implement the Directive by 6 August 2006.[110] The Directive does not apply to the UK, Ireland or Denmark.

Directive 2004/81 defines the conditions for issuing a limited residence permit, linked to the length of the judicial proceedings, to persons who cooperate in the fight against trafficking or the facilitation of illegal immigration.[111] The Directive defines trafficking and the facilitation of illegal immigration by reference to the EU acts concerning these issues, but the definition in the EU acts is not exhaustive.[112] Member States are obliged to apply the Directive to victims of trafficking in persons, including those who did not enter legally.[113] However, its application to minors is optional.[114]

The preamble sets out a safeguard clause on protection for refugees, persons with subsidiary protection and asylum seekers, along with human rights treaties, and also includes a non-discrimination clause.[115] On this point, it is conceivable that some victims might have a valid claim for international protection, if non-state persecutors (i.e. the criminal organisations which trafficked those victims) pose a sufficient risk of inflicting serious harm or persecution as defined by the EU Directive on qualification for refugee status or subsidiary protection.[116] Member States are free to provide for more extensive protection for persons covered by the Directive.[117]

Member States' authorities will usually trigger the application of the Directive by informing persons whom they believe could fall within its scope, although Member States have an option to decide if NGOs or associations specifically appointed by the Member State concerned can also trigger the process.[118] After that point, there is a reflection period for the persons concerned to decide if they wish to cooperate with the authorities; the starting point and length of this period are determined by national law.[119] During this period, expulsion orders cannot be enforced,[120] and the person concerned is entitled to minimum standards of treatment as regards subsistence, emergency medical treatment, translation and interpretation, and legal aid.[121] The reflection period does not create a right to subsequent residence,[122] and a Member State may end the period if the person concerned 'actively, voluntarily and on his/her own initiative' renews contact with the perpetrators, or on grounds of public policy or national security.[123] Following (or possibly before) the end of the reflection period, the national authorities shall consider the 'opportunity presented by' the continued stay of the victim, his or her intention to cooperate, and whether he or she has severed relations with the perpetrators,[124] before issuing a residence permit. However, the Directive does not appear to create a right to a permit if the conditions are met.[125] The permit must be valid for at least six months, and may be renewed if these conditions are still met.[126] Member States are encouraged to consider authorising the stay of the victim's family members on other grounds.[127]

The Directive also sets out rules on the treatment of the victims after the special permit is issued. Member States must continue to extend minimum standards regarding subsistence, emergency medical treatment, translation and interpretation, and (optionally) legal aid to victims, and must also give necessary medical or other assistance to victims with special needs and without sufficient resources.[128] If Member States apply the Directive to minors, they must take account of the best interests of the child, give access to education on the same basis as nationals (although this may be limited to the public education system), and establish the identity and nationality of, trace the family members of, and ensure legal representation for unaccompanied minors in accordance with national law.[129] Member States must define the rules for victims' access to the labour market, vocational training, and education during the period of the residence permit; this does not appear to grant them discretion over whether to allow such access, but only discretion as regards the extent of and procedures for exercising such access.[130] The persons concerned by the Directive must be given access to schemes designed to assist them to develop a normal social life, if such schemes exist, including courses to improve professional skills or to prepare for an assisted return to their country of origin. Member States may also provide for special schemes designed for the persons concerned, and may make the residence permit conditional on participation in either the general or special schemes.[131] Moreover, the subsequent Returns Directive provides that an 'entry ban' as defined by that Directive shall not be issued to victims of trafficking, although this is 'without prejudice' to the obligation to issue an entry ban if an obligation to return has not been complied with, and also subject to a derogation on grounds of 'public policy, public security or national security'.[132]

The permit shall not be renewed if the proceedings are over or if the conditions for its issue cease to be satisfied. After this point, normal immigration law applies,[133] but the preamble to the Directive states that Member States 'should consider the fact that' the person concerned already has a residence permit issued on the basis of this Directive if that person applies to stay on another ground.[134] The permit may also be withdrawn on grounds of: the person concerned 'actively, voluntarily and on his/her own initiative' renewing contact with the suspected perpetrators; the authorities' belief in fraudulent cooperation or a fraudulent complaint by the person concerned; public policy or national security; the person concerned ceasing to cooperate; and discontinuation of the proceedings. These grounds are non-exhaustive ('in particular').[135]

In 2008,[136] the Commission reported that the reflection period was not being applied in practice in most Member States. Residence permits were available for periods of between 40 days and one year, and most often for six months. Victims have access to the labour market in accordance with the Directive in every Member State except Poland. The available figures from nine Member States indicated that 2,676 victims had received permits, but 80 per cent of those were in Italy, which had a pre-existing and very generous status for trafficking victims. The Commission concluded that 'at EU level the situation is still largely unsatisfactory', but also noted that 'in countries . . . which have a significant number of assisted victims, figures on criminal proceedings are also higher . . . [t]herefore, further regulation might be necessary in order to ensure more effective victim support mechanisms'.

In 2010, the Commission issued a fully-fledged report on the application of the Directive.[137] In the Commission's view, there were some deficiencies in the definition of 'trafficking' by Member States. Two Member States used the option not to apply the Directive to minors. Some Member States did not sufficiently ensure that information was made available to trafficking victims. The length of the reflection period varied widely, although it was not clearly set out or mandatory in some Member States. One Member State did not prevent removals during the reflection period. Some Member States did not properly transpose the provision for a possible termination of the reflection period, or required additional documentation before a residence permit could be obtained. Nine Member States additionally permitted trafficking victims to stay even if they were not cooperating with the authorities. In some cases, the rules on support for victims were not adequately applied. The requirement to locate the family members of unaccompanied minors was not fully applied in several Member States. Only one Member State prevented access to employment for victims, while another imposed a licence requirement.

As for the impact of the Directive in practice, five Member States gave out more than 100 permits a year, while five gave out fewer than 20; the other Member States provided no or insufficient information. This was a small fraction of the overall numbers who were trafficked in some Member States. The Commission threatened to bring infringement proceedings against those Member States which were not applying the Directive correctly, and for the future suggested that there might be a need for amendments to the Directive as regards 'the possibility of issuing a temporary residence permit based on the vulnerable situation of the victim and not necessarily in exchange for cooperation with competent authorities', having 'a specified length of reflection periods for victims', 'strengthening the framework of treatment, in particular for minors', and a 'reinforcement of the obligation to inform victims of their rights'.

This evidence proves that the Directive, as it currently stands, was unable to avoid the inherent tension between trying to combat irregular immigration by encouraging the victims of trafficking and smuggling to testify, and the risk that the incentives offered to the victims would either be abused or have the result that the victims would be able to stay in the 'host' Member State longer than it would wish. Moreover, the Directive contains more limited provisions on the status of victims than the UN Protocol or the Council of Europe Convention on trafficking in persons.[138] In particular, the Council of Europe Convention requires some assistance to be given to all victims, whether or not they cooperate with the authorities, and lays down a minimum reflection period of 30 days.

It seems clear that the Directive has not made a significant contribution to its main goal of combating trafficking in persons. Possibly a revision of the Directive along the lines suggested by the Commission will change the situation.

Appraisal

While the UN Protocol suffers from a largely criminal-law focus on the trafficking issue, with limited provision on the status of and protection of victims, the Council of Europe Convention attempts an holistic interdisciplinary approach to the issue. It is too early to tell whether the Council of Europe Convention is effective at achieving its aims, since the process of monitoring their implementation has not yet led to any reported evaluations.

As for the EU, the legal framework suffers from only a partial application of the measures set out in the Council of Europe Convention, scattered across two main measures as well a number of general legal acts. Compared to the international measures on this issue, the agreed text of the Directive now corresponds to or goes further than the Council of Europe and UN measures as regards the definition of trafficking, prevention of the offence, jurisdiction and rules concerning victim protection, and assistance in the context of criminal law. The EU rules also go further in that they set specific possible sentences for the offences concerned. At least the EU measures, now including the Directive on criminal law measures, are more easily enforceable in the national courts and the Court of Justice than any international measures.

On the other hand, the Directive on the immigration status of victims appears, as noted above, to have had a modest effect, and there are a number of key provisions of the Council of Europe Convention in particular that are not reflected in EU law (as regards prevention, broader victim assistance, discouraging demand, identification of victims, and international cooperation). It seems likely that the international and regional legal framework needs to be further developed before it can play a decisive role in reducing human trafficking in practice. We still fall fowl to lessons in history that require us to re-examine why it is that our legislative arm with respect to the abuse of human rights, in the context of trading in human beings, falls wide of the mark.

Notes

1 K. Magliveras, *Combating Trafficking in Persons: The Role and Action of International Organisations* (Sakkoulas, 2007).
2 Neither the EU nor any non-European States have signed the Convention. Four Council of Europe States have not even signed the Convention: the Czech Republic, Liechtenstein, Monaco and Russia. The ten States which have signed but not ratified are: Andorra; Estonia; Finland; Germany; Greece; Hungary; Iceland; Lithuania; Switzerland; and Turkey. On the Convention, see A. Gallagher, 'Recent Legal Developments in the Field of Human Trafficking: A Critical Review of the 2005 European Convention and Related Instruments', 8 EJML (2006) 163.
3 Art. 4(a).
4 Art. 4(b).
5 Art. 4(c).
6 Art. 4(d).
7 Art. 4(e).
8 Art. 18.
9 Arts. 19 and 20.
10 Art. 21.
11 Art. 22.
12 Art. 23(1).
13 Art. 23(2).
14 Art. 24.
15 Art. 23(3).

16 Art. 23(4).
17 Art. 25.
18 Art. 26.
19 Art. 31(1).
20 Art. 31(2). There are reservations in force by Denmark, France, Latvia, Malta, Portugal, Slovenia, Sweden, the former Yugoslav Republic of Macedonia and the UK.
21 Art. 31(3).
22 Art. 31(4). It should be noted that the Council of Europe Convention on the transfer of proceedings (ETS 73) contains more detailed rules on this issue, but the list of parties to these two treaties only partly overlaps.
23 Art. 27(1).
24 Art. 27(2).
25 Art. 27(3).
26 Art. 28.
27 Art. 29.
28 Art. 30.
29 Arts. 5 and 6.
30 Art. 7.
31 Arts. 8 and 9.
32 Arts. 10–17.
33 Arts. 32–35.
34 Arts. 36–38.
35 Arts. 39–45.
36 It is not possible to derogate from this provision in times of emergency: see Art 15(2) ECHR.
37 This provision *is* subject to possible derogation pursuant to Art 15 ECHR; moreover, Art 4(3) ECHR lists forms of labour which are not covered by this proscription.
38 *Siliadin v France* (Reports of Judgments and Decisions 2005–VII). See H. Cullen, '*Siliadin v France*: Positive Obligations under Article 4 of the European Convention on Human Rights', 6 HRLR (2006) 585.
39 *Rantsev v Cyprus and Russia*, judgment of 7 Jan. 2010, not yet reported.
40 See generally A. Gallagher, 'Human Rights and the New UN Protocols on Trafficking and Migrant Smuggling: A Preliminary Analysis', 23 HRQ (2001) 975.
41 Art. 3. The Council of Europe Convention copied the definition in the Protocol, rather than the other way around.
42 Art. 4.
43 Art. 5.
44 Arts. 6–8.
45 Arts. 9–12. The latter three Articles are essentially identical to the matching provisions in the Council of Europe Convention.
46 Art. 15.
47 Dir. 2004/81 ([2004] OJ L 261/19). On the EU law framework in general, see H. Askola, 'Violence Against Women, Trafficking, and Migration in the European Union', 13 ELJ (2007) 204.
48 These comprise: Council conclusions on trafficking in persons ([2003] OJ C 137/1); Council resolution on the law enforcement response ([2003] OJ C 260/4); a Commission decision establishing an expert group of advisers ([2003] OJ L 79/25, replaced by [2007] OJ L 277/79); an Action Plan against human trafficking ([2005] OJ C 311/1); Council conclusions of Apr. 2006 (JHA

Council press release, 27–28 Apr. 2006); reports to the Council as regards trafficking for prostitution and the 2006 World Cup (Council docs 5008/07 and 5006/1/07, 3 Jan. and 19 Jan. 2007); Council conclusions of Nov 2007 (JHA Council press release, 8–9 Nov 2007); Council conclusions of June 2009 on an informal network of national rapporteurs (JHA Council press release, 4 June 2009). See also the Commission's communications on human trafficking (COM (2005) 514, 18 Oct. 2005 and COM (2008) 657, 17 Oct. 2008) and the reports and opinions of the expert group, online at: <http://ec.europa.eu/justice_home/doc_centre/crime/trafficking/doc_crime_human_trafficking_en.htm#Experts%20Group%20on%20Trafficking%20in%20Human%20Beings>, and the recommendations drawn up by the Commission for the 2007 Anti-Trafficking Day: <http://ec.europa.eu/justice_home/news/information_dossiers/anti_trafficking_day_07/documents_en.htm>.

49 [2001] OJ L 30/44 (signature); [2006] OJ L 262/44 and 51 (conclusion). See s. 3 above.

50 See s. 2.2 above.

51 [1997] OJ L 63/2.

52 [2002] OJ L 203/1. The other provisions of the Joint Action were replaced by a Framework Decision on sexual exploitation and child pornography ([2004] OJ L 13/44).

53 COM (2010) 95, 29 Mar. 2010; this replaced an earlier proposal for a new Framework Decision on this subject (COM (2009) 136, 25 Mar. 2009), which lapsed with the entry into force of the Treaty of Lisbon. On the 2010 proposal, see the comments by UNHCR, online at: <http://www.unhcr.org/4c0f932a9.html>, by a group of UN agencies and the ILO, online at: <http://www.lastradainternational.org/lsidocs/Joint%20UN%20letter%20ME Ps%20Directive%20Trafficking%20FINAL.pdf>, and by a group of NGOs, online at: <http://s3.amazonaws.com/rcpp/assets/attachments/1035_NGO_statement_for_EP_seminar_10_June_2010_original.pdf>.

54 Council doc. 10845/10, 10 June 2010.

55 Council doc. 17751/10, 17 Dec. 2010. The Directive is likely to be adopted formally in spring 2011, and Member States will have two years to implement it: Art. 22(1).

56 The exceptions are (for the Convention) the Czech Republic, Estonia, Finland, Germany, Greece, Hungary and Lithuania and (for the Protocol) the Czech Republic.

57 Romania had ratified the Convention before it joined the EU, but the Convention did not enter into force until after the date when it joined. As for the UN Protocol, the Framework Decision applied before the Protocol in 14 Member States: the exceptions are Bulgaria and Romania (which ratified the Protocol before joining the EU), as well as Cyprus, Denmark, Estonia, France, Latvia, Lithuania, Malta, Poland, Portugal, Spain and Sweden.

58 [2010] OJ C 56/7. The Member States which have not accepted the Court's jurisdiction over criminal law measures adopted before the entry into force of the Treaty of Lisbon are the UK, Ireland, Denmark, Poland, Bulgaria, Malta, Slovakia, and Estonia.

59 See the previous Art. 35 of the Treaty on European Union (TEU), which was repealed by the Treaty of Lisbon.

60 Ireland could also have opted out of the Directive, but chose instead to opt in. It is still possible for the UK to opt in at any point after the adoption of the Directive, or for Denmark to opt in later if the Danish public vote in a referendum to drop or modify their opt-out from EU Justice and Home Affairs

matters. On the UK reasons for opting out, and the case for the UK opting in, see S. Peers, 'Statewatch analysis: the new Directive on trafficking in persons', online at: <http://www.statewatch.org/analyses/no-113-trafficking.pdf>.

61 This is the necessary implication of Art. 21 of the agreed text, which only replaces the Directive as regards the Member States which participate in its adoption.

62 Art. 1(1), Framework Decision. However, exploitation for pornographic purposes is surely covered by 'other forms of sexual exploitation' in the Convention's and Protocol's definition. Also, the Framework Decision refers to the 'exchange or transfer of control' of a person, but this is surely covered by the Convention and Protocol as well, while the Framework Decision adds further definition as regards the concept of a 'position of vulnerability' (Art. 1(1)(c)).

63 Art. 1(2), Framework Decision.

64 Art. 1(3), Framework Decision; as in the Convention and Protocol, a 'child' is defined as any person under eighteen years of age (Art. 1(4)).

65 N. 55 above.

66 Agreed Art. 2(3). However, the explicit reference to 'pornography' as a form of exploitation will be dropped.

67 Agreed Art. 2(1).

68 Art. 18(4) of the agreed Directive; compare to Art. 19 of the Convention. The Directive will still not require Member States to criminalise the forgery of documents, et al., related to trafficking in persons; compare to Art. 20 of the Convention.

69 Art 9(1)(d) of Dir. 2009/52 on sanctions for employment of irregular migrants ([2009] OJ L 168/24); Member States must apply this Directive from 20 July 2011. This Directive does not apply to the UK, Ireland or Denmark. For more details on this Directive, see S. Peers, *EU Justice and Home Affairs Law*, 3rd edn (OUP, 2011), 546–557. The references in Directive 2009/52 to the Framework Decision on trafficking in persons will have to be understood as references to the Directive on the same issue, as regards the Member States participating in the latter: see Art. 21 of the latter Directive. Member States must also criminalise inciting and aiding or abetting such offences: Art 9(2), Dir. 2009/52. There is no provision on jurisdiction in Dir. 2009/52.

70 Art. 18(4) of the trafficking Directive will, however, have a broader scope in Ireland, since that Member State is not bound by Dir. 2009/52 (ibid).

71 Art. 2 of the Framework Decision; Art. 3 of the agreed Directive. The requirement to criminalise instigation goes further than the Council of Europe Convention or the UN Protocol: see Art. 21 of the Convention and Art. 5 of the UN Protocol. However, the UN Protocol does require States to criminalise 'organising or directing' trafficking (Art. 5(2)(c) of the Protocol), although the obligation to criminalise attempts is more limited (Art. 5(2)(a)).

72 Art. 3(1); the Convention contains the same rule (Art. 23(1)). There is no such provision in the UN Protocol.

73 Art. 4(1) of the Directive. The basic obligation to provide for 'effective' penalties, etc. is retained as regards inchoate offences (Art. 4(4) of the Directive). There is no reference in the Directive to the penalties which might be applicable if a Member State criminalises the use of services of trafficking victims, whereas Art. 23(1) of the Convention applies to such cases.

74 Compare to Art. 24 of the Convention, which lists 'aggravating circumstances' without specifying what higher penalties must apply.

75 Art. 3(2)(a), matching Art. 24(a) of the Convention.

76 Art. 3(2)(b). Art. 24(b) of the Convention states more simply that an offence committed against a child is always an 'aggravating circumstance'.

77 Art. 3(2)(c). This does not match Art. 24(c) of the Convention, which refers instead to offences committed by public officials.

78 Art 3(2)(d), referring to a 1998 Joint Action ([1998] OJ L 351/1) on organised crime, which has since been replaced by a Framework Decision ([2008] OJ L 300/42). Art. 24(d) of the Convention refers to acts committed within the framework of a criminal organisation, but without referring to a definition of that term. The UN Protocol does not provide for aggravating circumstances.

79 Agreed Art 4(2).

80 Agreed Art 4(3). This brings EU law into line with the Convention (Art. 24(c)).

81 Arts. 4–5, Framework Decision; Arts. 5–6 of the Directive. These provisions differ slightly from the Council of Europe Convention: compare to Arts. 22 and 23(2) and (4) of the latter. There are no equivalent provisions in the UN Protocol.

82 See Art. 25 of the Convention.

83 See the Framework Decision on this issue ([2008] OJ L 220/32), which Member States had to apply by 15 Aug. 2010. Moreover, the EU has put in place a framework to exchange information on criminal convictions in general, which is more advanced than the provisions of Council of Europe Conventions: see the Decision ([2005] OJ L 322/33) and the Framework Decision and Decision ([2009] OJ L 93/23 and 33; but note that Member States do not have to comply with the latter two measures until 27 April 2012).

84 Agreed Art. 7 of the Directive; compare to Art. 23(3) of the Convention.

85 Art. 3 of Framework Decision ([2005] OJ L 68/49).

86 See generally n. 69 above, Chapter 9.

87 Agreed Art. 8 of the Directive; compare to Art. 26 of the Convention. There is no such clause in the current Framework Decision.

88 Art 6(1), Framework Decision.

89 Art 6(2) and (4), Framework Decision.

90 Art 6(3), Framework Decision; compare to Art. 31(3) of the Convention (there is no jurisdiction rule in the UN Protocol). As between EU Member States, this provision is now largely irrelevant in light of the Framework Decision on the European Arrest Warrant ([2002] OJ L 190/1).

91 Compare to Art. 31(4) of the Convention.

92 [2009] OJ L 328/42, which Member States have to apply by 15 June 2012 (Art. 16); for analysis of this measure, see Peers, n. 69 above, 827–834.

93 Arts. 54–58 of the Schengen Convention ([2000] OJ L 239), which also apply to Norway, Iceland and Switzerland. Some Council of Europe Conventions contain similar rules. For details, see *Ibid.*, 834–854.

94 Agreed Art. 10(1). The current 'extradite or prosecute' rules will be dropped.

95 Agreed Art. 10(3).

96 Art 7(1), Framework Decision; compare to Art. 27(1) of the Convention.

97 Agreed Art. 9(1).

98 Agreed Art. 9(2) to (4).

99 Art. 7(2) and (3), Framework Decision on trafficking; on the Framework Decision on victims of crime ([2001] OJ L 82/1), see n. 69 above, 744–749.

100 Art. 11(2), Framework Decision on victims; compare to Art. 27(2) of the Convention.

101 Agreed Arts 11–17; compare to Arts. 28 and 30 of the Convention.

102 Art. 18; compare to Art. 5 of the Convention.

103 Art. 19; compare to Art. 29(4) of the Convention.

104 Art. 20.
105 COM (2006) 187, 2 May 2006.
106 The only relevant declaration available in the Council's register of documents concerns Hungary (Council doc. 13756/05, 26 Oct. 2005).
107 COM (2008) 657, n. 48 above.
108 For further statistics, see the impact assessment of the 2009 proposal for a new Framework Decision on this issue (SEC (2009) 358, 25 Mar. 2009), pp 7–12 and Annex I.
109 [2004] OJ L 261/19. See D. Haynes, 'Used, Abused, Arrested and Deported: Extending Immigration Benefits to Protect the Victims of Trafficking and to Secure the Prosecution of Traffickers' (2004) 26 HRQ 221 and H. Askola, *Legal Responses to Trafficking in Women for Sexual Exploitation in the European Union* (Hart, 2007).
110 Art. 17, Dir. 2004/81. All references in this subsection are to Dir 2004/81 unless otherwise indicated.
111 Art. 1.
112 Art. 2(b) and (c).
113 Art. 3(1).
114 Art. 3(3). The Directive defines 'minors' by reference to national law.
115 Recitals 4 and 7 in the preamble of the Directive.
116 Dir. 2004/83 ([2004] OJ L 304/12); there is a proposed new qualification Directive (COM (2009) 551, 1 Oct 2009), which is currently under discussion. See also Art. 11(6) of the agreed criminal law trafficking directive.
117 Art. 4.
118 Art. 5.
119 Art. 6(1)
120 Art. 6(2). Although the subsequent Returns Directive (Dir. 2008/115, [2008] OJ L 348/98) has created a *prima facie* obligation to expel irregular migrants, there is nonetheless a broad discretion for a Member State to refrain from issuing or to withdraw or suspend a return decision, or to postpone removal (Arts. 6(4) and 9(2), Dir. 2008/115). In any event, the entire Returns Directive is subject to more favourable provisions in other EU immigration and asylum law (Art. 4(2), Dir. 2008/115). This provision in Dir 2004/81 is obviously one example of a more favourable provision. Also, the obligation to postpone removal in Art. 6(2) entitles a Member State to permit the person concerned to work (see Art. 3(3), Dir. 2009/52, n. 69 above).
121 Arts. 6(2) and 7.
122 Art. 6(3).
123 Art. 6(4).
124 Art. 8(1).
125 See Art. 8(2).
126 Art. 8(3).
127 Recital 15 in the preamble.
128 Art. 9.
129 Art. 10. Art. 2(f) defines 'unaccompanied minors'.
130 Art. 11. The subsequent Dir. 2009/52 on employer sanctions for employing irregular migrants (n. 69 above) makes no express exception for victims of trafficking or smuggling who have such a permit, but it must be assumed that the granting of a residence permit pursuant to Dir. 2004/81 means that the person concerned is not an irregular migrant as long as that permit is valid (see Art. 2(b) and (d), Dir 2009/52).
131 Art. 12.

132 Art. 11(3), Dir. 2008/115 (n 120 above). Note that this protection will not apply if a victim falls outside the personal scope of the Returns Directive (see n. 69 above, pp. 563–575). Presumably the protection will also expire with the residence permit. However, Member States have considerable discretion on whether to issue or withdraw an entry ban in all such cases (Arts. 11(1) and (3), Dir. 2008/115).

133 Presumably the Returns Directive (ibid) would then normally apply, if the person concerned is within the scope of that Dir. This will trigger a *prima facie* obligation to issue a return decision (Art. 6(1) of that Directive), but Member States retain a broad discretion to grant an 'autonomous residence permit or other authorisation offering a right to stay for compassionate, humanitarian or other reasons' (Art. 6(4) of that Directive). As noted above, it is also possible that the person concerned might have a claim for international protection.

134 Recitals 15 and 18 in the preamble.

135 Art 14.

136 Communication on human trafficking (COM (2008) 657, 17 Oct 2008).

137 COM (2010) 493, 15 Oct. 2010.

138 See sections 2.1 and 3 above.

Chapter 4

Reparations

The universal periodic review and the right to development

Rohan Kariyawasam

> The right to development can only be compelling for those who find the principle on which it is based to be compelling.
>
> *(High Level Task Force on the implementation of the right to development, March 2010)*

Introduction

In the conference on reparations held at SOAS in 2008, I set out a proposal for the integration of the need to address the legacy of slavery in trade reform at a global level. Many advocates of trade reform promote the inclusion of a 'social clause' in the World Trade Organisation (WTO). Yet, there is a risk of having to compromise human rights principles if such principles are directly imported into the WTO, whose primary function it is to promote free trade and market access, and where these issues will take precedence over most concerns on human rights. As such, I suggest a different route for the purpose of addressing the legacy of the slave trade. The first step is to encourage states to acknowledge the events of the past and make real efforts to assess how these affect the present. This can be achieved (to some extent) by civil society pushing from the bottom-up to encourage political leaders to implement change. States, upon their acknowledgement of the facts, will in many cases out of political considerations create for themselves the benchmarks to achieve what they have promised the international community. This can be done through mechanisms, such as the *Universal Periodic Review* (UPR) discussed below. Commitments made through the UPR can be realised through the states' practices in the international trade arena. For instance, a state that has made a commitment at the UPR to address the legacy of the slave trade may enter into special bilateral or regional trade agreements with the countries affected by the legacy of slavery, granting the affected states preferential treatment on exported goods or access to specialised services, such as a technology transfer that could benefit capacity building for example. However, there are problems in using trade agreements of this sort which require a high level of commitment and resources and where the political will may be lacking.[1] Other, and perhaps more immediate forms of accommodation can be made, and also in line with trade, such as changes in domestic law to bring about the *Right To Development* (RTD), or a specific component of the RTD, such as a beneficial technology transfer (discussed below). The idea of enforcing the RTD has grown in recent years as the international community begins to recognise post-Doha that the concerns surrounding developing and least developing countries on development, subsidies and market access need to be seriously acted upon if any progress is to be made in future trade rounds. Both China and India can provide leadership in this area given their growing economic status. The next big push will be in trade in services. In this respect, a technology transfer will be crucial.

In previous work, I have argued for implementing the RTD – and specifically the Right To Development Tax Relief for a beneficial technology transfer (Kariyawasam 2006, 2008). In this chapter, I suggest how such a tax relief could be operationalised for the purposes of reparations. Countries (impacted by slavery) may have few tools to overcome the disadvantages inherited from colonialism and slavery. The advantage of using trade as a platform for reparations is that commitments by member states who have historically benefited from slavery can be quantified and measured concretely (viz., a tax relief system). Also, use of the UPR process takes place *outside* of the WTO structure. If the WTO alone is relied upon to achieve restitution for slavery (a most unlikely prospect) any progress in this area could be severely curtailed. And yet the tax relief I discuss in this chapter relies on a technology transfer, which is a trade issue and one that is covered by the TRIPS, a mandatory WTO covered agreement.

In addition, I emphasise the importance of the efforts being made by social movements and political pressure groups. Most states will not take any initiative for reparations unless there is a push from civil society from the bottom-up in those states to do so. As mentioned elsewhere in this book, the current administration in the USA is best positioned for providing the *political* leadership for the case for reparations. This chapter outlines how the UK could provide the *legal* means for a quantifiable measure of reparations and therefore act as a precedent for other countries, such as the USA and Canada. This is evidence of the interconnectedness of the various mechanisms for achieving restitution for the legacy of the slave trade.

The RTD tax relief as a form of reparations

As mentioned, this chapter looks to explain how a Right To Development Tax Relief can be used as a form of reparation for slavery. Other chapters in this book have explained the difficulties in establishing a case for reparations that can be litigated through the courts. For the various reasons given, which are better elaborated elsewhere, litigation does not look a very likely prospect. And yet many of the states that have suffered from the travesties of slavery still suffer from a lack of investment, manpower, technical skills, and a fully trained human capital base. A better argument for reparations (in my view) would be to encourage investment in affected states by also encouraging the historical trans-gressors to invest in technical skills, technology, research and develop-ment, education, health, and services. This could all be achieved through a beneficial technological transfer. I specifically mention 'beneficial' as any technology transferred would need to be *appropriate technology*. In order to be appropriate, technology must be connected to the place, resources, economics, culture, and the impact of its use (Soefstad and Sein, 2004). In this way, any technology transferred can be of real benefit to the receiving state.

It is possible to think of the right to development as a legally enforceable right and that this extends to both individuals and communities, and to states acting on behalf of both (Andreassen and Marks, 2010; Alston and Robinson, 2005).[2] The RTD can be seen as a vector of the individual human rights and one which is dependant on the effective implementation of a general set of social and economic rights within the country concerned. Also, it is not possible to envisage greater social and economic rights without also considering the enforcement of civil and political rights. Educating the human capital base is just as important as setting in place the right to a free press, the right to privacy, and the right to freedom of expression.

The aim of this chapter is to establish a mechanism for operationalising a beneficial technology transfer as a significant element under a general Right To Development and thereby to provide a means for reparations for the historical abuses of slavery. This chapter suggests that a RTD Tax Relief (discussed below) can be implemented and enforced through the UN's *Universal Periodic Review Mechanism* ('UPR'), established by the Human Rights Council ('HRC') in Resolution 5/1 of 18 June 2007.

The chapter sets out in outline a means for operationalising the RTD by providing for a *Technology Transfer Tax Credit* in WTO member state domestic law, and that would also be available to multinational corpor-ations (MNCs) registered for corporation tax purposes and who transfer appropriate technology to producers in DCs and/or LDCs, and specifically those countries impacted by the slave trade. The chapter argues that the UK, with a long tradition of providing aid to developing countries and with a relatively advanced tax collection regime, could provide leadership in operationalising the RTD, and developing a UPR reporting template to the HRC that could also be used as a template by other developed nations with a historical involvement in the slave trade. This could be achieved by implementing the tax credit scheme set out in this chapter, and then reporting on the performance of this scheme as part of the cycle of reviews envisaged under the UPR.

The right to development

The Senegalese jurist Keba M'Baye is widely credited with the initial idea of the 'Right To Development'. In 1972, at a lecture at the International Institute of Human Rights in Strasbourg, he argued: '*Every man has a right to live and a right to live better*' (M'Baye 1972: 503).

Over fourteen years later, the UN Declaration on the Right To Development (RTD), which states that the Right To Development is a human right,[3] was adopted by the UN General Assembly under resolution 4/128 on the 4 December 1986. Despite being in force for just under twenty years the Declaration, not being a legally binding instrument, has suffered from a lack of implementation and the political will required for international cooperation. Its evolution can be traced back to the transposition of *civil and political rights* (Articles 1 to 21 Universal Declaration of Human Rights)[4] and *economic, social, and cultural rights* (Articles 22 to 28 Universal Declaration of Human Rights) into two separate legally binding treaties: the *International Covenant on Civil and Political Rights* (ICCPR);[5] and the *International Covenant on Economic, Social, and Cultural Rights* (ICESCR).[6] As the (then) Independent Expert on the Right to Development, Arjun Sengupta, argued, 'it took many years of international deliberations and negotiations for the world community to get back to the original conception of integrated and indivisible human rights. The Declaration on the Right to Development was the result' (Sengupta 2000: 1). The Right to Development ('RTD') as a human right was subsequently reaffirmed in the Vienna Declaration adopted at the Second UN World Conference on Human Rights in Vienna, 1993.[7] Sengupta has described the RTD as (Independent Expert Report 2002: 5):

> . . . a composite right to a process of development; it is not just an 'umbrella' right, or the sum of a set of rights. The integrity of these rights implies that if any one of them is violated, the whole composite right to development is also violated. The independent expert describes this in terms of a 'vector' of human rights composed of various elements that represent the various economic, social and cultural rights as well as the civil and political rights. The realisation of the right to development requires an improvement of this vector, such that there is improvement of some, or at least one, of those rights without violating any other.

The UN Commission on Human Rights Independent expert on the right to development was subsequently replaced (in 2006) by a task force that could provide a broader base of expert advice on the implementation of the declaration on the right to development (HRC January 2010: paragraph 2). The task force was required to investigate criteria on the compliance of the *Millennium Development Goal* 8 (MDG 8-Global Partnerships) with the right to development (HRC January 2010: paragraph 2). According to the report on expert consultation by the high-level task force on the implementation of the right to development (sixth session, 2010), the task force has now reviewed 12 global development, aid and trade-based partnerships with a view to establishing *criteria* and *sub-criteria* in compliance with the right to development (discussed below). The aim of this exercise was to, 'Move the right to development from political commitment to development practice, using as a tool a set of criteria and operational sub criteria for the periodic evaluation of compliance with the right to development' (HRC January 2010: paragraph 4). Participants in the working group on RTD were clear that the primary addressees of these criteria were states and intergovernmental mechanisms and processes, such as the working group on the RTD, the Human Rights Council, the General Assembly, and the treaty monitoring bodies of the United Nations (HRC January 2010: paragraph 26).

These participants identified national institutions, academic institutions and civil society organisations as secondary audiences. In addition, they also recognised that under international human rights law, governments would be regarded as the duty bearers rather than the claimants of rights under the RTD. However, states also represented the *collective* interests of those people under their jurisdiction, which then gave them the right (potentially) to make claims under the RTD for their citizens (HRC January 2010: paragraph 28). The participants also made clear that the criteria that the task force were recommending would 'seek to provide greater content to the right to development and therefore must use terms which will last over time, while indicators may reflect current conditions and require revision to future use' (HRC January 2010: paragraph 30). The selection of the criteria and indicators would require close methodological scrutiny. These are discussed below.

RTD Criteria: Core Norm, attributes and indicators

The RTD draft criteria have now been published by the working group and high-level task force on the RTD (HRC March 2010: Annex). In the annex to the report, the task force set out a table listing the detailed criteria. The task force made clear the basic expectation of the RTD would be the 'Core Norm'. This Core Norm has three attributes (HRC March 2010: paragraph 2): '(a) States acting collectively in global and regional partnerships; (b)

States acting individually as they adopt and implement policies that affect persons not strictly within their jurisdiction; and (c) States acting individually as they formulate national development policies and programmes affecting persons within their jurisdiction' (HRC March 2010: Annex). Each of the three attributes is assessed by reference to several criteria, and these criteria in turn are referenced through a selection of sub-criteria. The sub-criteria are supported from a range of measurement tools listed in the footnotes to the Annex.[8] According to the high-level task force, the criteria and sub-criteria are meant to stay relatively stable, but the indicators are expected to change from time to time and as circumstances develop (HRC Add. 2: paragraph 13). With the criteria now at hand, the idea is to give states a tool by which their implementation of the RTD can be measured. However, not all states are happy with the draft criteria as outlined below.

Problems with indicators and recommendations

In the June 2010 report by the chairperson-rapporteur (Arjun Sengupta) (HRC June 2010), this makes clear that there are several problems or concerns with regard to the RTD criteria. For example some delegations felt that there was a lack of clarity on the three sub levels of the criteria. Also there were concerns on who would monitor the implementation of the RTD criteria and that there was a clear need to clarify the rights of peoples (HRC June 2010: paragraph 20). Others felt that the emphasis was slipping more to national efforts as opposed towards international cooporation, and that there was a need to emphasise shared responsibility and access to resources (thus rebalancing this with the commitments of the international community) (HRC June 2010: paragraph 22). There was concern also that the criteria seemed to be adopting a human rights-based approach to development. Some felt that the emphasis should be placed on strengthening the economic development capacity of states to promote and protect all human rights (HRC June 2010: paragraph 30). There was a perception that the criteria lacked an overall balance between national and international spheres of responsibility. Also that the criteria and corresponding sub criteria went beyond the contents of the RTD Declaration in looking at other issues, such as good governance and participation (HRC June 2010: paragraph 32).

The consensus was that the criteria would be circulated to governments and other entities so that they could be refined and further developed. Also, once agreement had been reached on a final set of criteria, the working group on the right to development would begin the process of developing a *reporting template* (HRC June 2010: paragraph 38). Although no definition for a reporting template was provided by the June meeting, I would imagine that such a template would basically allow member states to record their performance as against each of the agreed criteria and sub-criteria on the RTD. The reporting template could then be used within a human rights reporting mechanism, such as the UPR (discussed below), to monitor the actual implementation of member state commitments given in the reporting template on the RTD. In fact, the reference to the UPR has already been voiced by the Working Group on the RTD in two reports to the Human Rights Council. For example in its March report, the Working Group stated (HRC Add. 1 March 2010: paragraph 75) (HRC June 2010: paragraph 39):

> Second, governments have affirmed that the right to development must be treated on a par with other human rights. Other human rights, in the practice of treaty bodies monitoring them, are assessed using indicators. Unless the right to development is subject to assessment using indicators, it will not be on a par with other human rights. A similar argument applies to including this right in the universal periodic review.

The right to development tax relief

Having provided an overview to the RTD, the aim now is to show how one component of the RTD (i.e., a beneficial technology transfer) could be achieved by providing the means to incentivise the business community in states that have historically benefited from the slave trade (namely the UK, USA, Canada, etc.) to invest in states impacted by the slave trade. To incentivise the international business (MNCs) community to transfer appropriate technology to producers in the developing world, I would suggest a *Right to Development Tax Relief* ('RTD Tax Relief') that will operate in investor states and be administered jointly through the investor state's international development department and/or tax revenue department, and apply to any nationally registered MNC under relevant Company Act legislation in the investor state. To qualify for the RTD Tax Relief, MNCs will need to satisfy a minimum set of Technology Transfer Obligations (the 'Obligations'), which could be established by the WTO's Working Group on Trade and Transfer of Technology (WGTT), such Obligations to be annexed to the investor state's implementing legislation for the RTD Tax Relief (this is discussed further below with example to the UK). Examples of obligations could include: restrictions on the repatriation of IPR royalties from subsidiaries back to parents outside of the host (developing country) state; prohibitions on restrictions of *performance requirements* in favour of the host state;[9] prohibitions on *TRIPS Plus* provisions, etc. (Kariyawasam 2008).

Alternatively, the Commission on Intellectual Property (CIPR) suggests that the TRIPS Council should consider introducing *criteria* (note: confusingly these are not the same 'Criteria' referred to above with the RTD) to decide the basis on which Least Developed Countries (LDCs) should enforce the TRIPS obligations after 2016 (CIPR 2002: Chapter 8). In making this recommendation, the CIPR refers to a study completed by Lall and Albaladejo: 'Indicators of the Relative Importance of IPRs in Developing Countries' (UNCTAD 2001), which sets out various measures of scientific and technical capability in developing countries. Alternatively, the World Summit on the Information Society (WSIS) suggests in its Tunis Agenda an *ICT Opportunity Index* and a *Digital Opportunity Index* based on the work of the *Partnership on Measuring ICT for Development* (WSIS 2007). Both could help inform the creation of a set of Criteria or Obligations.

These Criteria (or Obligations) are a minimum set of legal terms on technology transfer, approved by the WTO's Working Group on Trade and Transfer of Technology, that would form the basis as to whether an MNC that included such terms in its technology transfer agreements with developing country producers/states would qualify for tax relief or not. This is a *legal test*, which if satisfied would qualify the MNC for a tax credit.

Under this proposed scheme, MNCs in investing states will notify their technology transfer agreements to the relevant investor state's international development department and/or tax revenue department[10] (as an example this is discussed more fully below with regard to the United Kingdom).[11] The appropriate scale for tax relief will be set by the investing state.

Any tax relief offered by a developed country to its MNCs as an incentive to offer a beneficial technology transfer to those states impacted by slavery will need to comply (in Europe for example) with EC rules on state aid and also with the WTO's Subsidies Agreement.[12] So for example, subsidies contingent upon the export of goods under the WTO are prohibited whereas services are allowed.[13] Here then we see an obvious restriction on how the RTD Tax-Relief could operate, namely that any technology transferred by MNCs to developing countries must be in the form of services only, for example technical know-how or consultancy services, and not in the form of goods (unless the rules were changed or agreed upon as a form of special and differential rights for DCs and LDCs, although this is unlikely). For DCs and LDCs therefore future negotiations under Article XV of GATS relating to subsidies must not stop the use of subsidies or tax-reliefs to encourage the transfer of technology to developing countries (Correa 2005: 253).

The significance of encouraging a beneficial technology transfer becomes more apparent if this can be directly linked to an improvement in development. A technology transfer to developing country producers (specifically slave-impacted states for example) can be either directly licensed or supplied as a form of foreign direct investment (FDI), usually through a commercial presence. Clearly technology has a role to play in helping to implement the UN's MDGs. In fact, as mentioned previously, the working party on the RTD has conducted extensive research on the connection of MDG 8 (Global partnerships) with the RTD (see below).

If the tax relief is to apply to MNCs, many of whom will be located in the developed world (and specifically in the context of the discussion on reparations to those developed countries with an historical role in the slave trade), a central question is whether these developed countries funding the relief should divert funds from ODA, or as part of a programme of Aid for Trade (AfT) in subsidising these already wealthy MNCs? This is a valid question, as funding such a tax relief (in this way) might seem morally reprehensible. I would argue (strongly) against diverting funds from ODA, but rather to the establishment of a dedicated tax relief funded by a state's treasury in line with other fiscal reliefs. We must recognise however the role of the private sector in being the gatekeepers of knowledge sourced from valuable R&D, who will be unwilling to give access to private property rights (IPRs) without some form of incentive, and also licensing intellectual property in states perceived to have weak IPR protection and enforcement regimes. And yet developing countries afflicted by the legacy of the slave trade need appropriate technology and many, particularly the LDCs, do not have the means to fund this where poverty is defined as less than US$1 a day.

Further, any attempt to solve social problems with technology must also address the *exclusion* of the illiterate community; the lack of basic education available in the appropriate language to help the most vulnerable and poor gain access to the appropriate technology; the lack of an efficient and adequate power supply; and the availability of food, clean drinking water, and sanitation. Unless these issues are addressed, any technology transferred by way of the private sector might lead to pockets of rapid economic growth but with the increased exclusion of the poorest.

This holistic approach is exactly what the RTD represents: the RTD is a vector of human rights and no one right (whether civil/political, economic, social or cultural) should be violated in favour of another. This has to be correct. In societies where there is disregard for the rule of law as well as low social cohesion and a state failure in the provision of basic human rights, such as subsistence, basic health care and a basic education, there is a risk that the role of the private sector in development could lead to uneven distribution and greater class polarisation, unless these gaps are effectively addressed. Also, there is a broader question here of the danger of responsibility for social obligations migrating from government – via government regulators or executive agencies – to the private sector, where accountability might be lower.

Joseph Stiglitz, a past chief economist of the World Bank, has called for economic growth to include objectives of sustainable development, egalitarian development and democratic development (note that the Articles of the World Bank prohibit its involvement in domestic politics). In pursuing these objectives Stiglitz calls for sound financial regulation, competition policy, and policies to facilitate the transfer of technology and transparency to make markets work that support development (Williamson 2000).

Reconciling the RTD tax relief with the RTD criteria

The criteria published by the Working Party on the Right To Development are a means by which the RTD can be operationalised in UN member states. These criteria are effectively a tool that member states can use to measure the implementation of the RTD in their territory. As mentioned above, the criteria (not the same criteria referred to in the section above on technology transfer) are set out in the Annex to the March 2010 report of the working group on the RTD (HRC Add.2 March 2010: 8). This Annex lists three *attributes* of the RTD: (1) is a 'comprehensive and human-centred development policy'; (2) is 'participatory human rights processes'; (3) is 'social justice in development'. It would now be useful to consider how the RTD tax relief as set out in the previous chapter can be reconciled against these attributes, criteria, sub-criteria and indicators of the RTD.

There are several criteria under which the RTD Tax Relief could fall. For example in attribute 1 – under 1(f) 'to promote and ensure access to adequate financial resources' – the sub-criteria at (1)(f)(i) is listed as 'domestic resource mobilisation' and the relevant indicator of this sub-criteria is 'effective taxation policies that ensure mobilisation of maximum available resources for fulfillment of human rights'. In the footnotes to the criteria, this indicator is defined as 'government revenue as a percentage of GDP'. It is unclear exactly what this means from the point of view of taxation, what is perhaps a more helpful criterion for the purposes of the RTD Tax Relief would be the next one down at 1(g) 'to promote and ensure access to the benefits of science and technology'. Here the relevant sub-criterion is listed as 1(g)(i) a 'poor technology development strategy', with the measurement indicator for this sub-criterion given as 'the existence of a policy framework for technology development targeted at poor people's needs'. Again the footnotes to the Annex describe this indicator as 'the existence of a national policy statement on science in technology'. This seems a little vague as a form of indicator upon which to measure the relevant sub-criteria.

Another relevant sub-criterion under 1(g) is 1(g)(iii) which is defined as 'manufacturing technology' with the relevant indicator being 'technology component of exports; performance requirement provisions in trade agreements'. However it is not clear from this definition whether this is in relation to goods and services, or just goods alone. The RTD Tax Relief will apply mainly to services (technology transfer in the form of know-how and technical assistance) given, as mentioned earlier, that the WTO

Subsidies Agreement places a restriction on goods, where subsidies that are contingent upon the export of goods are prohibited. Also of relevance under criterion 1(g), is sub-criterion 1(g)(iv), 'technology transfer, access and national capacity', where the relevant indicator is described as 'electricity consumption; Internet coverage; intellectual property and licensing, intellectual property and technology transfer provisions in trade agreements'.

The footnotes to the Annex define this indicator as 'bilateral trade agreements and regional trade agreements that include conditions tightening intellectual property rights protection beyond the agreed level of the TRIPS agreement'. This would imply that the technology transfer provisions are to be found in bilateral and regional trade agreements as well as private technology transfer agreements between licensor and licensee, or between a parent and a subsidiary through some form of FDI. Further the sub-criterion on information technology at 1(g)(vii) seems (to this author) to be an indicator that is too narrowly defined as 'access to telecommunications infrastructure'. Again the footnotes to the annexe define this indicator by reference to mobile telephone usage statistics only. This can be misleading, in that the telephone line density (the number of fixed lines per 100 population) could be much lower in some developing countries where mobile phone penetration is higher.

It is argued therefore that the RTD tax relief could fall either under criterion 1(f) on adequate access to financial resources, or under 1(g)(iv), the sub-criterion for technology transfer, access and national capacity.

Operationalising the RTD tax relief: the UK example

We have seen above how the RTD tax relief can be reconciled against each of the attributes, criteria, sub-criteria and indicators as developed by the high-level task force on the RTD. This section now looks at how the RTD tax relief can be implemented in national law. Given that the UK had a significant historical role in the slave trade, and a fairly well-developed tax collection machine, it would be useful to look at the implementation of the RTD tax relief under UK law, and that could form a precedent for other countries, such as the USA and Canada.

The company's wider duties and the technology transfer tax credit

The United Kingdom has recently amended its company law statute. Under the Companies Act 2006, at section 172, directors of companies now have statutory duties to have a due regard towards stakeholders and the *wider community* when considering companies' actions. Under section 172(1), directors have a duty to the company to act in good faith, to promote the success of the company for the benefit of its members as a whole. Directors must have due regard towards: the consequences of any decisions in the long-term,[14] company employees, suppliers and customers,[15] and the company's impact on the community and environment.[16] Also, directors must have due regard towards the high standards of business conduct and the need to act fairly between members of the company.[17] Section 170 of the act makes clear that this is a general statutory duty and replaces the common law rules, although s.170(4) also requires the court to have regard to the existing interpretation and development of common law principles (for example the laws of agency).

As directors of companies now have a statutory obligation to regard the wider community under UK law, the question is whether this obligation can be extended in developing countries where UK companies operate? If so, directors may also then need to consider the impact that their company is having on business partners, suppliers, and the local community overseas. Good corporate social governance would indicate that providing a beneficial technology transfer to producer partners in the developing world where UK companies operate would fall within the scope of such duties. In other words, though this is not a formal obligation to do so, that so long as a commercial incentive exists, that getting the UK company to provide beneficial technology transfer would satisfy and provide evidence for an effective corporate social governance scheme. Evidence of duties carried out under s.172(1)(c) and (d) in having regard to the need to foster the company's business relationships with suppliers, customers and others, and also having regard to the impact of the company's operations on the developing country community and environment respectively; evidence that could be published in a company's annual report for example and open to inspection by stakeholders, shareholders, and ethically-minded trust and investment funds. Dine (2010) has argued that the new UK Companies Law Act 2006 is a way to reform directors' duties. She argues that, 'Directors have a duty to have regard to a large constituency of companies. A radical structural reform could reform companies into an instrument of equality using a new concept known as a Post-concession system. Stakeholders would be assessed on the way that they run risks for their companies, not only economic risks but also psychological risks and the happiness of their constituents' (Dine 2010: 1). There is much to be said for this approach which resonates with a general desire to provide an appropriate technology transfer to those states impacted by slavery. But as mentioned above, there also needs to be a commercial incentive for doing so. This incentive could come in the form of an RTD Tax Credit, or in the case of UK implementing law (for example), this could be suitably renamed as a *Technology Transfer Investment Tax Credit*.

It has been well documented that a technology transfer is key to the implementation of the RTD (Kariyawasam 2008: Chapters 8/9). One way to incentivise multinationals to provide a beneficial technology transfer is to grant them tax relief to do so. As mentioned if there is a general duty under s.172 of the Companies Act 2006 for directors to have regard for the wider community, the need to do so would be further strengthened if there was a commercial incentive operating alongside.

Presently, under the UK Finance Act 2002, the Finance Act provides for a community investment tax relief. At s.57 of the Act, the community investment tax relief is defined as a tax relief to those companies providing finance to community development finance institutions on lending to enterprises in *disadvantaged* communities that are excluded from mainstream sources of finance.

There is no reason why an RTD tax relief (or in the UK, a *Technology Transfer Investment Tax Credit*) could not be based on a similar mechanism as established by s.57. Schedule 16 of the Finance Act defines a community investment tax relief and sets out the eligibility for that tax relief. Under the Finance Act, where a corporation makes an investment into a community development finance institution, the company is eligible to receive a tax credit of up to 5 per cent per annum of the amount invested in the community development finance institution and which may be claimed in the tax year in which the investment is made and in each of the four subsequent years.[18] Such relief could constitute a substantial amount for a public company and therefore a serious commercial incentive to act.

In a similar way, and subject to implementing legislation, a UK company that has a *qualifying* technology transfer agreement can register the agreement with the Department for International Development (DFID). So long as the agreement is qualifying in that it complies with a relevant set of criteria (as described above), the DFID in exercising duties delegated to it by the Secretary of State under the implementing legislation would be able to grant the transferor of technology a tax credit. In order to bring this into effect, the Finance Act 2002 would need to be amended by statutory instrument to allow for a new form of corporate tax relief certificate, which MNCs could then use to offset against corporation tax (for example). The regulatory amendment bringing this into effect (a statutory instrument) could then be notified under the United Nations UPR process as part of the UK's commitment to operationalise the RTD.

The UPR reviews take place in four-yearly cycles. The UK is next up for review in 2012 and then again in 2016. It is important to note however that the participants to the report of the working group on the RTD in its eleventh session (Geneva, 26–30 April 2010) indicated that it would 'not be appropriate to mainstream the right to development into the work of human rights treaty bodies and the universal periodic review before a reporting template was prepared' (HRC June 2010: 39). However, although this would be wise, in that it would provide for a consistent monitoring of implementation of the criteria for the RTD, there is no restriction as far as the UPR process is concerned in requiring such a template to be in place beforehand. Any domestic measure that implements human rights commitments covered by the UPR can be notified as evidence of a member states' improvement in human rights enforcement. The UPR is discussed next.

The Universal Periodic Review (UPR)

The universal periodic review is the UN process that involves reviewing the human rights records of all 192 UN member states once every four years. The UPR allows each state the opportunity to declare the steps they have taken to improving human rights within their territory and the steps that they intend to take to improve the position. Also, the UPR process allows states to share human rights practices that are considered the best practice developed globally. The UPR is a unique process which was established by the Human Rights Council (HRC) in March 2006 and following the resolution of the General Assembly (resolution 60/251). This resolution mandated the HRC to 'undertake a universal periodic review, based on objective and reliable information, the fulfillment by each state of its human rights obligations and commitments in a manner which ensures universality of coverage and equal treatment with respect to all states' (HRC April 2006: section 5(e)). On 18 January 2007 the HRC agreed an institution-building package, with one of its elements being the universal periodic review.

The reviews are conducted by the UPR working group, which consists of 47 members of the HRC (although any UN member state can take part in dialogue with the state under review). Each state review is assisted by a *troika* (a group of three states drawn from lots prior to each working group session). The review is based upon documents submitted to the UPR working group. These documents consist of: (1) information provided by the state under review, which can take the form of a 'national report'; (2) information from independent human rights experts and groups, known as the 'special procedures', human rights treaty bodies, and other UN entities; (3) information from other stakeholders including non-governmental organisations and national human rights institutions.

At the relevant review session of the working group, the state under review will present its national report as well as the answers to any written questions it has received in advance. Any questions that other member states wish to pose to the state under review will have been submitted in advance to the troika. At the review session, states can then take to the floor to ask questions and make recommendations about the documentation provided by the state under review. This is therefore a very effective technique in ensuring that that state is challenged on any promises it has made or where there are gaps in its response to questions.

A report is then prepared by the troika (in consultation with the state under review). This report, known as the 'outcome report', gives a summary of the review. The outcome report is adopted at a later meeting of the working group and no sooner than 48 hours after the country review. Following the adoption of the outcome report, the state is then required to implement any recommendations contained in the final outcome reports. When the time comes for the second review of the state under the UPR, the state under review will need to provide information on what they have done (or not done) to implement recommendations made during the first review (four years earlier) (Universal Periodic Review 2010).

In this way, the UPR can provide an effective means to check for implementation of the tax relief on a beneficial technology transfer as a component of the RTD.

Conclusion

This chapter has set out a means for operationalising the RTD and specifically with regard to a beneficial technology transfer as a means of reparations to countries impacted by the abuses of slavery. The UK has a well-documented role in the historical slave trade and this chapter has recommended operationalising one component of the RTD by means of an amendment to the UK Finance Act 2002, and creating a new tax relief for those companies in the UK who provide the transfer of appropriate technology to producers in countries impacted by the slave trade. As described above, in order to qualify for the tax credit, a UK company will need to submit its technology transfer agreement to the DFID for verification. The DFID could then confirm that the agreement is a qualifying agreement under the Finance Act (as amended) and issue that company with a tax credit certificate which it can then use to offset against corporation tax. It is suggested that, as part of the amendment to the UK Finance Act, this amendment includes a provision that the Secretary of State is able to delegate his powers for the purpose of verifying compliance with the requirement for approval of a technology transfer tax credit to DFID. This example follows a similar mechanism already established for a community development tax credit under the Finance Act.

As to whether the UK company's technology transfer agreement is a qualifying agreement, this will depend entirely on whether the agreement's clauses comply with any (yet to be established) criteria by the WTO's working group on the transfer of technology as suggested above. It is also important to remember that this tax credit would only apply for the supply of services as opposed to goods because of restrictions imposed by the WTO's subsidies and countervailing agreement on the export of goods.

The implementing legislation to establish the RTD tax relief (or technology transfer tax credit in the UK) could be seen as a provision that the UK government could then report on as part of its UPR obligation for the next cycle of reviews planned for 2012 – when the review for the UK arises again – or four years later in 2016.

It is suggested that the UK regime for such a tax credit for beneficial technology transfer agreements could form an important precedent for other countries implementing similar schemes, particularly in those countries that have benefited from the slave trade, such as the United States and Canada, both of which have advanced tax collection regimes and where similar schemes to that of the UK could be adopted.

Other countries (such as those impacted by slavery) interested in reparations through a technology transfer could then use the UPR process, and specifically the UPR working panel review sessions, to table questions and recommendations on the implementation of the scheme. If the UPR process is used in this way, this aspect of the RTD (technology transfer, under attribute 1 of the RTD criteria) could be swiftly achieved. This could be done whether or not the working group on the RTD has completed a reporting template for the RTD.

To make all of the above a feasible reality, civil society needs to assert its influence. On-line campaign groups, such as *Avaaz*, have been remarkably successful in pushing for changes in the law that will help the public good.[19] In a similar way, civil society needs to encourage political leaders to act from the bottom-up in helping to develop the case for reparations. By using a mechanism such as the UPR, and in requiring the governments of slave benefiting nations to foot the bill for instruments, such as tax relief schemes that incentivise the business community in investing in a technology transfer to states impacted by the slave trade, reparations can be both *quantifiable* and have a *direct effect* in the field to train and assist the afflicted state's human capital base.

In a report by the high-level task force on the implementation of the right to development, specifically the criteria and operational sub-criteria for the implementation of the RTD, the report states:

> the consultation concluded that the right to development, in spite of the political context in which it is subjected to contending priorities, enriches both substantive and procedural elements of international human rights law by addressing redistribution and equity questions at the national and international levels from the perspective of accountability and other principles, shared by the development and human rights agendas. The greatest challenge, in this regard, lies in defining whether and how human rights, in particular the right to development, can contribute to creating an enabling environment necessary for the constant improvement of the well-being of the people.
>
> (HRC January 2010: paragraph 32)

The implementation of the RTD tax relief is one way of overcoming this challenge and providing those nation states impacted by slavery with a form of reparations that can help build their services sector and allow them to trade more effectively within the world system.

Notes

1 In the case of the European Communities there are further restrictions to agreeing such treaties where shared competence to negotiate trade agreements exists between the European Commission and the individual EU member states. In this instance, private bilateral agreements by EU Member States (with a colonial involvement in slavery) with African countries impacted by slavery could provide for a technology transfer or an investment in services (as opposed to preferential tariffs being given on goods imported into the EU) as a means of reparations. A technology transfer is discussed further below. A further option would be to agree a negotiated preferential tariff through the European Commission in future bilateral or regional trade agreements made by the European Commission for goods imported from African states impacted by slavery. This would however require (unlikely) political consensus throughout the European Commission and Parliament, possibly achieved through individual member states' commitments by way of the UPR instrument.
2 This is a contentious issue and a discussion of the Right To Development lies outside the scope of this chapter. However, for a more complete analysis, please see: *Development as a Human Right: Legal, Political and Economic Dimensions* (2nd edition), Bard A. Andreassen and Stephen P. Marks (editors), Intersentia, 2010; *Human Rights and Development: Towards Mutual Reinforcement*, P. Alston and M. Robinson (editors), Oxford University Press, 2005.
3 Article 1 Declaration on the Right To Development (referred to throughout this chapter as the 'Declaration').
4 Adopted by UN General Assembly Resolution 217 (A) II on 10/12/1948.
5 General Assembly Resolution 2200A, adopted 16/12/1966, entering into force 23/03/1976.
6 General Assembly Resolution 2200A, adopted 16/12/1966, entering into force 03/01/1976.
7 Vienna Declaration and Programme of Action, adopted by the UN World Conference on Human Rights, 25 June 1993.
8 These footnotes for example point to a range of databases both at the National and international level that form the relevant indicators.
9 A performance requirement is an obligation that a host state might incorporate into a technology transfer agreement that requires (for example) the investing state to purchase a certain quantity of raw materials in the host state; recruit and train local people; invest in research and development in the host state, etc.
10 Both the development and tax revenue departments of the investor state could have *concurrent jurisdiction* (for example, as compared to similar provisions on concurrency to be found in national competition law frameworks, such as the United Kingdom's *Competition Act 1998*, allowing for both a sector-specific national regulatory authority and a separate competition authority to hear competition complaints) in order to call for and examine such agreements. The power to do so will be set out in the implementing legislation bringing the RTD Tax Relief into force in the relevant investor state's jurisdiction.
11 There may be issues of *State Aid* linked to the implementation of the RTD Tax Relief which will need to be examined, for example in Europe, under

Community competition rules on State Aid found in Articles 87 and 88 EC Treaty (now Articles 107 and 108 *Treaty of the Functioning of the European Union* 2008) and relevant case law specifically defining the meaning of aid in terms of its effect, for example preferential tax treatment (Case 173/73 *Commission v. Italy* [1974] ECR 709) and the application of the 'market economy investor principle' as set out in Case C-39/94 *Syndicat Francais de l'Express International (SFEI) v. La Poste* [1996] ECR I-2547; Cases C-278-280/92 *Spain v. Commission* [1994] ECR I-4103. The market economy investor principle asks whether the State is acting in a way that a private investor would in a market economy in providing loans or capital on similar terms to that of a private investor. Would a private investor invest in the same way? If so, the State may not be using public funds for State Aid under Article 107(1) Treaty of the Functioning of the European Union 2008. There may also be issues of State subsidies at the multilateral level given that the WTO has certain rules (Subsidy Rules under the WTO *Agreement on Subsidies and Countervailing Measures*) on States offering support to private industry. The analysis of State Aid/WTO subsidy rules is outside the scope of this chapter.

12 WTO Agreement on Subsidies and Countervailing Measures.
13 Article 3 Subsidies and Countervailing Measures Agreement, which applies to goods. See also Annex 1 to the agreement that lists the prohibitions on subsidies in the form of preferential tax regimes for domestic exporters (paragraph e, Annex 1).
14 s.172(1)(a) UK Companies Act 2006.
15 s.172(1)(b) and (c).
16 s.172(1)(d).
17 s.172(e) and (f).
18 Schedule 16, UK Finance Act 2002.
19 http://www.avaaz.org/, accessed December 2010.

Bibliography

Alston, P. and Robinson, M. (eds) (2005) *Human Rights and Development: Towards Mutual Reinforcement*. Oxford: Oxford University Press.

Andreassen, B.A. and Marks, S.P. (eds) (2010) *Development as a Human Right: Legal, Political and Economic Dimensions* (2nd edition). Intersentia.

CIPR (2002) Commission on Intellectual Property report on Intellectual Property and Development. Available at http://www.iprcommission.org/papers/text/final_ report/chapter8htmf (accessed December 2010).

Correa, C. (2005) Can the TRIPS Agreement foster technology transfer to developing countries? In K. Maskus and J. Reichman (eds), *International Public Goods and Transfer of Technology: Under a Globalized Intellectual Property Regime*. Cambridge: CUP.

Dine, J. (forthcoming) *Post-concession Companies Models*.

HRC (April 2006) Human Rights Council, A/RES/60/251.

HRC (January 2010) Human Rights Council, A/HRC/15/WG.2/TF/CRP.4

HRC Add.1 (March 2010) Human Rights Council, A/HRC/15/WG.2/TF/2/Add.1.

HRC Add. 2 (March 2010) Human Right Council, A/HRC/15/WG.2/TF/2/Add.2.

HRC (June 2010) Human Rights Council, A/HRC/15/23.

Independent Expert Report (2002) Fifth report of the Independent Expert on the Right To Development, Mr Arjun Sengupta, submitted in accordance with Commission Resolution 2002/69, at 5, p.6, U.N. Doc. E/CN.4/2002/WG.18/6.

Kariyawasam, R. (2006) 'Jekyll & Hyde and Equation 5: Enforcing the Right To Development through Economic Law'. In J. Dine and A. Fagan (eds), *Capitalism and Human Rights*. Edward Elgar.

Kariyawasam, R. (2008) 'International Development'. In R. Kariyawasam R. (ed.), *International Economic Law and the Digital Divide: A New Silk Road?* Cheltenham: Edward Elgar.

M'Baye, K. (1972) 'Le Droit au Développement comme un Droit de L'Homme', 5 *Revue Des Droits de L'Homme* (Hum. Rts. J), pp. 503–515.

Sengupta, A. (2000) '*The Right to Development as a Human Right*' Global Governance Watch at: http://www.globalgovernancewatch.org/resources/the-right-to-development-as-a-human-right (accessed December 2010).

Soefstad, L. and Sein, M. (2004) 'ICT and Development: East is East and West is West and never the Twain may meet'. In S. Krishna and S. Madon (eds), *The Digital Challenge: Information Technology in the Development Context*. Kent: Ashgate.

UNCTAD (2001) UNCTAD/ICTSD, Geneva 2001. Available at http://www.ictsd.org/unctad-icstd/docs/Lall2001.pdf (accessed December 2010).

Universal Periodic Review (2010) Available at http://www.upr-info.org/-UPR-Process.html (accessed December 2010).

Williamson, J. (2000) 'What Should the WB Think about the Washington Consensus?' *The World Bank Research Observer*, 15(2).

WSIS (2007) World Information Society Tunis Agenda. Available at http://www.itu.int/wsis/tunis/newsroom/stats/ (accessed December 2010).

Part II

Reparations as a legal strategy

Chapter 5

Formulating the case for reparations

Lord Anthony Gifford

In 1992, when I was building my Jamaican practice, I received a request from Dudley Thompson who was then Jamaican High Commissioner to Nigeria. He asked me if I would prepare a paper to be delivered to the First Pan African Conference on Reparations, to be held in Abuja, the capital of Nigeria. He wanted me to research the legal basis of the concept that African peoples should receive reparations for the damage done by the transatlantic slave trade and the institution of slavery in the Americas.

It was an awesome request. In essence he wanted me to write a legal opinion for the benefit of Africans and their descendants in the African diaspora – hundreds of millions of people spread over the continent of Africa, North and South America, the Caribbean and Europe – as to whether they had grounds to make a claim against the nations of Europe and the United States which had been enriched by the profits they had gained from trading in and owning slaves.

The conference was to bring together some of the most remarkable people I have ever known. Dudley Thompson, who defended Jomo Kenyatta in the 1950s, had been a friend for some years. His remarkable history included service in the Royal Air Force during the Second World War and practising law in colonial Kenya and Tanganyika. He became Minister of Security and later of Foreign Affairs in the Michael Manley administration in the 1970s. Throughout his life he had been an ardent Pan-Africanist and he had attended the Fifth Pan-African Congress in Manchester in 1945. When Manley was re-elected as Prime Minister in 1989, he appointed Dudley as Jamaica's diplomatic representative to the continent of Africa. There could be no more fitting appointment. From his High Commission in Lagos he acted, in effect, as the ambassador of the whole Caribbean to the whole of Africa. Then in his mid-seventies, he took on this task with incredible energy.

So when I received his request, I knew that it was something to be taken very seriously. I had learnt about the issue of reparations from another remarkable man who also had become my friend, Bernie Grant, the Member of Parliament for Tottenham in North London. We had become close during the time of the Broadwater Farm Inquiry which I had chaired in 1985–86. He was the most radical and outspoken of the four Black MPs elected in 1987. One of his initiatives was to found the African Reparations Movement in Britain. He had explained to me how there could be no real equality between Black and White people in Britain until Britain faced up to its infamous role in the transatlantic slave trade and was prepared to negotiate some form of reparation with Black people. When I moved to Jamaica the issue arose again, as a Committee on Reparations had also been formed in Jamaica in 1991 under the leadership of George Nelson. I had been invited to some of its meetings and had been asked to do some work on the legal issues, even before Dudley Thompson had contacted me.

The catalyst for awakening the concept of reparations in Africa itself was supplied by another larger-than-life individual, Chief Moshood ('M.K.O.') Abiola of Nigeria. He was a multimillionaire businessman who at the beginning of 1993 had been selected as one of the two candidates to be president of Nigeria. Nigeria was then under the control of the Armed Forces Ruling Council which had seized power in 1985. The head of state was General Ibrahim Babangida who had agreed to restore democracy through elections to be held in June 1993. Chief Abiola had for some years been pushing the case for reparations. He was chairman of the Group of Eminent Persons on Reparations to Africa and Africans in the diaspora, which had been set up by the Organisation of African Unity in a resolution passed in June 1991. He had led a delegation to Gorée Island in Senegal, the point of no return for the millions of many African captives who had been shipped across the Atlantic Ocean. Dudley Thompson was part of that delegation and had been appointed rapporteur of the Group of Eminent Persons.

Chief Abiola had the reputation of being a capitalist who retained a deep sense of honour and generosity. He had made a lot of money, but also used that money for the education and upliftment of his people. The cause of reparations was his supreme act of philanthropy. He spent large amounts of his own fortune in promoting the cause. The Pan-African Conference was also largely financed by him. I met him first in Jamaica when he came on a mission to promote the conference. He arrived in his personal Boeing 707 jet, but was very late. He had been delayed by the United States authorities who could not believe that a Black African was the owner of such a plane. He spoke with contemptuous wit about his experience that morning in Washington: 'Next time', he had told the Americans, 'I shall bring my 747.' His message to Jamaicans was encapsulated in a quote from a speech he made in 1992: 'While we demand reparations in order to enforce justice, to feed the poor, to teach the illiterate and to house the homeless, this crusade is also important because only reparations can heal our land, comfort our souls and restore our self-respect.'

Other members of the Group of Eminent Persons included Professors Ali Mazrui of Kenya and Ade Ajayi of Nigeria; Congressman Ronald Dellums of the United States; Dr M'Bow, the former director of UNESCO; the international singer Miriam Makeba; and Graca Machel whom I knew and greatly admired as a result of my links with Mozambique. These were the people who were organising the conference to be held in Abuja, Nigeria, from 27 to 29 April 1993.

I saw it as an exceptional honour that this group had asked me, a White British lawyer, to prepare a paper on the legal aspects of the issue. At the back of my mind there was also the knowledge that my own family had played a role in the destruction of Africa. The third Lord Gifford had been a senior officer in the force led by Sir Garnet Wolseley which had waged the Ashanti Campaign in Ghana in 1873–4.

In 1991 I had been visiting Ghana at the invitation of President Rawlings to take part in the process of drafting a democratic constitution for Ghana. I had visited Cape Coast Castle, where in the museum I had seen an engraving which depicted Lord Gifford subduing an Ashanti village. Later in the visit I went to Kumasi, capital of the Ashanti people, and had an audience with the Asantehema, the Queen Mother of the Ashantis. I made an apology for the crimes committed by my ancestor against the Ashanti people, and said that I came to Kumasi with a quite different spirit. She thanked me and said that 'the Ashanti bear no personal grudge against the British'. It was my small personal act of reparation.

I was not an expert in international law, so I took time on a visit to London to read some of the leading text books. I found that the concept of reparation was well established in international law. The Permanent Court of International Justice had defined the principle in 1928 in the Chorzow Factory case between Germany and Poland: 'Reparation must, as far as possible, wipe out all the consequences of the illegal act and re-establish the situation which would, in all probability, have existed if that act had not been committed.' Restitution in kind, and payment of compensation, were the main forms of reparation imposed by international law.

I recognised that there were formidable questions which any serious proponent of the claim for reparations had to answer. Was the slave trade contrary to international law? Were there any relevant precedents? Did it all happen too long ago? Who would be entitled to make the claim? Who would the claim be made against? What would be the components of the claim? And in which court or tribunal could it be made? These are basic questions which arise in the daily life of an advocate. But in the context of a slave trade covering several centuries and continents, and affecting tens of millions of Africans and African descendants, it was a challenge to try to answer these.

I started the paper with some biographical facts about my involvement in the struggles against colonialism and racism. I said that to me as a lawyer it was essential to locate the claim for reparations within a framework of law and justice. It should not be merely an appeal to the conscience of the White world. I noted that blatant racist advertising in Britain had not been stopped until laws were passed which forbade it, that apartheid in South Africa had begun to crumble as it became regarded as a crime against humanity and a threat to peace so that international sanctions could be imposed. These examples showed that the demand for justice and legality was an essential element in the struggle for a just cause.

I continued with words which I stand by today:

> So it is with the claim for Reparations. Indeed, once you accept, as I do, the truth of three propositions: (a) that the mass kidnap and enslavement of Africans was the most wicked criminal enterprise in recorded human history; (b) that no compensation was ever paid by any of the perpetrators to any of the sufferers; and (c) that the consequences of the crime continue to be massive, both in terms of the enrichment of the descendants of the perpetrators, and in terms of the impoverishment of Africans and the descendants of Africans; then the justice of the claim for Reparations is proved beyond reasonable doubt.

The slave trade was a crime against humanity

To answer the crucial questions, I developed the three propositions into seven. The first was that the enslavement of Africans was indeed a crime against humanity. I cited the Charter of the Nuremberg War Crimes Tribunal, which defined crimes against humanity as: 'Murder, extermination, enslavement, deportation and other inhumane acts committed against any civilian population ... *whether or not in violation of the domestic law where perpetrated.*' I referred to the Genocide Convention, which did not create a new international crime but gave it a new and more effective legal form. It recognised genocide as a crime against international law, and defined genocide as being 'acts committed with intent to destroy, in whole or in part, a national, ethnical, racial or religious group as such'. The invasion of African territories, the mass capture of Africans, the horrors of the middle passage, the sale and use of Africans as worse than beasts, the extermination of family life, culture and language, were all violations of these international laws.

I have never accepted the argument that because the slave trade was legal under the British laws of the time, it could not have been a crime against international law. The Nuremberg Charter dealt with that argument, which might have been used in the context of laws passed by the elected Nazi Government in Germany, in the words emphasised above. As international law experts have written, acts which are so reprehensible as to offend the conscience of mankind, directed against civilian populations, are crimes in international law and always have been. The criterion is the conscience of decent human beings (who in Britain were indeed outraged by the slave trade), not the standards of those who perpetrated the crimes.

Nor am I impressed with the comment that African societies themselves permitted slavery, or that many Africans helped the slave traders by capturing and selling the people who were transported. The peculiar cruelties of the transatlantic trade, and the subsequent conditions of slavery in the Americas, were infinitely worse than the indigenous African practices of enslaving prisoners of war or criminals. Africans did not treat each other as racially inferior, subhuman beings. Africans did not imprison each other in stinking dungeons or crowd each other into the holds of ships with less space than pigs in a sty. Africans did not work slaves to death because it was cheaper to replace them than to keep them alive.

Every book you can read about the transatlantic slave trade will confirm to you that its barbarities were not paralleled in history until Nazi Germany imposed its 'Final Solution' on the Jews. As for the culpability of the African slave dealers, it is a sad but inevitable fact that every large-scale criminal enterprise will attract collaborators. Some are seduced by greed, some are coerced by intimidation. The participation of Africans in the capture of their fellow Africans does not, to my mind, detract from the culpability of those who promoted and organised the trade. It was Europeans who created the transatlantic slave trade. It was Europeans who demanded an ever-increasing pool of slave labour to work in their plantations. It was Europeans who were determined to enrich themselves without regard to the suffering of those who created their wealth. It was Europeans who created the market for trafficking people on a massive scale – between 12 and 25 million captives snatched from their homes and families. In my assessment the transatlantic slave trade, and the institution of slavery in the Americas, were the ultimate crimes against humanity, because they depended on the denial of human status, on racial grounds, to a vast section of humanity.

Reparation is recognised by international law

My second proposition was that international law recognises that those who commit crimes against humanity must make reparation. I noted some of the modern examples of reparation. The Federal Republic of Germany had reached agreement for the payment of reparations to Israel, following a claim by Israel for the cost of resettling half a million Jews who had fled from Nazi-controlled countries. Austria also agreed to make reparation payments to Holocaust survivors. The governments which made the payments were not the perpetrators of the crimes, but they accepted responsibility for the crimes committed by their Nazi predecessors. Japan had made reparations payments to South Korea for acts committed during the occupation of Korea by Japan. The United States had passed the Civil Liberties Act in 1988, giving reparations to Japanese Americans who had been interned during the Second World War. The Act expressed an acknowledgment of the 'fundamental injustice' which the internees had suffered, apologised on behalf of the USA, and provided restitution to those individuals of Japanese ancestry who were interned.

I also drew attention to the steps taken to recognise the rights to restitution of indigenous peoples in different parts of the world, whose land had been plundered and whose people had been killed or degraded. In the United States, Canada, New Zealand and Australia, there have been settlements of various kinds, including a recognition of rights over land and financial payments. While these have been inadequate gestures, they still recognised that the surviving generations of indigenous peoples had the right to a measure of reparation for the crimes committed against their ancestors.

No limitation period

I continued with a third proposition which attacked the argument that it all happened too long ago. There is no legal barrier to prevent those who suffer the consequences of crimes against humanity from claiming repar-ations, even though the crimes were committed against their ancestors. I argued that in law the descendants who still suffer from the consequences of the crime have the right to restitution as much as the immediate victims.

Under the British Foreign Compensation Act, which provided for reparations for those whose property had been sequestrated in Egypt, a person who is the owner or the successor in title to the owner could make a claim. The descendants of those whose property, including works of art, was seized by the Nazis, have successfully made claims for the restoration of that property. To found a claim which is legally supportable, African claimants would have to show that they, the descendants of the transported captives, were continuing to suffer the consequences of the crime. I believe that the evidence of this is overwhelming.

I wrote in the paper: 'On the African continent, flourishing civilisations were destroyed; ordered systems of government were broken up; millions of citizens were forcibly removed; and a pattern of poverty and underde-velopment directly resulted, which now affects nearly every resident of Africa. In the Americas, the slavery system gave rise to poverty, landless-ness, underdevelopment, as well as to the crushing of culture and languages, the loss of identity, the inculcation of inferiority among Black people, and the indoctrination of Whites into a racist mindset – all of which continue to this day to affect the prospects and quality of Black people's lives in the Caribbean, USA, Canada and Europe.'

There is no limitation period in international law. The countries which were damaged by the international slave trade, in Africa and the Americas, had no means of pressing a claim, because slavery was accompanied by colonialism which continued into the second half of the twentieth century. Only then could any former colony speak with independence on behalf of its people. In 1993 I said: 'Indeed I would argue that now, as never before, is the right time for this claim to be made, as African leaders are speaking with a new confidence and operating new democratic structures.' I was thinking particularly of the two wealthiest countries in Africa, Nigeria and South Africa, both of which were then on the verge of a transformation to democracy.

Who are the claimants?

I argued that the claim would be brought on behalf of all Africans, in Africa and the diaspora, who suffer the consequences of the crime, through the agency of an appropriate representative. Hundreds of millions of people in different parts of the world have an interest in the issue of reparations. Some minds are so daunted by the practical problems that they will conclude that the claim is unrealistic. However, I wrote then: 'Difficulties of scale or procedures should not be obstacles to justice. The unwillingness of the White world to consider the claim is not a reason for giving it up, but rather a spur to mobilising awareness and support around the issues. Governments in Africa and the Caribbean should neither be excluded from nor have sole control over the prosecution of the claim. Many who still suffer the consequences of slavery, in the United States and Britain for example, had no government which could speak to them. So some form of appropriate, representative and trustworthy body would be required.'

Who are the defendants?

The claim would be brought against the governments of those countries which promoted and were enriched by the African slave trade and the institution of slavery. I concentrated on governments because they fostered the trade and allowed it to continue; because they represent the countries which were enriched by the trade; and because they would be responsible for the international conventions and agreements which a reparations package would require. I thought that trying to identify and make claims against individual companies, or the descendants of plantation owners or slave traders, would create many problems in international law. But in the case of works of art, stolen from Africa and held in individual collections, the principle of restitution demanded that they should be returned to the people from whose shores they were taken.

What would be claimed?

The components of the claim would be assessed and formulated in each region affected by the institution of slavery. I suggested that the concept of reparations would cover a wide spectrum of demands. The damage could be classified and researched under different headings. These were economic damage, cultural damage, social damage, psychological damage.

Another approach would be to look at the extent of the enrichment of the various slave-trading and slave-owning nations. Recognising that I did not know the answers to the difficult questions which were raised, I sketched the broad elements of a package which might include: an apology by the governments of the slave trading nations to Africans worldwide; the cancellation of debt; programmes of development in the inner cities where African descendants still suffer from the racism inculcated in the days of slavery; the rebuilding of the infrastructure of the African continent, once a land of well-developed trading networks; a facilitation of the return to Africa of those, including Rastafarians, who long to go to the continent from which their ancestors were taken. I suggested that the very process of formulating and negotiating the claim would be 'an educative process through which the horrors of the past will be re-examined'.

In what court could the claim be made?

The claim, if not settled by agreement, would be determined by a special international tribunal recognised by all parties. I noted that there was no court, national or international, which would be sufficiently competent to hear the claim for reparations. But in cases where reparations had been paid in the past, once the legitimacy of the claim was accepted, the necessary mechanisms were already established. A commission was set up to consider claims for reparations for American property confiscated in Iran. With the claim of the Japanese Americans, an Act of Congress had been passed. The payment of reparations by Germany to Israel had come about by voluntary agreement. I concluded that: 'The international recognition of the justice of the claim is a condition precedent to the setting up of any machinery.' In accepting the absence of any presently existing judicial body I was recognising that the reparations claim, while based on legal principle, could only be realised by political agitation and moral persuasion.

The Abuja Conference

The atmosphere at the conference in Abuja was dynamic. There were delegates from many parts of Africa, the United States, the Caribbean,

Brazil and Britain. President Babangida's message, read by his Vice-president, opened the conference. He spoke of the independence and civil rights struggles and continued: 'The reparations movement seeks to preserve and forward the gains of these earlier struggles, to make Africa progress into the next century and beyond, and to make our continent and its scattered people one and whole again. Reparations combine morality with logic and historical necessity by claiming the right of the injured to compensation. If history demonstrates that Africans have been injured by slavery and colonialism, and if morality demands that injury be compensated, then the logic of the reparations movement is established alongside its morality.' He warned the conference against seeing reparations as seeking revenge or proceeding in anger and ill-will. The reparations movement had no element of racism, but called upon men and women of all races to help put an end to the hatred and contempt that had divided the human race over the past six hundred years.

It was heady stuff. Chief Abiola, chairing the conference with panache, pledged that if he was elected president in June he would take the case for reparations to the United Nations: 'Our legs have been broken by slavery and colonialism, and we must insist that these legs be mended.' He concluded that the claim for reparations was not about vengeance, rather it was about justice: 'It is justice we demand; by the grace of God, it is justice we will get.'

There were messages from the presidents of Senegal and Cuba. The Secretary General of the Organisation of African Unity, Salim Ahmed Salim from Tanzania, said that this was a crusade which went beyond financial considerations: 'It will be the overwhelming mobilisation in pursuit of justice, time and space and for the dignity of man.' Dudley Thompson gave a speech which vibrated with his passionate Pan-Africanism. He quoted from Dr W.E.B. Dubois' speech to the First Pan-African Congress, held in Paris in 1919: 'The problem of the 20th century is the problem of the colour line.'

He also acknowledged the Black leaders who had inspired him: Marcus Garvey, Kwame Nkrumah, Jomo Kenyatta, George Padmore, Toussaint L'Ouverture, Franz Fanon, Martin Luther King, Nelson Mandela. In his person, and through his achievements, Dudley symbolised the re-uniting of African peoples. Pan-Africanism, he said, was not a plea for charity: 'It is the burden of this Conference to show that the reparations aspect of Pan-Africanism rests on a basic philosophy as old as justice itself; it rests not only on an unassailable moral ground, but on ancient and modern precedents.' He quoted from Dr King's dream that 'one day the sons of former slaves and the sons of former slave owners will be able to sit down together at the table of brotherhood'.

I befriended one of the delegates from Brazil, and helped her to translate her message from Portuguese, learning at the same time how Afro-

Brazilians suffered from 'an ideology of the desirability of whiteness', which had led to 'the negation of our racial identity'. I listened to Dr Ronald Walters of Howard University who led the USA delegation, who spoke of the struggle for reparations as 'yet another chapter in the decolonisation of the African mind'.

My own paper was well received by the delegates, but not I think by the European diplomatic observers who clamoured to have copies. I remembered a recent exchange with a leading Foreign Office diplomat whom I had first met when he was the high commissioner to Ghana. On hearing that I was preparing a paper on reparations he had reacted with consternation and told me, only half in jest, that the British government should get reparations for their role in suppressing the slave trade after the Abolition Act had been passed.

I believe that what disturbs the British profoundly about the concept of reparations is that it changes the whole basis of the dialogue between Black and White, North and South, Europeans and Africans. Instead of African pleas for aid to be dispensed by a benevolent and kindly Europe, the Abuja conference demanded justice from a Europe which had committed crimes. British imperial history has often been characterised by hypocritical assertions of moral superiority by the colonisers. They went into Africa on a 'civilising mission' and committed barbarities. They brought 'Christian values' to the Caribbean and allowed slaves to be whipped and worked to death. They portrayed emancipation in 1838 as a gift from Britannia to grateful slaves, forgetting that it was only through slave rebellions in the Caribbean and popular demonstrations in Britain that the ending of slavery was finally conceded by a ruling class which had resisted all demands for it during the previous forty years. They also paid £20 million in compensation to the slave owners (roughly 40 per cent of Britain's national budget at the time) and not a penny to the slaves.

The Abuja declaration, passed at the end of the Conference, challenged this version of history. It declared that the damage sustained by African peoples was 'not a thing of the past, but is painfully manifest in the damaged lives of contemporary Africans from Harlem to Harare, in the damaged economies of the Black world from Guinea to Guyana, from Somalia to Suriname'. It drew attention to the historic precedents of reparations paid to Jews and Japanese Americans. It observed that compensation for injustice could be paid both in capital transfer and in other forms of restitution. It declared the delegates' conviction that the claim for reparations was well grounded in international law, and urged the OAU to set up a legal committee on the issue.

In a generous recognition of the unity of Africans, it exhorted African states to grant entrance rights to all persons of African descent, and the right to obtain residence. It urged those countries which were enriched by slavery to give total relief from foreign debt. It called for a permanent

African seat on the Security Council of the United Nations. It emphasised that 'what matters is not the guilt but the responsibility of those states and nations whose economic evolution once depended on slave labour and colonialism'. It called for the return to Africa of stolen artefacts and traditional treasures. It recommended the setting up of national reparations committees in Africa and the diaspora. Finally, it called upon the international community 'to recognise that there is a unique and unprecedented moral debt owed to the African peoples which has yet to be paid – the debt of compensation to the Africans as the most humiliated and exploited people of the last four hundred years'.

I wish that I could say that the Abuja conference led to the case for reparations being speedily put on the world agenda, as the framers of the Abuja Declaration had intended. In fact the exhilaration of Abuja was followed within two months by the disaster of the aborted Nigerian elections. Everything looked set for the return of democracy in Nigeria. The run-off was between two presidential candidates who were both representative of business interests. Between the two, Chief Abiola appeared to be the more popular. But after the elections were held on 12 June 1993, the government refused to publish the results. These were eventually leaked on 18 June by the Campaign for Democracy. Chief Abiola had comfortably defeated his rival industrialist, winning 19 out of 30 states. On 23 June President Babangida announced that the elections had been annulled. The National Electoral Commission was suspended and no further challenges were allowed through the courts of law. President Babangida stepped down in favour of an interim Head of Government, but the real power lay with General Sani Abacha, Minister of Defence, who in November 1993 took power and reinstated military rule. Chief Abiola, who declared himself to be the lawful president, went into hiding and was arrested in June 1994. He remained in prison in humiliating solitary confinement during the whole of General Abacha's military rule, until the general died in May 1998. A month later Chief Abiola also died, still in prison.

The aborting of the election and the imprisonment of Chief Abiola dealt a bitter blow to the campaign for reparations. He was the continent's most vocal spokesman on the issue and as President of Nigeria he would have had the authority to raise it internationally. Working with Dudley Thompson as Jamaican High Commissioner, he would have brought together African and Caribbean nations and the broader African diaspora. The campaign would have had the required resources behind it; after he had gone there was no one able and willing to fund meetings or publications or other initiatives. It was a tragedy for the wider interests of Africa, since I believe that Chief Abiola had the moral stature and political support which would have changed Nigeria's standing in the world.

As I watched these events unfold, I wondered why they had happened. I never heard any convincing reason for the annulment of the elections. It was an extreme action which shattered Nigeria's image around the world. It seemed so unnecessary and wrong. I suspected then, and indeed still suspect, that some part in this was played by Britain and the United States, between them the biggest outside influences on Nigeria. The coming to power of Chief Abiola was threatening to them, not because of anything in his economic or social programmes, but because of his dominant and determined role in the movement for reparations. The demand for justice which he had proclaimed from the podium at Abuja would have vibrated ominously through the Foreign and Commonwealth Office and the State Department. Had they persuaded General Babangida, in spite of his enthusiastic message to the Conference, that Chief Abiola would not be an acceptable President of Nigeria? It would be another eight years before the issue of reparations would be mentioned at an international conference in Africa. If the motive for the removal of Chief Abiola had been to set back the cause of reparations, those who planned it had succeeded, at least for a limited time.

Presenting the case in the House of Lords

I came back from Abuja to Jamaica. The Jamaica Committee on Reparations was revived and I went to some of its meetings. One evening I was challenged by Ibo Cooper, the musician. He berated me for confining my advocacy of reparations to audiences in Africa and the Caribbean. He said that if I really believed in it, I should be speaking to my own people in Britain who most needed persuading. I mulled over this conversation for a long time, and saw that he had a point. I had a ready-made platform in the heart of Britain's Parliament, and it was time that I used it.

Since setting up a residence in Jamaica I had been an absentee member of the House of Lords. I had made only one speech there, protesting about the treatment of Jamaicans at Gatwick Airport. But I was still a member with full rights, including the right to initiate debates. I knew that by putting down a question on the House of Lords order paper, I would be able to get a hearing in a matter of months. So in the Parliamentary Report for 14 March 1996, it was printed that at 9.18 p.m. 'Lord Gifford rose to ask Her Majesty's Government whether they will make appropriate reparations to African nations and to the descendants of Africans for the damage caused by the slave trade and the practice of slavery'. In the gallery were various friends, including Bernie Grant M.P. and the Jamaican historian Richard Hart, as well as high commissioners from Africa and the Caribbean. I had invited them to give me moral support in what I knew to be unfriendly territory.

I summarised the horrors of the transatlantic slave trade and the consequences which continued to flow from it: poverty, landlessness, the new shackles of debt, and the persistence of the philosophy of racial superiority which 'continues to poison our society today'. I referred to the historic precedents, and added a new one which I had just learned about. In November 1995 the Queen had personally signed the Waikato-Raupatu Claims Settlement Bill in New Zealand. Through this Bill the New Zealand Government apologised for the seizure of Maori lands by British settlers in 1863 and paid substantial compensation both in land and money to the Maori people. The presence of the Queen symbolised the recognition of an ancient grievance. It was a telling example of how, over a century after the illegal act, effective reparation can be made.

I went through some of the elements of an appropriate reparations package: an apology at the highest level; the cancellation of debt; the return of treasures and works of art; programmes of development in Africa and the Caribbean; and promoting equal rights and justice within the countries of the West. I ended with a plea that all of us would be healed if we moved in this direction: 'As we move to the next millennium, none of us can deny that there is a growing divide between north and south, between black and white, across frontiers and within frontiers. It is in the interest of all of us to recognise that the reasons for that divide lie in a shameful past. If we realise that, we will be on the way to doing something to repair the wrong which was done, even though it may cost heavily in terms of pride and revenue. The steps to be taken will bring a happier world for all our children.'

Immediately a Conservative Lord, Lord Burnham, intervened with a question: 'My Lords, before the noble Lord sits down, can he tell the House which country first stopped the slave trade?' I saw the old trick. To offset my condemnation of Britain for the crimes of slavery, he wanted me to praise Britain for ending the crime. I was not quite sure of the answer to the question, so I answered guardedly: 'My Lords, after carrying it on and profiting massively from it, the slave trade was stopped by the nations of Europe. I pay tribute to the ancestor of the noble Lord, Lord Wilberforce, who played a leading part in stopping the trade. However, no compensation was paid when it was stopped and the unredressed grievance remains with us today.'

Richard Hart in the gallery managed to pass down a note. It corrected the assumption behind Lord Burnham's question. At a later stage in the debate, when another Lord, Viscount Falkland, was trumpeting the achievements of the British abolitionists, I intervened to say: 'My Lords, the noble Viscount is interesting and erudite in his history, but I am sure that he will accept that it was the Danes who were the first European nation to abolish the slave trade. We followed them six years later.' I was glad that I had not fallen into the trap which Lord Burnham had set for me.

My reference to Wilberforce was a courteous recognition of the presence in the House of the present Lord Wilberforce, an eminent law lord and descendant of William Wilberforce M.P. As president of Anti-Slavery International, which campaigns against modern slavery, he made a speech in the debate. He was not satisfied with the legal case for reparations. He said that in the cases which I had cited the guilty party was clear – the German state in the case of the Jews – and there were 'identifiable victims of the wrong and direct and assessable consequences'. He did not find those conditions satisfied in the case of the African slave trade. However he accepted that there was a moral responsibility to mitigate the consequences of slavery. He referred to the low prices for commodities and the burden of debt, 'which is itself a form of slavery'. He ended by saying that 'the case now is not one of guilt but of morality'.

The strongest speech in my support came from Lord Judd, speaking for the Labour opposition. He was kind enough to say that I spoke in the tradition of Thomas Clarkson and William Wilberforce. He said that it was not only slavery but also colonialism which had brought a tragic aftermath. He traced the connection between Belgian colonial policies and the genocide in Rwanda. Then he spoke eloquently about the costs of structural adjustment in Africa. He described how the burdens of debt were crippling Uganda, Zambia, Tanzania and other countries. He described as 'unproductive madness' how billions of pounds of development aid were diverted into servicing a multilateral debt.

The government's response

Lord Chesham replied to the debate on behalf of the Conservative government. Predictably, he said that while slavery was 'a moral outrage', the government did not accept that there was a case for reparations. But for the first time the government of a former slave-trading nation was obliged to set out the reasons for being against reparations. He said that first, slavery was practised by Arabs and Africans as well as Europeans. Second, African leaders were active participants in the slave trade. Third, it was not the British government which traded in slaves but individual traders and companies. Fourth, there was no evidence that the effects of slavery were still being felt by Africans now living in Africa and the diaspora. Fifth, racism was not just a black and white problem, but that it occurred between different ethnic groups all over the world. Sixth, it would be impossible to say which Africans should benefit from reparations.

Lord Chesham described the payment of reparations by Germany and Japan and Iraq as 'a red herring'. As for the Queen's apology to the Maoris, the situation was entirely different: 'It was not a question of slavery but one of the possession of land resulting from war'. At this I said to myself so what? Both were crimes against international law and the suffering caused by the slave trade was on a much vaster scale, thereby requiring greater atonement.

Part of Lord Chesham's response was intended to push the blame for the slave trade onto other people. The Arabs and the Africans were involved. It was not the government but the individual traders. Other ethnic groups practised racism. Lawyers call it the '*tu quoque*' (you too) defence. I was not impressed, especially since the early British slave trading ventures were conducted by the Royal African Company under a Charter signed by King Charles II in 1672. The trade was sanctioned by British law and tenaciously supported by the British Parliament until its abolition in 1807. It was a distortion of history for Lord Chesham to say that the 'responsibility for British involvement in the transatlantic slave trade does not rest on the shoulders of the British government'.

I was interested by Lord Chesham's fourth reason. He was, I believe, profoundly wrong to claim that there was no evidence of the slave trade having damaging effects on African people today. Living in Jamaica I can see the evidence daily, in terms of poverty, underdevelopment, the inequality of resources, family breakdowns, and the frequency with which disputes are settled with violence. The persistence of racism and racial discrimination against Black people in the United States and Britain arises directly from the doctrines of racial superiority which were used to justify the trade. As to Africa, the slave trade robbed it of millions of its strongest people. Walter Rodney, in his classic work *How Europe Underdeveloped Africa* (1973, Howard University Press), shows how the population of Africa stagnated between 1650 and 1850 while that of Europe and Asia grew almost threefold. To me there can be no doubt that the systematic squeezing of Africa for the extraction of profits for Europe was the ruination of a continent that boasted some of the most civilised kingdoms of the world in the pre-slavery era.

However, the corollary of Lord Chesham's fourth reason was that if the evidence could be shown, at least a moral case could be made out. I have no doubt that those who run Britain are well aware of the moral strength behind the arguments for reparation. They know that the history of the British plantations in the Americas, and how they were supplied with labour, is shameful. They try to deny the connection because to admit it would logically entail measures of compensation being implemented. Lord Chesham's statement was a challenge to the proponents of reparation to gather the evidence and prove him wrong.

I found the debate to be very instructive. I was impressed by the approach of Lord Wilberforce, that the issue was moral rather than legal. Although I still consider that the case for reparations is based on the principles of international law, I do not argue that it is a kind of super-litigation which could be brought before some court at some time. Rather it is a question of facing up to a fundamental injustice which permanently affected the relationship between African and European people. The process of facing up to what was done in the past, and its consequences, will necessitate measures of atonement and reparation to level the playing field. I see it as a healing process, not a conflict.

The World Conference against Racism

In 2001 the United Nations convened the World Conference against Racism, Racial Discrimination, Xenophobia and Related Intolerance. It was to be held in Durban, South Africa. In the preparations for the conference new life was breathed into the reparations issue. For how could the world discuss racism without mentioning the causes? Several African governments insisted that the past must be included on the agenda. In a 'non-paper' prepared in advance of the conference by the group of African nations, some key themes were inserted into the conference's draft resolutions: 'Remembering the past, unequivocally condemning its major racist tragedies, and telling the truth about history are essential elements for international reconciliation'; 'An explicit apology should be extended by States which practised, benefited or unjustly enriched themselves from slavery and the slave trade' ; and those who benefited were urged 'to assume full responsibility through, *inter alia*, enhanced remedial development policies, programmes and concrete measures'. This was a call for reparations in all but name.

The United States responded with a 'non-paper' of its own: 'We would like the World Conference against Racism to focus on the current form and manifestations of racism as it was intended to do by the UN General Assembly, rather than to apportion blame for past injustices or seek to exact compensation for these acts'. The USA agreed that slavery and the slave trade 'must be acknowledged, discussed, learned from and condemned', but also that 'we simply do not believe that it is appropriate to address this history – and its many and vast aspects – through such measures as international compensatory measures'. The USA was 'willing to join others in expressing regret for involvement in those historical practices', however 'we are not willing to agree to anything that suggests present-day liability on the part of one state to another for that historical situation'.

I had not been to South Africa since the historic democratic elections of 1994. Since then the work of the Truth and Reconciliation Commission had started and ended. I had followed the reports of the TRC with admiration. Under the chairmanship of Archbishop Tutu, it had shown the world that it was possible for gross injustices to be exposed and confronted. The new South Africa seemed to be the right place in which the world would meet and talk about the evils of racism.

The exciting part of the conference was taking place outside the conference hall, in the Forum of Non-Governmental Organisations which was based in a nearby cricket stadium. There was a buzz of activity as thousands of participants in different tents discussed the vast spectrum of topics that were to be addressed at the conference. I raised my voice from the floor at a meeting on reparations and also addressed a meeting which was organised by the International Association of Democratic Lawyers. I was touched when Congressman John Conyers, who year after year had tabled a motion in Congress calling for a commission to study Reparations for African-Americans, came to the meeting and praised my speech. Also at the meeting was South African law lecturer Max du Plessis, who had written an academic paper on the issue of reparations for slavery and colonialism. Quoting extensively on my paper and House of Lords speech, he concluded, like Lord Wilberforce, that legal claims would fail, but that the call for reparation, in some form, 'surely has a legitimate moral grounding'.

I was not part of the intense negotiating that took place behind the scenes on the wording of the Conference Final Declaration. I have heard that the Caribbean delegations, especially from Jamaica and Barbados, played a pivotal role in this. The United States had walked out of the conference, expressing displeasure about the way in which two key issues – the rights of Palestinians, and reparation – were being dealt with. But the European governments, led by the British and the French, were there to prevent the Declaration from containing anything too radical. The alliance of African and Caribbean delegations pushed for a clear statement that the transatlantic slave trade had been a crime against humanity.

The Final Declaration stated that 'we profoundly regret the massive human suffering' caused by slavery and the slave trade. It acknowledged that the slave trade and slavery 'are a crime against humanity and should always have been so' (fudging the issue as to whether it was a crime against humanity at the time). It noted 'that some States have taken the initiative to apologise, and have paid reparation, where appropriate, for grave and massive violations committed'. Those who had not taken such initiatives were urged 'to find appropriate ways to do so': 'We are aware of the moral obligation on the part of all concerned States and call upon these States to take appropriate and effective measures to halt and reverse the lasting consequences of those practices'.

The Conference Declaration reeked of compromise and imprecise language. That was inevitable, given the conflicting interests of the different participants. What was important was that there was a successful attempt to face up to the connection between the horrors of the past and the racism and poverty of today. There was plenty in the Declaration, and its accompanying Programme of Action, for activists to work on. Much more was said on the subject of reparation than the former slave-owning states would have liked.

The decade after Durban

The impact of the Durban Conference has been limited. A follow-up conference held in Geneva in 2009 attracted little attention. The new US government under President Obama did not attend. And yet the issue of reparations still refuses to go away.

In the USA there have been significant advances. The National Coalition of Blacks for Reparations in America (NCOBRA) has grown into a powerful movement and has achieved significant successes. In January 2005 the bank J. P. Morgan Chase came under pressure from the City of Chicago to declare its historical links to slavery if it wished to do business with the City. It revealed that its predecessor banks in Louisiana had allowed 13,000 slaves to be used as collateral on loans. In 1,250 cases the borrowers defaulted and this collateral was seized by the bank. J.P.Morgan apologised and created a $5 million scholarship for African-American students in Louisiana. While the response of the company has since been criticised as inadequate, the precedent is being followed in other cities in the USA. American lawyers have also been at the forefront of the campaign, bringing a number of lawsuits against companies whose predecessors were involved in slavery. These suits have so far failed, on the basis that too long a time has passed; but they have proved to be an important focus for publicity and mobilisation.

In the United Kingdom the two hundredth anniversary of the abolition of the slave trade was marked by many events which raised consciousness, even if the focus was too markedly on the achievements of the British abolitionists and not on the criminal nature of the trade or on the resistance of the slaves which accelerated the movement to emancipation. Prime Minister Tony Blair made a 'non-apology'. In an article in the *New Nation* newspaper he wrote: 'the bicentenary offers us a chance not just to say how profoundly shameful the slave trade was – how we condemn its existence utterly and praise those who fought for its abolition, but also to express our deep sorrow that it ever happened, that it could ever have happened, and to rejoice at the different and better times we live in today'. The *New Nation* believed that the Prime Minister 'deliberately went out of his way to say as much as he could without contravening the advice he received from the Foreign Office that ruled out an outright apology for slavery on the grounds that it would open up the government to possible legal action for reparations'.

The Church of England did better, voting to apologise to the descendants of victims of the slave trade. Its General Synod recognised that a church organisation, the Society for the Propagation of the Gospel, had owned the Codrington Plantation in Barbados, where slaves had the word 'SOCIETY' branded on their backs with a red-hot iron. The church had been compensated when its slaves were emancipated. Now the Archbishop of

Canterbury shared in the apology for the evil that had been done in the church's name.

Australia showed that a government could make a proper apology for its past offences, when in 2008 Prime Minister Kevin Rudd said that the country was sorry for all the indignities and injustices suffered by aboriginal Australians. He called it 'a first step by acknowledging the past'. The debate over reparations to the aboriginal communities continues.

It may well be that the steps which will turn out to be the most significant and far-reaching, on the issue of slavery reparations, are those which have been taken in the Caribbean. The effort to make real the promises made in the Durban declaration was first made in Barbados. Barbados, taking the lead in the Caribbean, had set up an official Commission for Pan African Affairs, which sponsored the Africa and African Descendants Conference in October 2002. In March 2007 the then Prime Minister, Owen Arthur, made a stirring speech in Hull in which he described reparations as 'a matter, not of retribution, but of morality. We need to bring equity to the emancipation process, and closure to the criminal activity that was racial chattel slavery'.

In August 2007 Mr Arthur opened the African Diaspora Global Conference with a speech under the title 'History will not forget us': 'Mankind has yet to properly make amends for the crimes committed against Africa and her children'. He described the unrepaired wrong as 'the festering sore of a monstrous historical crime whose pervasive damage has been left largely unaddressed and unrepaired, which will not fade away but rather get worse'. A declaration was drafted by reparations supporters and accepted by the conference. The declaration posited that 'the movement for reparations has entered a new stage, in which specific claims are being discussed, formulated and presented to the former colonising and enslaving states'.

Since then Jamaica has picked up the baton, with a series of initiatives designed to bring the claims for reparations closer to reality. A major work of public education was done in 2007 by the Jamaica Bicentenary Committee, chaired by Professor Verene Shepherd. In the same year the Jamaican Parliament debated a motion moved by Mr Mike Henry, asking that 'the nations due to make reparations be called upon to provide compensation by way of cash and/or debt relief'. All the participants supported the motion, including the leader of the Opposition Mr Bruce Golding.

In 2008 there was a change of government in Jamaica and Mr Golding became Prime Minister. In May 2009 he announced the formation of a National Commission on Reparations. Its task was to receive submissions and testimonies, evaluate research, and carry out public consultations 'with the aim of guiding a national approach to reparations'. Crucially, the Commission was also to 'recommend the form or forms that such reparations may take', bearing in mind the recommendations of the Durban Conference and other factors. The chairman is Professor Barry Chevannes, distinguished Jamaican scholar. I have been honoured to be chosen as a member of the commission.

The commission is pursuing is role, slowly but resolutely. It has begun consultations in Jamaica and plans to hold meetings and take evidence in the UK. I see it as a historic initiative. It moves the issue away from rhetoric and aspiration towards a new phase in which a claim can be planned, formulated and pursued. The commission does not have an easy task. It must neither be tokenistic nor unreal. It must identify forms of reparation which relate to the undoubted present day damage that the slavery history has caused. It will have to take into account the needs of other countries in the region, especially Haiti which was forced to pay compensation to the government of France. Its work will, I hope and believe, form another milestone on the road to a real reconciliation between Africa and Europe, Black people and White.

Chapter 6

Litigation and political action to address historic injustices in the United States

Problems and prospects

Dinah Shelton

Throughout history, humans have migrated, often violently invading and subsequently supplanting or integrating with earlier settlements. Empires have been built and dismantled, civilisations have emerged, lived and died. Across the millennia, the human record is replete with episodes of genocide, slavery, torture, forced conversions, and the mass expulsions of overrun peoples. The existence, boundaries and multi-ethnic populations of modern states are largely the result of acts and omissions that would be unlawful if done today – and some of which were unlawful at the time. Indigenous peoples have lost their traditional lands, and members of many communities have been killed, excluded and subject to discrimination by invaders who enriched themselves through privilege and the suppression of pre-existing societies. Such events, even from centuries ago, remain alive in memory and the consequences of past injustices continue into the present, manifest in on-going inequality, discrimination and racism.

The differences between widespread historical violations and individual claims have posed formidable obstacles to reparations. In the United States, the litigation model based on the remedial paradigm of individual perpetrator, individual victim and proven quantifiable losses, has proven unable to adjust itself to group claims for historical wrongs. In addition, procedural barriers, including statutes of limitations and the principle against the non-retroactivity of law, have been coupled with the political problem that the real cost of full reparations entails the loss of economic and social advantages enjoyed by the powerful.

Reparations for the past and present wrongs are due, however, even if it may be difficult to determine their appropriate nature and sweep. First, as already mentioned, many abuses continue today and violate existing human rights norms that are binding on all states, entitling their victims to access justice and substantive redress. Reparations claims help to determine the moral and political significance of past actions, identifying arguments that are relevant and contributing to the emergence of a common set of values by which to judge the acceptability of present and future acts, as well as accountability for the past.

Second, some historical acts were illegal under national or international law at the time they were committed. The victims have been unable to secure redress for political reasons, because evidence was concealed or procedural barriers prevented them from presenting claims. In such circumstances the lapse of time should not prevent reparation for harm caused by the illegal conduct.

Third, states, communities, businesses and individuals have unjustly profited from many of the abuses, garnering wealth at the expense of the victims. The economic disparities created have continued over generations, often becoming more pronounced over time. As one author has put it:

> Not seeking financial restitution, in the face of documented proof that financial giants worldwide are sitting on billions of dollars in funds made on the backs of . . . victims, which they then invested and reinvested many times over . . . amounts to an injustice that cannot be ignored.
> (Bazyler 2002: 41)

In the USA, reparations claims point to the ways in which the majority in modern America have benefited from slavery and subsequent *de jure* and *de facto* discrimination, not to mention the land clearances and genocide of Native American tribes. Failure to acknowledge and account for US history would be to reject the continuing experiences of a large segment of the population, with the implication that both they and what happened to them are somehow not worthy of notice.

Fourth, many claims have a compelling moral dimension because acknowledged wrongs were committed during or after the emergence of the concept of the equal and fundamental human rights of all persons (Olick and Coughlin 2003: 37). Human rights were part of positive law in states in Europe and North America by the end of the eighteenth century, and at least partially recognised in other countries from the same period. If human rights are truly inherent and universal then they should apply not only territorially but also temporally, and also provide a basis by which to judge the often savage treatment meted out to indigenous and enslaved peoples in a direct contravention of the stated norms. The payment of damages is symbolic of the moral condemnation of the abuses that occurred. It may also be asserted in equity that present generations have a responsibility for the past. Every individual is born into a society or culture that has emerged over time and that shapes each person, making the past part of the present and giving that society's individuals an historic identity. International law, in recognising that institutions or collective entities such as states have a continuity over time, provides that a change of government does not absolve a state of the responsibility for wrongful conduct.

Finally, reparations acknowledge the suffering of victims and the legacies of that suffering in contemporary society. This acknowledgement in itself can be restorative and promote reconciliation: 'The discourse of universal human rights is tied directly to a politics of regret because its advocates believe that only gestures of reparation, apology, and acknowledgment can restore the dignity of history's victims and can deter new outbreaks of inhumanity' (Olick and Coughlin 2003: 42).[1] On a practical level, '[u]nrighted wrongs can leave victims uncompensated, under-deter harmful conduct, and foster social resentment' (Rowe 2001: 158).[2] At worst, that resentment may re-emerge in internal and international armed conflicts.

With these supporting rationales, historical wrongs have been the subject of a growing number of legal and/or political claims for reparations.[3] Litigation, activism, social pressure and legislation have all succeeded in part, but none entirely. The issues, actors, legal regimes and models for affording reparations involve complex factors that must be evaluated in each case. Legal actions may seek to invoke state responsibility in international law (inter-state claims); national or international human rights law (individuals or groups filing complaints against a state or state agent); criminal law (a state or the international community prosecuting an individual perpetrator); or national tort law (individuals or groups seeking remedies against individual perpetrators). Substantive legal claims may be based on violations of human rights; state responsibility for a breach of inter-state obligations; violations of humanitarian law; infringements of constitutional guarantees; or acts contrary to national legislation such as theft, murder, or other personal injury. Equitable claims may assert unjust enrichment or breach of trust. Forms of reparations can include apologies, prosecutions, commemorations, memorials, rehabilitation, compensation, affirmative action, restitution, land reform, law reform, and various types of truth commissions.

This chapter provides an overview of the claims asserted in US courts and legislatures and the responses to them – from apologies and compensation to rejection – and indicates the primary legal barriers to reparation. It also examines the legal bases for claims in national law and equity. The conclusion finds that the synergies produced by activism, litigation and legislation have produced the greatest success in a direct relationship with how recent the events are to the present. Living direct survivors have been clearly favoured over descendants who claim to suffer the continuing effects of distant wrongs.

US litigation

Litigation to address slavery, the taking of indigenous lands, lives and cultures, and other domestic injustices began early in US history and has continued to the present day.[4] Increased efforts to obtain reparations began in the 1990s,[5] in part as a result of the successful efforts by Japanese-

Americans to obtain reparations for their wrongful internment and loss of property during World War II.[6] The Civil Liberties Act of 1988, which provided for reparations, led other groups to begin organising themselves to seek redress.[7] A further stimulus came after the reunification of Germany allowed new cases to be filed in the USA against Germany and German companies for Nazi-era abuses. While many of the lawsuits were dismissed on procedural grounds, they often served to build a historical record of injustice, creating public pressure to negotiate settlements or take legislative action to ensure redress for the aging survivors.[8] Third, the growing number of cases brought against human rights violators from Ferdinand Marcos to Argentinean general Suarez-Mason, under the jurisdiction of the Alien Tort Statute,[9] led many to observe a disparity between the treatment of violators from outside the United States and the treatment of those within. For these reasons, and the growing attention being paid to human rights law generally, reparations litigation has considerably expanded. This next section looks at some of the major cases and claims in relation to transatlantic slavery. For reasons of space other areas of claims in US courts, principally indigenous land and cultural claims, and foreign claims in reference to the Holocaust, are not examined here.

Slave reparations

Current slave reparations claims are based on centuries of uncompensated slave labour and the current inequalities in education, income, and opportunity between Whites and Blacks. Slavery reparations claims often seek to account for an acknowledgment of the fact that US wealth and institutions were founded on this 'peculiar institution'. The most common strategy that has been used is litigation, although some scholars and activists would argue that it is divisive and disabling to take a confrontational posture (Miller 2004: 46). The litigation demand is usually based upon claims founded in tort or unjust enrichment, placing all African Americans into a claimant group and the rest of society into debtors.[10]

Slavery litigation against the government has not yet been successful. In *Cato v. United States*, 70 F.3d 1103 (9th Cir. 1995), two groups of individual plaintiffs filed almost identical complaints against the USA seeking $100 million in damages for slavery and subsequent discrimination, for an acknowledgment of such discrimination as well as an apology. The district court dismissed the case prior to service of process, stating 'Discrimination and bigotry of any type is intolerable, and the enslavement of Africans by this Country is inexcusable. This Court, however, is unable to identify any legally cognisable basis upon which plaintiff's claims may proceed against the United States. While plaintiff may be justified in seeking redress for past and present injustices, it is not within the jurisdiction of this Court to grant the requested relief. The legislature, rather than the judiciary, is the appropriate forum for plaintiff's grievances.' The primary reason given for the decision was that the USA had not waived its sovereign immunity. The Ninth Circuit, on appeal, added that the plaintiffs lacked sufficient standing to represent all African-Americans in a generalised grievance based on the 13th Amendment, and that as the 'complaint neither identifies any constitutional or statutory right that was violated, nor asserts any basis for federal subject matter jurisdiction or waiver of sovereign immunity, it was properly dismissed'. The court distinguished Indian cases because of the 'fiduciary responsibilities running from the United States to Indian Tribes because of specific treaty obligations.'

In order to avoid problems of government immunity, litigation against corporations who utilised or benefited from slavery began 'after it had become manifestly apparent no federal reparations could be expected in the foreseeable future' (Kornweibel 2006: 219). The consolidated cases in the *African American Slave Litigation* had 18 defendants: five major financial institutions, five insurance corporations, four railroads, three tobacco companies, and one textile firm (Kornweibel 2006: 220). In one of the original cases that was later consolidated, *Carrington v. FleetBoston Fin. Corp.*, No. 02-CV-01863 (EDNY filed Mar 26, 2002), and *Farmer-Paellmann v. FleetBoston Fin Corp.*, No. 02-CV-01862 (EDNY filed Mar. 26, 2002), the claims included conspiracy; a demand for accounting; human rights violations; conversion; and unjust enrichment. A companion case in California, *Hurdle v. FleetBoston Fin. Corp.*, No. CGC-02-412388 (Cal. Super. Ct. filed Sept. 10, 2002), invoking Ca. Unfair Competition Law, Cal. Bus. & Prof. Code sec. 17200 (West 1997), invoked the state statute prohibiting 'unlawful, unfair or fraudulent business act or practice'. The statute offered a considerable advantage in providing a broad standing for consumers to act as private attorneys general.

Unjust enrichment also provides a useful basis for litigating reparations claims because the doctrine does not require that the act on which the claim is based was legally wrongful when committed, only that it was unfair or unjust (Sherwin 2004). Thus, a claim can cover conduct that was morally wrong though permissible at the time if the plaintiff has a moral claim to the enrichment the defendant obtained. Restitution can even be claimed from those who innocently obtained a benefit to which they were not entitled. Based on this theory, class actions seeking slavery reparations were brought against corporate defendants who were alleged to have participated in or supported the institution of slavery, seeking compensation and restitution for the value of labour converted from slaves and the disgorgement of profits from slavery.

The consolidated case was dismissed for lack of standing (and alternative grounds, including justiciability and statute of limitations) and an amended complaint was filed thereafter as the Second Consolidated and Amended

Complaint and Jury Demand, *In re African-Am. Slave Descendants' Litig.*, MDL No. 1491 (N.D. Ill. April 5, 2004). Emily Sherwin has outlined the difficulties with the case: 'Slave descendants must establish that those who profited from slavery did so at the descendants' expense. Not only is ancestry difficult to trace, but there is no guarantee that descendants would eventually have enjoyed assets or advantages lost to their ancestors' (2004: 1452). The plaintiffs were not themselves victims of slavery nor were the current corporate owners those who had committed the wrongs, even if they are currently benefiting from earlier wrong-doing.

Defenses and litigation hurdles

There are numerous procedural barriers to litigation recovery in the United States. Problems include: (1) linking past harm to present claimants; (2) identifying a baseline from which to measure harm; (3) identifying present claimants, i.e. issues of standing; and (4) identifying wrong-doers today. There are also time barriers, based on statutes of limitations and laches. Governments have rejected some claims on the basis that there was nothing illegal about their acts at the time they were committed or have invoked their sovereign immunity, as in, for example, *Sampson v. Federal Republic of Germany*, 250 F.3d 1145 (7th Cir. 2001) and *Princz v Federal Republic of Germany*, 26 F.3d 1166 (D.C.Cir. 1994), cert. denied, 513 U.S. 1121 (1995). Besides the issue of retroactivity addressed below, they may claim that existing civil rights laws are reparations and point out the impossibility of accurately calculating damages or compensation.[11] For slavery claims these issues translate into objections that all slaves have been dead for at least a generation because the events happened over one hundred years ago; White Americans living today did not enslave, especially those who immigrated to the US after 1865; slavery did not cause the present ills of African-Americans (i.e., no causation); it is impossible to determine who should pay and who should get how much. These are problems that arise due to utilising traditional tort law, which looks to individuals who are at fault for specific acts of wrongdoing resulting in injuries to identifiable victims whose injuries are quantifiable. While some of these objections may resonate with slavery claims they do not apply to *de jure* segregation, because these claimaints are still alive and suffering from the discrimination they endure.

   The 7th circuit opinion by Judge Posner in *Am Slave Descendants Litig.* 375 F.Supp.2d 721 (N.D. Ill. 2005), aff'd as modified in 471 F.3d 754, 759 (7th Cir. 2006), upheld the lack of standing for tort and unjust enrichment, in part because of the causality issue: 'It would be impossible by the methods of litigation to connect the defendants' alleged misconduct with the financial and emotional harm that the plaintiffs claim to have suffered as a result of that conduct.' He saw a fatal disconnect between slaves and plaintiffs because 'the causal chain is too long and has too many weak links for a court to be able to find that the defendants' conduct harmed the plaintiffs at all, let alone in an amount that could be estimated without the widest speculation'. He dismissed the plaintiffs' economic analysis of continuing injury as 'aggregate effects, not affecting particular individuals' (at 750) adding that there would be 'no way' to determine that a given African-American today, was any worse off due to the conduct of one or more of the defendants. Posner left open two possible exceptions where a claim might survive. First, prove a violation of the law prohibiting the transport of slaves after 1850, establish standing, establish a private right of action for slaves or their descendants, identify the ancestors, quantify the damages and find a reason to toll the statute of limitations. Second, bring an action based on the current law for fraud or consumer protection violations, on the grounds that plaintiffs bought products they would not have bought but for the concealment of the manufacturer's involvement in slavery.

Indigenous claims generally fare no better. The litigation obstacles may in fact be even greater, because in addition to problems of standing, proximate causation, the time bar, laches, *res judiciata*, the exhaustion of remedies, an *ex post facto* application of laws, and sovereign immunity, there is the political question doctrine that applies to relations between the US government and tribes. The political question doctrine coupled with a recognition of Congress's 'plenary power' to decide Indian issues precludes a judicial redress for harm even when in violation of treaties. Indian real property also lacks the full protection of Constitutional law as it is considered US trust territory. The entire legal structure is antithetical to the communally-based claims of native tribes.

The defendants in the Holocaust litigation raised similar objections. In a noteworthy act the judge sat on the case for a year rather than decide all the various motions, while public pressure built for a settlement through media stories about aging Holocaust victims. The most prominent victim was paid separately during the litigation and died the following year. It also came out that one of the Swiss banks was illegally shredding World War II documents.[12] The threat of sanctions by the US government also played a strong role, which unfortunately cannot work when the USA itself is the defendant. The settlement came two weeks before the threatened start of sanctions and a week before the bank rating agency reported that UBS might lose its highest rating if the sanctions were imposed (Bayzler 2004: 66).[13]

Art restitution cases involve their own defences. Art dealers argue that a full recovery of Nazi stolen art could disrupt the international art market, especially for French Impressionists (Bayzler 2004: 164). Also many of the present owners are bona fide purchasers.[14]

Historic wrongs in general raise the problem of long-passed statutes of limitations or laches and the fact that intervening events and contingencies can obscure the causes of harm.[15] Statutes of limitations and laches doctrines are deemed to promote efficiency and certainty by ensuring that claims are fresh and reasonably connected in time and space to a particular act. The older the claim, the more problematic it is to resolve.[16] An equitable tolling of the statute may be appropriate in many cases since one basis for tolling is the absence of an actual and effective remedy and many plaintiffs can introduce credible assertions of insurmountable legal barriers to obtaining redress (Hylton 2004). Courts can also examine the facts to determine when courts became available to plaintiffs, and indeed courts have done so in cases of violations committed by other governments. In *Barrueto v. Larios*, 205 F.Supp.1325 (S.D. Fla. 2002), an Alien Tort Statute case from Chile brought in the Southern District of Florida in 2002, the court tolled the statute of limitations, concluding that evidence of murder had been hidden by the Chilean government and that the pre-1990 concealment of the cause of death tolled the running of the statute of limitations until 1990.[17]

Another problem in reparations litigation is how to apportion responsibility and redress.[18] The notion of personal responsibility, including a ban on bills of attainder in the common law, posits that it is unjust to require individuals or companies today to pay for the acts of their predecessors, over which they had no control and in which they did not participate.[19] Legal theories need to be constructed to explain who bears the responsibility; how such wrongs should be redressed; and who is entitled to reparations. Standing normally requires some relationship between the wrong-doer and victim. There must be some harms that are transmitted from victim to victim across generations. Identifying such harms becomes an essential part of reparations litigation. Federal standing[20] requires an actual injury that has been caused to the plaintiff by the defendant and that there is something the defendant can do to redress the injury. Thus, it is premised on a relationship between the parties that caused the injury. Where there are presently injured parties this is usually not a problem, but standing can be an insurmountable barrier when cases are based on being a descendant of the persons directly injured ('hereditary or genetic standing'). In some instances a third type of standing may be based on being a 'private attorney general', thereby enforcing the law without any direct relationship.

Some types of claims are more easily transferred across generations than others. With slavery litigation the following must be asked: (1) who if anyone can represent all African-American descendants of slaves? and (2) what is the plaintiff's relationship to the alleged injury that the law recognises? In general, some type of current injury must be shown as a result of the injury to the original victims. In the litigation already brought, the plaintiff asserted that the present injury lay in the vestiges of slavery, racial inequalities and psychic scars on African-Americans. That plaintiff sought unjust profits from those companies which had enslaved or engaged in the slave trade. The district court noted that there was little to connect the plaintiff to the defendants, because she made no specific allegation that an ancestor had been on one of the defendants' ships or insured or had worked for a railroad. She could have alleged specific harm nonetheless as an African-American generally because (1) slavery determined an enduring social stigma for Blacks, with an accompanying economic loss;[21] (2) she suffered enduring psychological harm; and (3) companies were unjustly enriched. Her arguments echoed comments by Justice Marshall in *Bakke v. Regents of the University of California* at 400–01:

> For several hundred years Negroes have been discriminated against, not as individuals, but rather solely because of the color of their skins. It is unnecessary in 20th century America to have individual Negroes demonstrate that they have been victims of racial discrimination; the racism of our society has been so pervasive that none, regardless of wealth or position, has managed to escape its impact. The experience . . . has been different in kind, not just in degree, from that of other ethnic groups. It is not merely the history of slavery alone, but also that a whole people were marked as inferior by the law. And that mark has endured.

The Supreme Court recently has rejected racial preferences as remedies for past discrimination, holding that the Constitution prohibits any discrimination (defined as preference) based upon membership in a racial group (*Adarand Constructors Inc v. Pena*, 515 U.S. 200 (1995)). Where once Justice Warren looked to psychological harm of the group in *Brown v. Board of Education*, and ordered remedial action, recent jurisprudence considers racial classifications injurious no matter what the effects (even beneficial) on the individuals classified, even to remedy past harm. Justice Thomas has stated that to tie past discrimination to present disadvantage itself inflicts a psychological injury by creating an 'ideology of victimhood' – blaming the circumstances rather than taking personal responsibility. Thus, as also noted in *Adarand Constructors Inc v. Pena* at 108, any race-based demand for remediation based on a continuing pattern of discrimination is evidence of a psychological injury that keeps those injured from fighting and succeeding against the odds. We are thus forced to look at individualised injury,[22] thereby placing significant obstacles in the way of group remedies despite the history of slavery and segregation. The consequence is, as Miller puts it, that 'once the racially constituted status quo is established, it cannot be changed using further racial criteria' (Miller 2004: 104).

The most common political objection to reparations for historical injustices is the general principle of the non-retroactivity of the law. This ground of opposition assumes, of course, that the acts were lawful at the time they were committed. The judicial resolution of a reparations claim for historical injustice requires a determination of the law as it was applicable to events that commenced or were concluded long ago. International dispute resolution bodies have expressed the notion of inter-temporality – that the rights and duties of parties are determined by the law in force at the time a claim arises.[23]

The United States Supreme Court sometimes gives a retrospective application to its constitutional rulings or to statutes, weighing the merits and demerits of a retroactive application of the law by looking to the prior history of the rule in question, its purpose and effect, and whether a retrospective operation will further or retard its operation.[24] The court permits a retroactive application of rules that are deemed 'absolute prerequisites to fundamental fairness'.[25] Accordingly, the judgment on whether a particular statute has acted retroactively should be informed and guided by considerations of fair notice, reasonable reliance, and settled expectations.

In the absence of a clear indication on the part of a law-making body, most national and international courts will presume non-retroactivity,[26] but they may 'find' a new rule to govern prior conduct where necessary in order to resolve a dispute.[27] Implicit in the presumption of non-retroactivity is the notion of fundamental fairness, the idea that individuals may legitimately rely on legal norms in force (Fallon and Meltzer 1991). As noted in *Landgraf v USI Film Prods.* 511 US 244, 265 (1994): 'Elementary considerations of fairness dictate that individuals should have an opportunity to know what the law is and to conform their conduct accordingly; settled expectations should not be lightly disrupted. For that reason, the principle that the legal effect of conduct should ordinarily be assessed under the law that existed when the conduct took place has timeless and universal appeal.' Yet reliance may not be legitimate if the rule is openly contested, in transition, or patently unjust (Meltzer 1988).

Finally, indigenous land claims have met with a test imposed by some states, and perhaps acknowledged by the Inter-American Court, that the indigenous people retain their links to their traditional lands in order to recover them. In effect, this means that the more successful a state has been in dispossessing the indigenous, the less likely it is that they will be able to recover their lands. While the court has progressively interpreted the right to property to include collective or communal rights to indigenous lands as a form of property, as for example in *Mayagna (Sumo) Awas Tingni Community v Nicaragua* 79 IACtHR (ser. C) (2001), 10 IHRR 758 (2003), it has indicated that a state should take a case-by-case approach to balancing the communal ancestral rights of the indigenous people to the present-day private property rights of non-indigenous landowners. While there is certainly a recognition of indigenous claims to lands, the court insisted in *Yakye Axa Indigenous Community v Paraguay* (2005) 125 IACtHR (ser. C) at para 149 (trans Pasqualucci 2006: 300), that '[t]his does not mean that whenever there is a conflict between the territorial interests of individuals or the State and the territorial interests of the members of indigenous communities, the latter will prevail over the former'. If a wrongful taking is demonstrated, compensation may have to be a substitute for restitution.

A first response: apology

Despite the formidable hurdles to reparations, in recent years legislatures and companies, among others, have issued formal apologies for the commission of past wrongs (Cunningham 1999: 285; Gibney and Rox-strom 2001). On 8 September 2000, the director of the US Bureau of Indian Affairs formally apologised for the agency's participation in the clearing of western tribes (Gover 2000).[28] Washington State adopted Senate Resolution 8729 on 27 February 2006 to apologise for the cross-border seizure and lynching of a 14-year-old Native American boy suspected of killing a shopkeeper. The resolution acknowledged the failure of authorities to act, seeking remembrance and 'to ensure that such a tragedy will neither be forgotten nor repeated'. The United Methodist Church in the United States also apologised to Native Americans in the State of Wyoming for a massacre led by a Methodist minister. Perhaps most far-reaching, in 1993, on the centenary of the conquest of the Kingdom of Hawaii, the United States Congress passed Public Law 103-150, known as the Apology Bill, which states: 'the indigenous Hawaiian people never directly relinquished their claims to their inherent sovereignty as a people or over their national lands to the United States, either through their monarchy or through a plebiscite or referendum'. The measure expressed the commitment of Congress to acknowledge the ramifications of the overthrow of the Kingdom of Hawaii.[29]

An apology can serve different purposes.[30] It can acknowledge the suffering of others, as when expressing sorrow over the death of a loved one ('I am sorry for your loss'). It can express regret and solidarity over events that are outside the control of the speaker ('I am really sorry about the miserable weather we are having'). It can also be an acceptance of fault leading to redress ('I am sorry I lost your book'). It is only in the last instance that an apology may carry with it legal implications, establishing a causal link between the action of the speaker and the injury suffered. The possibility that an apology may serve to buttress legal claims can make government officials reluctant to express regret over historical injustices.

The US Congress's Apology Bill for Hawaii, for example, contains language that effectively acknowledges Hawaii's right to self-determination. In many circumstances, the exact meaning of apology and the sincerity with which an apology is given are difficult to discern. Unless the sincerity and meaning are clear, an apology may exacerbate rather than mitigate the sense of injury.

Some apologies have been accompanied by specific measures of redress. J.P. Morgan Chase, for example, apologised in January 2005 for the actions of its corporate predecessors in (1) the acceptance of nearly 13,000 slaves as collateral and (2) the ownership of approximately 1,250 people when the loans went into default. The company said: 'We apologise to the African-American community, particularly those who are descendants of slaves, and to the rest of the American public for the role that Citizens Bank and Canal Bank played' (Flahardy 2005). The bank pledged $5 million for college scholarships for Black students from Louisiana. It is important to note that this apology was not entirely forthcoming without pressure having been applied: in October 2002, the Chicago City Council passed an ordinance that required companies who do business with the city to search all available records for their corporate connections to slavery.

The federal government has promulgated several apologies over the past decade. President Clinton apologised for non-consensual medical experimentation on Black airmen (Clinton 1997). More recently, in 2005, the US Senate issued an apology for its failure to enact anti-lynching legislation.[31] The bill noted that more than 200 bills on the subject were introduced in Congress in the first half of the twentieth century and none were passed, while nearly 5000 persons were lynched between 1882 and 1968 with 99 per cent of all perpetrators escaping punishment. The resolution explains that the apology is justified because 'only by coming to terms with history can the United States effectively champion human rights abroad'; it then adds that 'an apology offered in the spirit of true repentance moves the United States toward reconciliation and may become central to a new understanding, on which improved racial relations can be forged'. It 'expresses the deepest sympathies and most solemn regrets of the Senate to the descendants of victims of lynching, the ancestors of whom were deprived of life, human dignity, and the constitutional protections accorded all citizens of the United States'; it also 'remembers the history of lynching, to ensure that these tragedies will be neither forgotten nor repeated'. The bill was co-authored by Senator Landrieu of Louisiana and Senator George Allen of Virginia. Senator Landrieu began the debate on the bill by individually naming the lynching victims from Louisiana, together with the date and place each one occurred. This history was recounted state by state, from Illinois (Obama) to the Deep South.

The Senate issued a second apology in July 2008, in a bill Apologizing for the Enslavement and Segregation of African-Americans.[32] The text was based on measures that had been adopted by legislatures in former slave states. The text acknowledged the injustice, cruelty and inhumanity of slavery and Jim Crow laws and apologised to African-Americans on behalf of the people of the United States for the wrongs committed against them and their ancestors: it also 'expresses its commitment to rectify the lingering consequences of the misdeeds committed against African-Americans and to stop the occurrence of human rights violations in the future'.

During 2007, prior to the Senate action, states throughout the South adopted legislation acknowledging the wrongs of slavery and Jim Crow and apologising to African-Americans. Virginia's Joint Resolution was one of the first. It expressed regret and sorrow for the state's former slavery industry and its harms to African-Americans, as well as – uniquely – for the state's exploitation of Native Americans.[33] Passed during the four hundredth anniversary of the first permanent English settlement at Jamestown, the resolution referred to 'transgressions of fundamental principles and moral standards of liberty and equality', including 'the maltreatment and exploitation of Native Americans and the immoral institution of human slavery'. It recognised Native Americans as the 'first people' who aided the settlers and acknowledged Native efforts to protect their land and culture even while Virginia's laws segregated them and deprived them of their rights. It also recognised that the Racial Integrity Act of 1924 made anyone with 'one drop' of African blood an African and thereby denied the existence of many self-identified Native Americans, destroying their ability to now be recognised by the federal government and gain benefits: 'Whereas the most abject apology for past wrongs cannot right them; yet the spirit of true repentance on behalf of a government and, through it, a people, can promote reconciliation and healing, and avert the repetition of past wrongs and the disregard of manifested injustices . . .' The resolution cited 'dehumanising atrocities' and said that the contributions of Native Americans and African-Americans should be 'embraced, celebrated and retold for generations to come'.

Similar apology legislation was adopted in Maryland,[34] North Carolina,[35] Alabama,[36] Florida,[37] and New Jersey.[38] New Jersey is one of the few to see the potential implications of the apologies and put in its operative second paragraph: 'It is the intent of the Legislature that this resolution shall not be used in, or be the basis of, any type of litigation.'[39]

Other forms of legislated reparations

Political initiatives have thus developed alternative models of relief, looking at broader goals than monetary compensation. In some instances, groups have negotiated reparations that include restitution (Frantz 1998). The 1971 Alaska Native Claims Settlement Act granted indigenous Alaskans land as well as monetary relief.[40] The Aleutian and Pribilof Islands Restitution Act[41] established a restitution fund for losses suffered during World War II.

Several states[42] and local communities[43] have passed disclosure ordinances, requiring businesses in their jurisdictions to search and reveal records of their involvement in slavery, the slave trade, or the Holocaust. These measures make all corporations who were involved potentially liable if they fail to report. They also place an onus on the government to compile and publish the information. California's law is illustrative here. It requires the commissioner of insurance to request and obtain information from insurers doing business in California regarding any records of slaveholder insurance policies issued by any predecessor company during the slavery era,[44] including the names of any slaveholders and slaves described in the records. Some 1357 insurance carriers are subject to the regulation. The compliance response rate in the first year was 92 per cent. Aetna, one of the largest insurers in the state, initially submitted the names of 16 slaves and then added other names it had found. New York Life Ins. Co. reported that its predecessor wrote slave life insurance policies from 1846 to 1848. In addition to expressing its profound regret, it reported on 484 slaves' lives insured by their owners. Only Providence Washington was able to report that in 1799, its shareholder meeting voted that no insurance would be issued on behalf of the company on any vessel or property involved in the slave trade.

One of the most far-reaching local efforts to provide reparations occurred in the State of Florida which legislated[45] a redress for the 1923 Rosewood Massacre, when mob violence destroyed an African-American town, killing some residents and forcing all others to leave. The state established an official 'truth commission' which issued a report, followed by an acknowledgement, an admission of responsibility, the payment of compensation of up to $150,000 to the victims, a scholarship fund, and a research fund for future generations (Jones et al. 1993).[46] Representative John Conyers has proposed a similar national truth commission to investigate wrongs inflicted by slavery,[47] but thus far without success.

Inadequate legislative measures can generate their own litigation. Like Rosewood, the 1921 Tulsa riots[48] involved the destruction of an African-American community, deaths and detention. From 31 May to 1 June white rioters, including some acting with the authority of the Chief of Police and members of the Oklahoma State National Guard, entered the Greenwood district of Tulsa, popularly called the Black Wall Street. More than 8,000 persons were forced to flee; 300 were murdered; and over 1,200 residences were burned to the ground. Those who stayed were put in detention camps and remained there over the winter (Ogletree 2004).

Eighty years later the state of Oklahoma created the Oklahoma Commission to Study the Tulsa Race Riot of 1921. The Commission was given the power to publish new information discovered through a search of the historical records and to make recommendations (Churchwell 2001). The commission recommended payment of reparations to the survivors and descendants. The failure of the city and state to respond led to a lawsuit being filed on behalf of 120 survivors. The state did set up an education fund which critics said provided no more help to victims than had previously been available.[49] The case was dismissed as untimely.[50]

In sum, most reparations have come about through negotiations or the political process, rather than through litigation. The fact that lawsuits do not produce an immediate judgment that is favourable to reparations does not mean, however, that they lack value in bringing attention to the legitimacy and moral dimensions of the claims at issue. In fact, many lawsuits have been a precursor to negotiated or legislative settlements.

The remedies

One problem with historic injustices in particular is the counter-factual – we cannot know what would have been the situation absent the wrong (Roht-Arriaza 2003). It is also impossible to determine the value of lost real and personal property due to slavery or other historical injustices. Avoiding individualised compensation, it may be possible to foresee collective reparations as development or preferential access. Randall Robinson among others, has argued for community-based reparations rather than an individualised grant of $20,000 to each of 20 million living descendants of slaves, which would result in a politically unlikely US$400 billion in expenditures.

Professor Alfred Brophy, like Rep. Conyers, suggests a Congressional investigation or a truth commission (Brophy 2006). He like many other US reparations scholars believes it will be legislation and not litigations that provides reparations. Such reparations may include a broad range of programmes, such as apologies, truth commissions, civil rights legislation, and payments to communities and individuals. Some say that Lyndon Johnson began a reparations programme with his Great Society programme of civil rights legislation, referred to as 'the most important reparations program ever undertaken' (Brophy 2006: 825).

A legislative resolution means taxpayers must pay for programmes involving disbursement. Such a spreading of responsibility across the community may be seen to diminish individual culpability, but this is appropriate when the individuals responsible can no longer be identified. Those who favour compensation for slavery argue that there are bases to measure the amounts due: (1) the value of slaves' services that are still retained; (2) the money needed to bring the African-American poverty rate to the non-Hispanic white American poverty rate; (3) difference in per capita wealth of racial groups; or (4) the amount needed to bring educational performance, health care and wealth to parity. Overall, the measures tend to ask to what extent do those who benefited continue to do so and to what extent are there harms that are still traceable to the institution of slavery?

One reason for the very different approaches is that some take as a starting-point the violations committed while others focus on the consequences suffered: 'Consequences have a temporal quality that does not correspond to the events or crimes that give rise to them. They have a cumulative character' (Magarrell 2003). Such consequences include 'deterioration in mental health, disability, interpersonal violence, sexual exploitation, land conflicts, loss of jobs and opportunities, economic dependence, political stigmas, political isolation, and loss of cultural identity, etc.' (Magarrell 2003). Mixing a socio-economic entitlement with reparations can end up simply providing something that is already considered a right, such as health plans, access to post-secondary education, and housing.

Today many reparations scholars and activists in the United States see reconciliation rather than compensation as the conceptual foundation for reparations, (Yamamoto et al. 2007), while also retaining a focus on the role of justice in social healing. Reparations are part of the larger project of social healing that moves from recognition to responsibility to reconstruction, repairing the damage to group members and building new relationships as focal points for fostering interest convergence among groups. There is also a newfound desire to globalise reparations practice by building on the experiences of other societies.

Conclusion

As is well known, the right to a remedy is part of international law, contained in global[51] and regional[52] human rights treaties and other instruments.[53] International and national legal doctrine suggests that historical claims may warrant reparations in two circumstances. First, when the acts were illegal at the time committed and no reparations have been afforded.[54] Second, reparations are justified where a reliance on the earlier law was not reasonable and expectations were not settled because the law patently conflicted with the fundamental principles then in force.[55] The benefit unjustly obtained may then be claimed by those who suffered or their descendants.

Cases involving unlawful acts present fewer problems than historical injustices based on actions that were lawful at the time they were done. In the latter instances, the question of whether or not to give retroactive effect to the law and afford reparations involves a balancing of the equities, the strength of the claims, the need for reconciliation, and the practicalities of devising appropriate reparations between appropriate entities and persons. When it is clear that there was considerable debate over the morality or legality of historical acts, it may be more justified to award reparations because the reliance on the law at the time was probably not settled and those acting would have had some notice of the likelihood of change to bring the law into conformity with basic constitutional principles and emerging norms of human rights.

Even where the claims lack a firm legal foundation, experience thus far suggests that reparations may still take place via the political process. Many factors will affect the likelihood of reparations being afforded for past injustices, most of them linked to the amount of time that has passed. First, it is more likely that reparations will be afforded if the perpetrators are identifiable and still living. Similarly, and secondly, the victims should be identifiable and mostly still alive or their immediate descendants present. The size of the group will also affect the amount, if not the fact of reparations; the larger the group and its claim, the more difficult it is to obtain redress. Thirdly, demands for reparations will probably only succeed with political pressure and strong, cohesive support from the victims themselves. Perhaps most importantly, the substance of the claim must be one that presents a compelling human injustice that is well documented. The claim will be even stronger where there is continued harm and a causal connection between present harm and the past injustice. The claims of Japanese Americans to reparations for their World War II internment succeeded in part because (1) the evidence was clear – there was a specific executive order, the enforcement of which led to harm; (2) the existing law was violated; (3) the provable facts showed the violation of law; (4) the claimants were easily identifiable individuals who were not too numerous; (5) the causation between the act and harm was easy to show; (6) damages were fixed and limited; and finally (7) payment meant finality (Yamamoto 1998).

For most claimants, reparation is a moral issue involving a formal acknowledgement of an historical wrong, a recognition of continuing injury, and a commitment to make redress. Reparations are pursued because they are powerful acts that can challenge the assumptions underlying past and present social arrangements. At the same time, they must avoid 'entrenched victim status, image distortion, mainstream backlash, inter-minority friction and status quo enhancement'(Yamamoto 1998). A key issue is to determine which solutions to past abuses are most likely to provide a secure future while affording justice to the victims of that abuse. The alternatives range from doing nothing to a full social welfare or insurance system or public and private compensation or other assistance.

At their best, reparations may involve restructuring the relationships that gave rise to the underlying grievance and address the root problems leading to the abuse and systemic oppression.[56] This brings the notion of reparations close to the current idea of restorative justice as a potentially transformative social action. It also provides a reason for why legislatures may be better suited to determine reparations: they are not bound by precedent and legal doctrine and can instead fashion equitable remedies. Remedies thus become part of a healing process that may avoid the creation of future historical injustices.[57]

Notes

1   Op cit p. 42. (ibid).
2   'Symposium: Debates over Group Litigation in Comparative Perspective: What Can We Learn from Each Other?' (2001) 11 Duke J. Comp. & Int'l L. 157, at 158.
3   See, generally Ulrich and Krabbe Boserup (eds) 2003, Shelton 2004.
4   For a history of slave reparations efforts in the U.S., see Brophy 2002b at 109. Brophy documents the numerous injuries were inflicted in addition to the horrors of slavery itself. These included lynchings, the denial of political rights, and *de jure* discrimination. While slaves were not afforded the compensation promised at emancipation, Congress compensated some masters who lived in Washington, DC, during the Civil War for their slaves who were freed.
5   One plaintiff successfully sued Mobil Oil Company for polluting its drinking water in the 1940s and won in 1993. *Cyril v. Mobil Oil Corp.* 11 F3d 996 (10th Cir. 1993).
6   Shortly after the Japanese attack on Pearl Harbor that led the USA into the War, Exec. Order No. 9066, 7 Fed. Reg. 1407 (Feb. 19, 1942) ordered the immediate confinement of approximately 120,000 Japanese-Americans. Those who resisted, like Fred Korematsu, were convicted of crimes. In the 1970s, the Japanese American Citizens League began a movement for reparations. The Commission on Wartime Relocation and Internment of Civilians Act, Pub. L. No. 96-317, 94 Stat. 964 (1980), was passed to vacate the conviction of Fred Korematsu, but only in 1988 did Congress pass an act affording reparations. It included an acknowledgment and apology as well as a public education fund and restitution to individual Japanese. Civil Liberties Act of 1988, Pub L. No. 100–383, 102 Stat. 903, 50 U.S.C.A. App. sec. 1989b-1989b-9 (West 1988) (expired 1998). Of those who remained alive, 82,219 received redress; 1,500 could not be located, and 28 refused to accept compensation. The total amount of reparations foreseen, paid from general tax revenues, was $1,250,000,000. By a subsequent amendment in 1992, the amount was increased to $1.65 billion.
7   *Obadele v. United States*, 52 Fed. Cl. 432 (2002) was filed under the Civil Liberties Act, which provided payments to Japanese American internees of World War II. Plaintiffs sought slavery reparations and argued that the Act rested on an unconstitutional racial classification. The court upheld the constitutionality, but noted that 'the Plaintiffs have made a powerful case for redress as representatives of a racial group other than American of Japanese ancestry'. *Obadele*, at 442.
8   In addition to the cases discussed in the text, an example is provided by *Cruz v. United States*, 219 F.Supp.2d 1027 (N.D. Cal. 2002), a class action brought on behalf of *braceros*, Mexican workers brought to the USA to work on farms during a period lasting from World War II through the 1960s. Ten per cent of

the wages were deducted to be given to the workers on their return to Mexico, but none ever received the funds. The lawsuit dismissed, but in 2002 the US House of Representatives rather inadequately passed a resolution of gratitude for the *braceros*' efforts during WWII.

 9 The Alien Tort Statute, 28 U.S.C. § 1350, permits an alien to file a claim in federal court for a tort committed in violation of a treaty of the United States or in breach of the 'law of nations'.

10 Miller argues that this binary system is over-inclusive because not all or perhaps even the majority of whites are descended from slave-owners or those who benefited and many African Americans are not descendants of slaves (Miller 2004).

11 See *Vigil v. United States*, 293 F.Supp. 1187 (D.C. Colo. 1968, aff'd 430 F.2d 1357 (10th Cir. 1970), in which Mexican-Americans promised reparations by the USA in 1848 Treaty of Hidalgo ending the Mexican-American War were denied reparations on the ground that it would be impossible to fairly assess the damages.

12 A bank security guard discovered the effort to destroy documents and turned over what he could rescue to a Jewish group who gave them to the Zurich police. The guard was fired and the bank sought to have him prosecuted for violating Swiss bank secrecy laws. He was forced to flee Switzerland after death threats and may have been the first Swiss national to obtain political asylum in the USA (Bayzler 2002: 64).

13 Note that it is doubtful that the sanctions would have been legal under US law, because many were being imposed by state and local governments in opposition to the federal administration. The case was settled before any opposition to them could be tested in court. The fact that the sanctions were against private parties might have affected the outcome in favour of upholding them, but this cannot be certain.

14 Choice of law can also make for very different substantive obligations on the part of the claimant and the purchaser. See e.g. *Goodman v. Searle*, No. 96-C-6459 (N.D. Ill. Filed Jan. 27, 1998), a case involving a Degas painting. It was found when the owner loaned it to New York's Metropolitan Museum for a show in 1994. The defendant claimed the original owner had sold it which the plaintiffs denied; the defence also relied on statute of limitations or laches. New York law gives three years to file from demand and refusal. Other states require good faith efforts to discover stolen art, or a reasonably diligent search. The issue of choice of law was never resolved, as the case was settled by having shared ownership with a buyout.

15 Note that prior to the Civil Rights Act of 1988, litigation by Japanese-Americans was dismissed on statute of limitations grounds. See *Hohri v. United States*, 847 F.3d 779 (Fed. Cir. 1988) (dismissing class action filed on behalf of the 120,000 Japanese Americans interned during World War II on statute of limitations grounds). See also Soifer 1998.

16 The Tulsa case was dismissed in March 2004 on these grounds, although commentators have demonstrated that there were no effective remedies (Brophy 2004).

17 See also *Forti v. Suarez-Mason*, 672 F.Supp. 1531 (N.D. Cal. 1987) (impossibility of relief in Argentine courts gives a basis for tolling).

18 On this issue, generally see Miller 2004.

19 See, for example, the comments of Representative Henry Hyde, Republican member of the United States Congress: 'The notion of collective guilt for what people did (200-plus) years ago, that this generation should pay a debt for that generation, is an idea whose time has gone. I never owned a slave. I never

oppressed anybody. I don't know that I should have to pay for someone who did generations before I was born' (Merida 1999: col 1).

20 Federal rules don't apply in state cases, where courts are not bound by standing limitations imposed on federal courts.

21 *Bakke v. Regents of the University of California*, 438 U.S. 265, 396 (1978 Marshall, J., concurring), suggested that when one race has been historically discriminated against on the basis of race alone, then race-based group-oriented remedial measures are justified so long as they do not unnecessarily stigmatise or impact members of other populations. Justice Marshall notably said: 'At every point from birth to death the impact of the past is reflected in the still disfavored position of the Negro.'

22 See also *Gratz v. Bollinger* 539 U.S. 244 (2003) and *Grutter v. Bollinger*, 539 U.S. 306 (2003).

23 See *Island of Palmas Case (United States v the Netherlands)*' (1928) 2 UNRIAA 829, in which the arbiter Huber declared that inchoate claims of sovereignty arose upon discovery of new lands, based on the law at the time of discovery, but that the maintenance of sovereignty depended upon how the law and facts evolved. Thus the original title could be divested according to legal developments, based on the distinction between the creation of rights and the continued existence of rights. See also 'Legal Consequences for States of the Continued Presence of South Africa in Namibia (South West Africa), notwithstanding Security Council Resolution 276 (1970), Advisory Opinion' [1971] ICJ Rep. 16.

24 See, for example *Linkletter v Walker* 381 US.618, at 629 (1965) (no retroactive application of criminal statutes is permitted); *Boule v City of Columbia* 378 US 347, 363 (1964) (retroactive application of criminal statute to conduct not criminal at the time it was undertaken denies due process).

25 See *Teague v Lane* 489 US 288 (1989) at 314–315; *Stovall v Denno* 388 US 293 (1967) at 297.

26 See, for example, Luneberg 1991.

27 See, for example, '*Trail Smelter* Case (*U.S. v Canada*)', (1941) 3 UNRIAA 1911, acknowledging that 'No case of air pollution dealt with by an international tribunal has been brought to the attention of the Tribunal nor does the Tribunal know of any such case. The nearest analogy is that of water pollution. But, here also, no decision of an international tribunal has been cited or has been found.' Despite this lack of precedent, the tribunal was able to determine that Canada was liable for damage caused by the lawful activities of the Trail Smelter, drawing upon analogies from inter-state cases in federal states.

28 In 1830, Congress passed the Indian Removal Act to force all Native Americans to relocate west of the Mississippi River. As a result of forced relocation, killings, assimilation, and sterilisation, the estimated population of 10 million Native American at European arrival has declined to approximately 2.4 million (Glauner 2002).

29 S.J. Res. 19, 103d Cong. (1st Sess. 1993), acknowledging the 100th Anniversary of the Jan. 17, 1893 overthrow of the Kingdom of Hawaii. Public Law 103–150. The resolution notes that from 1826–1893 the United States recognised the independence of the Kingdom of Hawaii, with full and complete diplomatic recognition, and bilateral treaties. The history is further recounted including the overthrow of the Hawaiian government 'in violation of treaties between the two nations and of international law' and through an abuse of authority by US representatives in support of the overthrow. President Cleveland at the time called it a 'substantial wrong' that 'requires we should endeavor to repair' and called for a restoration of the monarchy. Lobbying by the American settlers paid

off, however. The operative paragraphs of the resolution: 'acknowledges the historical significance of [the centenary of the illegal overthrow which resulted in the suppression of the inherent sovereignty of the Native Hawaiian people'. It apologises to the Native Hawaiians and 'expresses its commitment to acknowledge the ramifications of the overthrow of the Kingdom of Hawaii', to allow for reconciliation. Perhaps most importantly, it recognises that 'the indigenous Hawaiian people never directly relinquished their claims to their inherent sovereignty as a people or over their national lands to the United States . . .'

30 See, for example, O'Hara and Yarn 2002 (providing multifactored analysis of apology in litigation) and Robbennolt 2003.

31 S. Res. 39, 109th Cong. (2005). Congressional Record S6364, June 13, 2005: 'apologising to the victims of lynching and the descendants of those victims for the failure of the Senate to enact anti-lynching legislation'.

32 H.Res. 194. adopted 29 July 2008 without debate.

33 S.J. Res. 332, 2007 Reg. Ses (Va. 2007) of Feb. 24, 2007, 'Acknowledging the involuntary servitude of Africans and the Exploitation of Native Americans, and calling for reconciliation among all Virginians.'

34 S.J. Res. 6, 2007 REg. Sees. (Md. 2007). 'Slavery in Maryland' resolution adopted 3 April 2007 ('expressing profound regret for the role that Maryland played in instituting and maintaining slavery and for the discrimination that was slavery's legacy'. It was a climate of oppression and created a legacy that 'has afflicted the citizens of [the] state down to the present'.

35 S.J Res. 1557, Res 2007-21, Sess. 2007 (N.C. 2007), 4/12/2007. Senate joint resolution entitled 'A joint resolution expressing the profound regret of the North Carolina General Assembly for the History of Wrongs Inflicted upon Black Citizens by means of slavery, exploitation and legalised racial segregation and calling on all citizens to take part in acts of racial reconciliation.' The resolution noted that the government ensured that slavery was 'embedded in constitutional provisions and laws' in the state, where at time of US independence, three in ten persons owned slaves. The resolution recounts that a 1826 law prohibited free Blacks from entering the state; an 1830 law prohibited anyone from teaching a slave to read or write; and an 1835 law prohibited free Blacks the right to vote. It notes slave contributions to agriculture, public facilities and 'the creation and accumulation of wealth'. Although many Blacks were in the legislature during reconstruction, by the beginning of the twentieth century, North Carolina had enacted laws to prevent them from participating in public life, and again prohibiting them from voting and segregating into unequal schools. The operative paragraph after the apology called on all educational and other institutions and associations to learn the lessons of history and to promote racial reconciliation as well as recommit to equality and non-discrimination.

36 H.J. Res. 321, Sess. 2007 (Ala. 2007) expressing 'profound regret' for the state's role in slavery.

37 Concurrent resolution S2930, 3/27/08: 'Expresses profound regret for the involuntary servitude of Africans and calls for reconciliation among all Floridians: even though the laws permitting such injustices have been repealed, it is important that the Legislature express profound regret for the shameful chapter in th[e] state's history and, in so doing, promote healing and reconciliation among all Floridians.'

38 Assembly Concurrent Resolution No. 270, Nov. 8, 2007, expressing New Jersey's profound regret for its role in slavery and apologising for wrongs inflicted by slavery and its after effects in the United States. The resolution notes

that NJ had as many as 12,000 slaves, one of the largest populations of captive Africans in the northern colonies, and that it was the last northern state to emancipate its slaves, passing a gradual emancipation in 1804. It was also one of very few to accept the Fugitive Slave Act of 1850: 'Our nation acknowledges the crimes and persecution visited upon other peoples during World War II lest the world forget, yet the very mention of the broken promise of "40 acres and a mule" to former slaves or the existence of racism today evokes denial from many quarters of any responsibility for the centuries of legally sanctioned deprivation of African-Americans of their endowed rights or for contemporary policies that perpetuate the existing state of affairs . . .' The resolution calls on-going discrimination and racism 'the vestiges of slavery' and seeks both remembrance and a celebration of contributions as well as recognition and reconciliation. While it acknowledges the wrongs and that slave descendants 'continue to suffer from the effects of Jim Crow laws, segregation, housing discrimination, discrimination in education, and other ills', it also expressly denies that the resolution can be the basis of litigation.

39 Similarly, Virginia's original draft, proposed by the great-grandsons of slaves, used the word 'atonement', which was changed to 'acknowledging with profound regret' the enslavement and exploitation. The word was omitted because lawmakers thought it might generate claims for reparations.

40 43 USC s 1601 (1998). The Alaskan Native Claims Settlement Act awarded US$1 billion and 44 million acres of land that had been wrongfully seized.

41 50 USC app. 1989c.

42 Cal. Ins. Code sec. 13810 (West 207) (requiring insurance companies that do business with the state to disclose past ties to slavery); Illinois: 215 Ill. Comp. State 5/155-39 (2007).

43 Chicago: Slavery Era Disclosure Ordinance, Chi., I'll. Mun. Code 2-92-420 (2002) (in response, Lehman Brothers said they owned at least one slave when it was legal); Los Angeles: Cal. Admin. Code ch. 1, art. 15 (2003); Detroit, Mich., City Code ch. 18 sec. V, div. 7 (2004); Phil. Pa. Coe sec. 17-104(2) (2004).

44 California Department of Insurance Slavery Era Insurance Registry Report to the California Legislature, based on SB 2199, enacted as Ca. Ins. Code sec. 13810 et seq.

45 1994 Fla. Sess. Law. Serv. 94–359 (West).

46 See also Finan 1995.

47 H.R. 40, first proposed in 1989. Commission to Study Reparations for African American Act, H.R. 40, 108th Cong. (2003). Chicago, Detroit, DC, Cleveland, and Dallas have gone further and adopted resolutions urging Congress to investigate reparations for slavery (Bryan 2002).

48 For a history of the incident see, Brophy 2002a; Ellsworth 1982.

49 Okla. Stat. Ann. Tit. 70 sec. 2621–2627 (authorizing Tulsa Reconciliation Education and Scholarship Program. See also Okla. Stat. Ann. Tit. 74, sec. 8000.1 (West 2002) (making legislative findings); Okla. Stat. Ann. Tit. 74, sec. 8201.1 (West 2002) (creating race riot memorial committee); Okla. Stat. Ann. Tit. 74, sec. 8205 (West 2002) (certifying riot survivors); Okla. Stat.Ann. tit. 74, sec. 8221–8226 (West 2002) (creating Greenwood Area Redevelopment Authority).

50 *Alexander v. Governor of State of Oklahoma*, 382 F.2d 1206 (10th Cir. 2004), cert. denied, 125 S.Ct. 2257.

51 See, for example, Art 8, UDHR ('Everyone has the right to an effective remedy by the competent national tribunals for acts violating the fundamental rights granted him by the constitution or by law'). The International Covenant on Civil and Political Rights contains three separate articles on remedies, addressing the

right of access to an authority competent to afford remedies and the right to an effective and enforceable remedy in Art 2(3), while Arts 9(5) and 14(6) provide that anyone unlawfully arrested, detained, or convicted shall have an enforceable right to compensation or be compensated according to law. The Convention on the Elimination of Racial Discrimination, Art 6, and the Convention on the Elimination of All Forms of Discrimination against Women, Art 2(c), contain broad language on remedies. The United Nations Convention against Torture refers in Art 14 to redress and compensation for torture victims. Several treaties refer to the right to legal protection for attacks on privacy, family, home or correspondence, or attacks on honour and reputation. See International Covenant on Civil and Political Rights, Art 17; Convention on the Rights of the Child, Art 16; American Convention on Human Rights, Art 11(3); European Convention on Human Rights, Art 8; African Charter on Human and Peoples Rights, Art 5. Non-treaty texts include the Universal Declaration of Human Rights, Art 12 and American Declaration of the Rights and Duties of Man, Art v Among treaties adopted by the specialised agencies, the ILO Convention No 169 Concerning Indigenous and Tribal Peoples in Independent Countries refers to 'fair compensation for damages' (Art 15(2)), 'compensation in money' (Art 16(4)) and full compensation for 'any loss or injury' (Art 16(5)).

52 European Convention for the Protection of Human Rights and Fundamental Freedoms, Art 13; American Declaration of the Rights and Duties of Man, Art XVII; American Convention on Human Rights, Arts 1(1), 8, 10, 25; African Charter on Human and Peoples' Rights, Arts 7, 21, 26.

53 The Universal Declaration of Human Rights provides that '[e]veryone has the right to an effective remedy by the competent national tribunals for acts violating the fundamental rights granted him by the constitution or laws.' UDHR, Art 8. Two texts of the European Union address access to justice and compensation for victims of crimes. See Council Framework Decision of 15 March 2001 on the standing of victims in criminal proceedings (2001/220/JHA, [2001] OJ L82 and Council Directive 2004/80/EC of 29 April 2004 relating to compensation to crime victims, [2004] OJ L261/15. The most sustained effort on the topic was the work of the former UN Sub-Commission on Promotion and Protection of Human Rights and the UN Commission on Human Rights to elaborate international principles on reparation for victims of human rights violations adopted by the General Assembly in 2005. Basic Principles and Guidelines on the Right to Remedy and Reparation for Victims of Gross Violations of International Human Rights Law and Serious Violations of International Humanitarian Law, Commission on Human Rights, Res. 2005/35 of 19 April 2005 (adopted 40–0 with 13 abstentions).

54 Traditionally, states could and often did renounce claims on behalf of their nationals in time of war and peace. With the widespread recognition of the right to a remedy as a human right, it is open to question whether such waivers continue to be valid in international law without alternative means of redress.

55 See eg *Altmann v Republic of Austria* 317 F.3d 954 (2002) (giving retroactive application to the expropriation exception to the Foreign Sovereign Immunities Act, 28 USC s 1605(a)(3) on the ground that Austria could not have had any settled expectation that the State Department would have recommended immunity for the wrongful appropriate of Jewish property in the 1930s and 1940s).

56 Yamamoto 1998 criticises the view of reparations as forward-looking and is sceptical of their potential for creating a new social arrangement, but he also rejects the notion that they are irrelevant to the process.

57 See Ratner 1999; Hesse and Post (eds) 1999; Christie 2000.

Bibliography

Bazyler, M. (2002) 'The Holocaust Restitution Movement in Comparative Perspective', *Berkeley Journal of International Law*, 20: 11–44.

Brophy, A.L. (2002a) *Reconstructing the Dreamland: The Tulsa Riot of 1921*. New York: Oxford University Press.

Brophy, A.L. (2002b) 'The World of Reparations: Slavery Reparations in Historical Perspective', *Journal of Law and Society*, 3: 105.

Brophy, A.L. (2004) 'Norms, Law and Reparation: The Case of the Ku Klux Klan in 1920s Oklahoma', *Harvard Blackletter Law Journal*, 20: 17–48.

Brophy, A.L. (2006) 'Reconsidering Reparations', *Indiana Law Journal*, 81: 811–849.

Bryan, C.W. (2002) 'Precedent for Reparations? A Look at Historical Movements for Redress and Where Awarding Reparations for Slavery Might Fit', *Alabama Law Review*, 54: 599.

Christie, K. (2000) *The South African Truth Commission*. New York: St Martin's Press.

Churchwell, T.D. (chair) (2001), *Report by the Oklahoma Commission to Study the Tulsa Race Riot of 1921*, Oklahoma City, OK: Oklahoma Historical Society. Online. Available at HTTP: <http://www.okhistory.org/trrc/freport.pdf> (accessed 1 December 2010).

Clinton, W.J. (1997) *Remarks by the President in Apology for Study Done in Tuskegee, May 16, 1997*, Online. Available at HTTP: <http://www.cdc.gov/tuskegee/clintonp.htm> (accessed 1 December 2010).

Cunningham, M. (1999) 'Saying Sorry: The Politics of Apology', *The Political Quarterly*, 70: 285–293.

Ellsworth, S. (1982) *Death in a Promised Land: The Tulsa Riot of 1921*. Baton Rouge: Louisiana State University Press.

Fallon, Jr, R. H. and Meltzer, D.J. (1991) 'New Law, Non-Retroactivity, and Constitutional Remedies', *Harvard Law Review*, 104: 1733.

Finan, E. (1995) 'Delayed Justice: The Rosewood Story', *Human Rights*, 22: 8.

Flahardy, C. (2005) 'Chicago Forces J.P. Morgan to Disclose Slavery Ties', *Inside Counsel*, March.

Frantz, C.D. (1998) 'Getting Back What was Theirs? The Reparations Mechanisms for the Land Rights Claims of the Maori and the Navajo', *Dickinson Journal of International Law*, 16: 489.

Gibney, M. and Roxstrom, E. (2001) 'The Status of State Apologies', *Human Rights Quarterly*, 23: 911.

Glauner, L. (2002) 'The Need for Accountability and Reparation 1830–1976: The United States Government's Role in the Promotion, Implementation and Execution of the Crime of Genocide against Native Americans', *DePaul Law Review*, 51: 911.

Gover, K. (2000) 'Remarks of the Assistant Secretary, Indian Affairs, Department of the Interior, at the Ceremony Acknowledging the 175th Anniversary of the Establishment of the Bureau of Indian Affairs', *American Indian Law Review*, 25: 161.

Hesse, C. and Post, R. (eds) (1999) *Human Rights in Political Transitions: Gettysburg to Bosnia*, Cambridge, MA: MIT Press.

Hylton, K. N. (2004) 'A Framework for Reparations Claims', *Boston College Third World Law Journal*, 24: 31.

Jones, M.D., Rivers, L.E., Colburn, D.R., Dye R.T. and Rogers, W.W. (1993) *The Rosewood Report: A Documented History of the Incident which Occurred at Rosewood, Florida, in January 1923, submitted to the Florida Board of Regents 22 December, 1993*, Online. Available at HTTP: <http://www.displaysfor-schools.com/rosewoodrp.html> (accessed 1 December 2010).

Kornweibel, Jr, T. (2006) 'Reparations and Railroads,' *Thomas Jefferson Law Review*, 29: 219.

Luneberg, W.V. (1991) 'Retroactivity and Administrative Rulemaking', *Duke Law Journal* 1991, 1: 106–165.

Magarrell, L. (2003) 'Reparations for Massive or Widespread Human Rights Violations: Sorting out Claims for Reparations and the Struggle for Social Justice', *Windsor Yearbook of Access to Justice*, 22: 91.

Meltzer, D.J. (1988) 'Deterring Constitutional Violations by Law Enforcement Officials: Plaintiffs and Defendants as Private Attorneys General', *Columbia Law Review*, 88: 247.

Merida, K. (1999) 'Did Freedom Alone Pay a Nation's Debt? Rep. John Conyers Jr. Has a Question. He's Willing to Wait a Long Time for the Right Answer', *Washington Post*, 23 November.

Miller, E.J. (2004) 'Reconceiving Reparations: Multiple Strategies in the Reparations Debate,' *Boston College Third World Law Journal*, 24: 45.

Miller, E.J. (2004) 'Representing the Race: Standing to Sue in Reparations Lawsuits,' *Harvard Blackletter Law Journal*, 20: 91.

O'Hara, E.A. and Yarn, D. (2002) 'On Apology and Consilience', *Washington Law Review (Seattle)*, 77: 1121.

Ogletree, Jr, C.J. (2004) 'Tulsa Reparations: The Survivors' Story', *Boston College Third World Law Journal*, 24: 13.

Olick, J.K. and Coughlin, B. (2003) 'The Politics of Regret: Analytical Frames', in J. Torpey (ed.), *Politics And The Past*. Lanham, MD: Rowman & Littlefield.

Pasqualucci, J.M. (2006) 'The Evolution of International Indigenous Rights in the Inter-American Human Rights System', *Human Rights Law Review*, 6: 281–322.

Ratner, S. (1999) 'New Democracies, Old Atrocities: An Inquiry in International Law', *Georgetown Law Journal*, 87: 707–748.

Robbennolt, J.K. (2003) 'Apologies and Legal Settlement: An Empirical Examination', *Michigan Law Review*, 102: 460.

Roht-Arriaza, N. (2003) 'Reparations Decisions and Dilemmas', *Hastings International and Comparative Law Review*, 27: 157.

Rowe, Jr, T.D. (ed) (2001) 'Symposium: Debates over Group Litigation in Comparative Perspective: What Can We Learn from Each Other?', *Duke Journal of Comparative and International Law*, 11: 157.

Shelton, D. (2004) *Remedies In International Human Rights Law* (2nd edition). New York: Oxford University Press.

Sherwin, E. (2004) 'Reparations and Unjust Enrichment', *Boston University Law Review*, 84: 1443.

Soifer, A. (1998) 'Redress, Progress and the Benchmark Problem', *Boston College Law Review*, 40: 525.

Ulrich, G. and Krabbe Boserup, L. (eds) (2003) *Reparations: Redressing Past Wrongs, Human Rights In Development Yearbook 2001*. The Hague: Kluwer Law International.

Yamamoto, E. (1998) 'Racial Reparations: Japanese American Redress and African American Claims', *Boston College Law Review*, 40: 477.

Yamamoto, E.K., Kim, S.H.Y. and Holden, A.M. (2007) 'American Reparations Theory and Practice at the Crossroads', *California Western Law Review*, 44: 1.

Table of cases

Adarand Constructors Inc v. Pena, 515 U.S. 200 (1995).
Alexander v. Governor of State of Oklahoma, 382 F.2d 1206 (10th Cir. 2004), cert. denied, 125 S.Ct. 2257.
Altmann v Republic of Austria, 317 F.3d 954 (2002).
Am Slave Descendants Litig., 375 F.Supp.2d 721 (N.D. Ill. 2005), aff'd as modified in 471 F.3d 754, 759 (7th Cir. 2006).
Bakke v. Regents of Univ. of Cal., 438 U.S. 265, 396 (1978 Marshall, J., concurring)).
Barrueto v. Larios, 205 F.Supp.1325 (S.D. Fla. 2002).
Boule v City of Columbia, 378 US 347, 363 (1964).
Carrington v. FleetBoston Fin. Corp., No. 02-CV-01863 (EDNY filed Mar 26, 2002).
Cato v. United States, 70 F.3d 1103 (9th Cir. 1995).
Cruz v. United States, 219 F.Supp.2d 1027 (N.D. Cal. 2002).
Cyril v. Mobil Oil Corp., 11 F3d 996 (10th Cir. 1993).
Farmer-Paellmann v. FleetBoston Fin Corp., No. 02-CV-01862 (EDNY filed Mar. 26, 2002).
Forti v. Suarez-Mason, 672 F.Supp. 1531 (N.D. Cal. 1987).
Goodman v. Searle, No. 96-C-6459 (N.D. Ill. Filed Jan. 27, 1998).
Gratz v. Bollinger, 539 U.S. 244 (2003).
Grutter v. Bollinger, 539 U.S. 306 (2003).
Hohri v. United States, 847 F.3d 779 (Fed. Cir. 1988).
Hurdle v. FleetBoston Fin. Corp., No. CGC-02-412388 (Cal. Super. Ct. filed Sept. 10, 2002).
Island of Palmas Case (United States v the Netherlands) (1928) 2 UNRIAA 829.
Landgraf v USI Film Prods., 511 US 244, 265 (1994).
Landgraf v USI Film Prods., 511 US 244, 265 (1994).
Linkletter v Walker, 381 US.618, at 629 (1965).
Mayagna (Sumo) Awas Tingni Community v Nicaragua, 79 IACtHR (ser. C) (2001), 10 IHRR 758 (2003).
Obadele v. United States, 52 Fed. Cl. 432 (2002).
Princz v Federal Republic of Germany, 26 F.3d 1166 (D.C.Cir. 1994), cert. denied, 513 U.S. 1121 (1995).
Sampson v. Federal Republic of Germany, 250 F.3d 1145 (7th Cir. 2001).
Stovall v Denno, 388 US 293 (1967).
Teague v Lane, 489 US 288 (1989).
Trail Smelter Case (U.S. v Canada) (1941) 3 UNRIAA 1911.

Vigil v. United States, 293 F.Supp. 1187 (D.C. Colo. 1968, aff'd 430 F.2d 1357 (10th Cir. 1970).

Yakye Axa Indigenous Community v Paraguay (2005) 125 IACtHR (ser. C) (translation by Jo M Pasqualucci, in 'The Evolution of International Indigenous Rights in the Inter-American Human Rights System' (2006) 6 Hum. Rts. L. Rev. 281, at 300).

Table of legislation

Commission to Study Reparations for African American Act, H.R. 40, 108th Cong. (2003).

The Alien Tort Statute, 28 U.S.C.

The Commission on Wartime Relocation and Internment of Civilians Act, Pub. L. No. 96-317, 94 Stat. 964 (1980).

Exec. Order No. 9066, 7 Fed. Reg. 1407 (Feb. 19, 1942).

12 Stat. 376, 538 (1861).

Civil Liberties Act of 1988, Pub L. No. 100-383, 102 Stat. 903, 50 U.S.C.A. App. sec. 1989b-1989b-9 (West 1988) (expired 1998).

Ca. Unfair Competition Law, Cal. Bus. & Prof. Code sec. 17200 (West 1997).

Legal Consequences for States of the Continued Presence of South Africa in Namibia (South West Africa), notwithstanding Security Council Resolution 276 (1970), Advisory Opinion [1971] ICJ Rep. 16.

S.J. Res. 19, 103d Cong. (1st Sess. 1993), acknowledging the 100th Anniversary of the Jan. 17, 1893 overthrow of the Kingdom of Hawaii. Public Law 103-150.

S. Res. 39, 109th Cong. (2005). Congressional Record S6364, June 13, 2005. 'Apologizing to the victims of lynching and the descendants of those victims for the failure of the Senate to enact anti-lynching legislation.'

H.Res. 194. adopted July 29, 2008 without debate.

S.J. Res. 332, 2007 Reg. Ses (Va. 2007) of Feb. 24, 2007, 'Acknowledging the involuntary servitude of Africans and the Exploitation of Native Americans, and calling for reconciliation among all Virginians.'

S.J. Res. 6, 2007 REg. Sees. (Md. 2007). 'Slavery in Maryland' resolution adopted April 3, 2007 'expressing profound regret for the role that Maryland played in instituting and maintaining slavery and for the discrimination that was slavery's legacy.'

S.J Res. 1557, Res 2007-21, Sess. 2007 (N.C. 2007), 4/12/2007.

H.J. Res. 321, Sess. 2007 (Ala. 2007) expressing 'profound regret' for the state's role in slavery.

Concurrent resolution S2930, 3/27/08: 'Expresses profound regret for the involuntary servitude of Africans and calls for reconciliation among all Floridians': 'even though the laws permitting such injustices have been repealed, it is important that the Legislature express profound regret for the shameful chapter in th[e] state's history and, in so doing, promote healing and reconciliation among all Floridians'.

Assembly Concurrent Resolution No. 270, Nov. 8, 2007, expressing New Jersey's profound regret for its role in slavery and apologising for wrongs inflicted by slavery and its after effects in the United States.

43 USC s 1601 (1998).
50 USC app. 1989c.
Cal. Ins. Code sec. 13810 (West 207).
Illinois: 215 Ill. Comp. State 5/155-39 (2007).
Chicago: Slavery Era Disclosure Ordinance, Chi., I'll. Mun. Code 2-92-420 (2002).
Los Angeles: Cal. Admin. Code ch. 1, art. 15 (2003).
Detroit, Mich., City Code ch. 18 sec. V, div. 7 (2004).
Phil. Pa. Coe sec. 17-104(2) (2004).
California Department of Insurance Slavery Era Insurance Registry Report to the California Legislature, based on SB 2199, enacted as Ca. Ins. Code sec. 13810 et seq.
1994 Fla. Sess. Law. Serv. 94–359 (West).
Okla. Stat. Ann. Tit. 70.
Okla. Stat. Ann. Tit. 74.
Convention for the Protection of Human Rights and Fundamental Freedoms ('European Convention on Human Rights'), European Treaty Series No. 5 (1950).
American Declaration of the Rights and Duties of Man, OAS Res. XXX, reprinted in Basic Documents Pertaining to Human Rights in the Inter-American System, OAS/Ser.L/V/I.4 Rev. 9 (2003); 43 AJIL Supp. 133 (1949).
American Convention on Human Rights, OAS Treaty Series No. 36; 1144 UNTS 123; 9 ILM 99 (1969).
African Charter on Human and Peoples' Rights, OAU Doc. CAB/LEG/67/3 rev. 5; 1520 UNTS 217; 21 ILM 58 (1982).
Universal Declaration of Human Rights, GA res. 217 A (III), adopted 10 December 1948.
International Covenant on Civil and Political Rights, GA res. 2200 A (XXI), adopted 16 December 1966.
Basic Principles and Guidelines on the Right to Remedy and Reparation for Victims of Gross Violations of International Human Rights Law and Serious Violations of International Humanitarian Law, Commission on Human Rights, Res. 2005/35 of 19 April 2005.

Chapter 7

Two hundred years after the abolition of the transatlantic slave trade, could there be a juridical basis for the call for reparations?

Kwesi Quartey

Many of us have tended to believe that the transatlantic slave trade which took place between 1450 and 1807 when it was abolished by the British parliament was perhaps a series of sporadic events carried out by a few bad people. Others have argued that it was so long ago that the less said about it the better; that the apology first by President Clinton in Accra and the regretful non-apology by Prime Minister Tony Blair should be the end of the matter. Indeed some academics such as Professor Niall Ferguson have taken Prime Minister Blair to task for having the temerity to issue what was in effect a non-apology, one that the British authorities have suffered to let slip from the lofty moral heights of Empire and Monarchy.

I would like to examine the facts of history and hope to let them speak for themselves. I intend in this chapter to examine the history and legal organisation of the slave trade as a business, for that was indeed what it was – the main international business of the day. In the process I shall attempt to make a comparison of how the two most successful trading (i.e., slave trading) nations, Britain and the United Provinces (the contemporary name for what is now the Netherlands), carried on their lucrative international business through their respective vehicles that had been created to facilitate this business on the Guinea coast, i.e., the coast of West Africa.

We shall therefore briefly examine the Royal African Company of Adventurers to Africa and its rival organisation, the Dutch West Indian company, in their operations in West Africa.

I would also like to examine the juridical infrastructure, i.e., the various Acts of Parliament, the legal bases of the operations, as well as questions of state responsibility and state succession that arise in International Law. Questions of criminal responsibility might intrude into the discussion when we examine, as we must, when a nation's main economic activity leads, foments or is contributory to situations that can only be characterised as the large-scale murdering of a race.

How did the trade begin?

There are several accounts of how the transatlantic slave trade began. Slavery and trading in slaves had always existed in Africa. It is said that Sir John Hawkins first sailed to Africa in 1562, thereby inaugurating the British slave trade. However, the Portuguese had arrived before him. In his book *History of Christianity in Ghana*,[1] Dr Hans Debrunner, a historian of Christianity, recounts the arrival of Don Diego d'Ajambuja. According to him, Don Diego landed in Elmina on 20 January 1482 'with all his people dressed but with hidden arms in case of need'. On a small hill stood a tall tree and onto this the royal Portuguese banner was hoisted. There then followed the memorable encounter between Don Diego and Chief Kwamena Ansah of Elmina. D'Ajambuja spoke at great length about the King of Portugal's love for the soul of Kwamena Ansah. Only at the end of the long speech did d'Azambuja mention his intention to build a fortress. As politely as he could Kwamena Ansah tried to evade this unwelcome building. He told them that 'friends who meet occasionally remain better friends than if they were neighbours' and with peace between them his people might be more ready to hear about the God whom he wished to know. Trading began sporadically; alluvial gold was found which gave the name of the town as El Mina de Oro – later Elmina. However, it was the discovery of America that was to change things dramatically.

According to the late Eric Williams,[2] the first post-independence Prime Minister of Trinidad and Tobago, in his classic work *Capitalism and Slavery*,[3] when Christopher Columbus discovered the new world in 1492, he set in motion a long chain of events. Legend has it that on his way to the new world he stopped over at Elmina Castle[4] for a few days to re-provision his fleet. And on his second journey he took some sugar cane from Las Palmas to plant, which is how sugar cane cultivation in the Americas started. The Native Americans, who the Spanish first encountered, were brutally subjected to this harsh degrading labour. Unused to such work, they died in such numbers that the Bishop of Chiapas suggested the use of negroes, who were thought to be more sturdy and able to withstand this forced labour. Thus the transatlantic slave trade to West Africa began. The rest, as they say, is history.

Organisation of the trade

After an abortive beginning in 1607, the Dutch West Indian Company[5] was finally established in 1621. It was granted a monopoly of the trade with America, the West Indies and West Africa from the Tropic of Cancer to the Cape of Good Hope. Supreme authority was vested by the Dutch

Parliament in a council made up of 19 people. The chairman was appointed by the Estates General, i.e. parliament. Part of the capital was constituted from public funds. The United Provinces undertook to supply soldiers and work materials.

The Royal Africa Company was set up by royal charter as a monopoly on 20 September 1672. King Charles II issued the charter of the Royal Africa company 'for the further encouragement of the undertakers in discovering the golden mines and settling of plantations, being an enterprise so laudable and conducing to so worthy an end as the increase of traffic and merchandise wherein this nation hath been famous . . .'[6]

The charter continues: 'And further our more special grace do hereby grant unto the society of the Royal African Company of England and their successors, and none others, to be prepared and furnished with ordnance, artillery and ammunition . . . and shall hereafter have, use and enjoy all mines of gold and silver which are or shall be found . . . in South Barbary, Guinea or Angola for the buying, selling, bartering and exchanging goods, wares and merchandise, gold, silver, negroes, slaves good to be rented or found in any of the towns, etc. . . . and to import any redwood, elephants teeth, negro slaves, etc.'

It concludes as follows: 'We do hereby, for us, our heirs and successors, grant and give full power and authority under the said Royal African Company of England and their successor to enter into any ship, vessel and attack, arrest, take and seize all manner of ships, vessels, negro slaves etc.' The authority comes direct from the Crown, the monarch of England: '. . . provided . . . That we our heirs and successors shall have and may have, take and receive two thirds of all the gold mines which shall be found, seized, possessed in the part and places aforesaid . . .' In law, indeed in the law of England, this is incitement to plunder, rapine and mass murder.

To this end, a contract (*Asiento*) was signed in 1701 between the sovereigns of England and Spain. Its heading was crystal clear as to its purposes. It stated quite openly:

> Contract for Blacks or Negroes made by the King of Spain and agreed with Her Majesty of Great Britain for herself and such of her subjects as she shall appoint to be contractors.
>
> Part 1 – With licence from Her Majesty the contractor takes upon them the Asiento or Agreement to import negro slaves into the Spanish West Indies, and to establish this necessary trade for the united and reciprocal benefit of their Majesties and the subjects of both crowns and the contractors oblige themselves to import in the space of ten years forty eight thousand negroes of both sexes.[7]

The *Asiento* contracts

Spain (which then had more colonies in America than anybody else) depended on other countries to supply slaves to the Spanish colonies. The country could afford to outsource the business supply to Great Britain. The privilege of supplying these slaves to the Spanish colonies, called the *Asiento*, became one of the most coveted prizes in international diplomacy.[8]

During the brief occupation of Cuba, thousands of slaves were introduced there by Britain. During the whole of the eighteenth century, Britain furnished the sugar planters of France and Spain with half a million negroes. The story of this period in the slave trade is also mainly the story of the rise of Liverpool – from a fishing hamlet to becoming the second major city in the British Empire.

According to Eric Williams, the purchase of slaves called for business sense and shrewd discrimination. An Angolan negro was considered worthless; Koramatin slaves from the Gold Coast were good workers but too rebellious; Mandingos from Senegal were said to be too prone to theft; the Ibos were said to be timid; while those from Whydah were the most docile. The era of identifying distinguishing characteristics, and exacerbating tribal differences in order to divide and rule, had begun.

There was competition for slaves, between England, Holland and France. Anglo-French warfare in the eighteenth century was essentially a conflict of rival commercial interest on the African coast. The struggle was fought out in the Caribbean, in Africa, in India, in Canada, and on the banks of the Mississippi, for the privilege of looting India as well as for the control of certain vital and strategic commodities – negroes, sugar, tobacco, fish and fur. Of these commodities, the most important were negroes and sugar, because tea, coffee, sweets and rum could not be produced without slave labour, i.e., the labour of captive Africans transported from a host Africa. The outstanding issue was the control of the *Asiento*. This privilege was conceded to England by the Treaty of Utrecht in 1713 as one result of her victory in the war of the Spanish succession. War with France gave England almost total control of the African coast and the slave trade.[9]

John Hippisley, governor of the Cape Coast Castle, writing about the population of Africa in 1764, was able to say that 'the extensive employment of our shipping in, to and from America, the great brood of seamen consequent thereon, and the daily bread of the most considerable part of our British manufacturing are owing primarily to the labour of negroes *the negro trade and the natural consequences resulting from it may justly be esteemed an inexhaustible fund of wealth and power to this nation*' (author emphasis).

As Governor of the Cape Coast Castle he was bullish on the future of the African slave Trade. He wrote that '*Africa not only can continue supplying the west indies with the quantities she has hitherto, but if necessity required it, could spare thousands, nay millions more, and go on doing this to the end of time*' (author emphasis). British prices for slaves were considerably lower than those prevailing in the French Islands, noted John Laud Sheffield in his observation on the commerce of the American States 'as to the supply of negroes, we have a decided superiority in the African trade . . .'[10]

How the slaves were acquired

In the Abstract of Evidence delivered before the Select Committee of the House of Commons[11] in 1790 and 1791, it was stated in Chapter 1 that the trading of slaves along the River Senegal was chiefly with negroes who had gained them through war . . . and also by kidnapping (i.e., lying in wait near a village, where there was no conflict, and seizing whomever they could).

It also stated that kidnapping was so generally prevalent that self-preservation had become the first principle of the natives – to never go unarmed while a slave vessel was on the coast for fear of being taken.

Was there resistance?

Europeans continue to state that Africans gleefully sold their kith and kin to them: this is false because the records show that Africans always resisted the transatlantic slave trade. Consider this letter written by the agent of the Dutch West Indian Company on the coast, Van Woolwerf, to his Board of Directors in Holland. It is dated 31 January 1687, at Cape Coast. This is from the Dutch archives taken from Elmina to The Hague and translated by Van Danzig.

> On 26th December, the 'Portugalise Handelaer', a slave ship, arrived, which I have dispatched today with 525 pieces of slaves, 368 men and 139 women. As before, there is great abundance of slaves here, but there is also great famine, with the result that I have not been able to supply this ship with as much millet as I would have desired.
>
> The negroes, who as I have mentioned earlier, are here not at all polite, have torn up the noble company's flag, on the day that the ship 'Cromantyn' left. On many occasions it is custom, and one is even obliged, to have such a flag on the beach for the reputation of the noble company.
>
> This event is therefore a serious matter, and the English and the French at Fida were quite happy about it, as they concluded, as can be understood, that our presence in this country is no longer brooked . . .

> I have therefore, on my own costs, prosecuted and eradicated the flag violator on behalf of H.E. the General, and sent him to Elmina per canoe; the General has publicly sentenced him [to death] and decapitated him and has sent the severed head on board the company ship 'Goude Tyger', hither. As an example of the punishment for such wantonness I have put it on top of a pole here at the lodge . . .[12]

This is one example of the cynical brutality inflicted on our ancestors at Cape Coast, for the crime of expressing disgust at the slave trade. These are facts, as told from the Dutch archives.

More can be found in another letter discovered in the Dutch Archives and dated 29 September 1730, again at Cape Coast. This letter is from a Dutchman named Hertogh to a Mr Pranger of the Dutch West Indian Company in the Netherlands. It goes as follows:

> in the night of 26 to 27 September (1730) at about 1' o'clock, a heavy fire broke out near the noble company's lodge. As a result of the strong wind it came dangerously close, and I did my utmost to save the company's goods and to extinguish the fire as I could; but when the fire reached the powder house [i.e., the gunpowder] in the crom, it exploded immediately, and it was as if fire rained down from the sky. Within a few moments, the lodge and the entire Crown caught fire on all sides, and I just managed to save myself with the captain, the Assistant, and the Master. I had already bought 145 slaves for the ship 'Waartwyl' of whom I had embarked 90 in the day before the fire. As yet I cannot give your Highness any precise information about what happened to the others, but I know many of them were miserably burnt alive, and others who managed to escape, may have hidden anywhere. Most of the company's goods are, however, quite safe . . .
>
> (Cape Coast, 26 to 27 September, 1730[13])

The middle passage

Adam Smith, in *The Wealth of Nations*, his classic work on political economy, states without equivocation that the discovery of America and also the Cape route to India were the two greatest and most important events recorded in the history of mankind. The discovery of America opened up a new and inexhaustible market for European commodities. It also opened up the market for African slaves and gave rise to an enormous increase in world trade. Eric Williams argues that for Britain that trade was primarily a triangular trade. Writing in 1718, William Wood, author of *A Survey of Trade* (London), described the transatlantic slave trade – otherwise known euphemistically as the African Trade – as the '*spring and parent from whence the others flow'*. A few years later Malachi Postleth-wayt described the slave trade as the 'First Principle and Foundation of the Rest, The Mainspring of the Machine which sets every wheel in motion'.

In this triangular trade, Eric Williams writes:

> England, France and Colonial America supplied the export and the ships; Africa the human merchandise; the plantations, the colonial raw materials. The slave ship sailed from the home country with a cargo of manufactured goods. They were exchanged at a profit on the coast of Africa for negroes, who were then traded on the plantation at another profit, in exchange for a cargo of colonial produce to be taken back to the home country. The triangular trade gave a triple stimulus to British Industry. The negroes were purchased with British manufactures; transported to the plantation in British ships, they produced sugar, cotton, melons and other tropical products, the processing of which created new industries in England, while the maintenance of the negroes on the plantation provided another market for British industry, New England agriculture and the Newfoundland factories. By 1750 there was hardly a trading or manufacturing town in England which was not in some way connected with the triangular or direct colonial trade. *The profits obtained provided one or the main stream of that accumulation of capital in England which financed the industrial revolution.*[14] [author emphasis]

That was how the West Indian Islands became the hub of the British Empire and also vital to the grandeur and prosperity of England. It was the negro slaves who made these sugar colonies the most precious ever recorded in British history. Malachi Postlethwayt, says with disarming frankness they were 'The fundamental prop and support of the colonies', 'valuable people – [he makes a rare concession to their humanity here] whose labour supplied Britain with all plantation produce'.

He then goes on to conclude that the British Empire was a 'magnificent superstructure of American commerce and naval power on an African foundation'. The roots of the special relationship lie deep, having been generously fertilised by African flesh and blood, and sweat and tears. The British Empire, out of which evolved the Commonwealth of Nations and in many ways the current international globalised economic system, was indeed constructed on an African foundation.

In what condition were African slaves transported to the new world and the West Indies? According to PM Eric Williams, in his classic *Capitalism and Slavery*, the space allotted to each slave on the Atlantic crossing measured five and half feet in length by 16 inches in breadth. The slaves were packed like rows of books on shelves, chained two by two, right leg and left leg, right hand and left hand – each person had less room than a man in a coffin. The emphasis was on profit not comfort.

Dr Alexander Falconbridge who was a surgeon on a slave ship kept a diary. He described the scene in the ship's hold quite vividly and with all the accuracy that was typical of his profession.

Here he outlines the condition of slaves in the hold of the slave ship:

> In all the slaves' quarters were to be found three or four large buckets, of a conical form . . . in which were where necessary, the negroes have recourse; chained as they were together, one may doze off and wake up to find your partner in misery dead, but you will still have to carry him with you when you are forced by nature to reach for the bucket in time of dire necessity . . .[15] [W.C.s were still very much in the future, and in any case, not for African slaves]. Many were too sick or disheartened to run the gauntlet, many simply had no strength to move.

They simply let nature take its course.

According to Professor of History at York University, James Walvin, 'with the lavatory buckets overflowing and slaves defecating where they lay, the floor was so covered with blood and mucus which proceeded from them in consequence of the flux (dysentery), it resembled a slaughter house. It is not in the power of human imagination, to picture oneself in a situation more dreadful or disgusting.' All of this was being compounded by the continuous motion of the ship: so deep were the groans, and so powerful was the stench, that you could smell a slave ship from more than a mile away. Sharks certainly knew where a decent meal could be obtained and they would follow a slave ship all the way to America.

Resistance and rebellion

In a situation such as this, the possibility of rebellion was never far from the minds of the slaves. However, it was even more prevalent in the minds of the slave captains. The truth was that violence and brutality begat even more violence and more brutality.

Slave traders developed a variety of theories about what caused revolts and how to prevent them. After William Snellgrave, a slave captain, had crushed a rebellion on his ship in 1721, he interrogated the leaders as to why they had rebelled. They replied that Snellgrave 'was a great rogue to buy them in order to carry them away from their own country; and that they were resolved to regain their liberty if possible'. To guard against revolt, slave traders were advised to identify those slaves who seemed the most indifferent to their liberty and to give them preferential treatment in order to turn them into informers. Women were also routinely raped. John Newton, who was inspired to write the hymn *Amazing Grace*, recounted how he once saw a woman with her baby where the child continued crying after her mother had been warned several times. When the infant continued to cry a member of the crew angrily grabbed it from the mother and casually tossed the child overboard. The mother in her anguish followed after her baby, thus becoming a welcome target for the sharks which had developed the habit of following slave ships. In this kind of atmosphere, revolt or the threat of revolt was omnipresent.

When faced with the threat or reality of a shipboard uprising, most captains on slave ships followed the theory that brutal intimidation was the best course of action. Jean Barbot, a French slave captain who was also an author, believed that if a rebellion occurred the captain should spare no effort to suppress the insolence and as an example to the others should sacrifice the lives of the most mutinous: 'This will terrify the others and keep them obedient. The way of making it clear to them, I mean the punishment that scares the African the most, is cutting up a live man with an axe and handing out the pieces to the others.' In this sordid business, the French and the British competed in every department.

The Africans believed that dismemberment prevented the spirit of the person from returning home after death. Thus, European slave traders not only executed rebellious slaves, they also wanted to prevent their spirits from returning home. The Europeans tried to control both the flesh and the spirit. By so doing, they hoped to intimidate the African captives sufficiently to prevent future acts of rebellion. But the human spirit would not be subdued, and there were several successful rebellions. A *Boston Newsletter* dated 25 September 1729 reported 'we have an account from Guinea by way of Antigua that the ship Clare Galley, whose Captain was called Murrell had departed the Guinea coast, Cape Coast, to be precise headed for South Carolina. Within 10 leagues, the Negroes rose up and making themselves masters of the gunpowder and fire arms, the captain and the crew took their long boat, and escaped ashore near Cape Coast castle. The negroes sailed the ship within a few leagues of Cape Coast Castle and made their escape.'[16]

Slavery and the law

The nature of the slave trade was that it was underpinned by violence, rape, fraud and murder: it therefore needed the most iniquitous laws to sustain it. Parliament was not found wanting in this regard. In February 1764 the Planters Parliament of Bermuda, under the authority of the British parliament, enacted 'An Act for the Better Government of Negroes, Mullatos and Indians, Bond and Free and for the most Effectual Punishing Conspiracies and Insurrections of them'.

The law provided that, 'where a negro or Indian or Mullato gave false testimony . . . every such offender shall, without trial be ordered . . . to have one ear nailed to a tree, and there to stand for the space of an hour, and then the said ear be cut off; and thereafter the other ear in like manner be cut off at the expiration of the other half hour.' That was an Act of the British parliament for the better governance of negro slaves in Bermuda.

One of the most shocking legal cases was *Gregson v Gilbert* (1781), otherwise known as the case of *The Zong*. *The Zong* was a slave ship owned by a large Liverpool slaving company. In 1781 it went from Liverpool to Cape Coast and from there with a cargo of 470 slaves headed for Jamaica. Twelve weeks into its voyage it had lost 60 Africans and seven of its 17 man crew. Luke Collingwood, the Captain, called his officers together and suggested to them that the sick slaves should be thrown overboard because water was getting short. This would allow the shipping company to claim their loss from the insurers. The reasoning was simple – if the slaves died a natural death it would be the owner's loss, but if they were thrown into the sea alive (like cargo) it would be the underwriters' loss. On 29 November the first batch of 54 were pushed overboard. The next day 42 were drowned and on the third day 26 more were thrown into the sea. This was done in full view of the other slaves on deck. A total of 131 Africans were coolly murdered from the deck of the Liverpool slaver. No-one would have heard of this affair had it not been for the claim for insurance. The *Zong* case came up for hearing in Guildhall in London when Gregson, the ship's owner, claimed for the loss of his slaves (£30 each) from the underwriters, Gilbert. The insurance company behaved like typical companies today.

They refused to pay. At the trial the jury sided with the ship's owner, ordering the insurance company to pay compensation for the dead slaves. The slave owners were represented by John Lee, the Solicitor-General. He argued that to bring a criminal prosecution as was being suggested by some people would be madness – the slaves were property. This may have seemed outrageous, but in essence it was true. The legal system hinged on the concept of the slave as a thing – a chattel, a piece of property. It was a concept which contained an inherent contradiction – for how could a human being be a thing? This contradiction has continued to haunt the British establishment to this day.

Lord Mansfield, the Chief Justice, accepted the point. 'There was no doubt,' he reasoned in his judgment, '(though it shocks one very much), that the case of the slaves was the same as if horses had been thrown into the sea.' That was English Law. After years of stubborn resistance, parliament finally decided to appoint a committee to investigate this odious yet profitable business. The road to abolition had begun.

The road to abolition: the collection of evidence

The Parliament of Great Britain decided to hear evidence in relation to the slave trade, in consequence of the numerous petitions which had been sent out. The slave merchants and planters also brought several witnesses on behalf of the continuance of the slave trade. These were heard and examined in the years 1789 and 1790.

The document produced after all the evidence was heard and presented to parliament was entitled 'An Abstract of the Evidence delivered before a Select Committee of the House of Commons in the years 1790 and 1791 on the Part of the Petitioners for the Abolition of the Slave Trade'. In the preface, some of the information that emerged illuminated what went on. A few examples should suffice here.

- *Bahamas Islands* (1784): A law was enacted that 'if any slave shall absent him or herself from his or her owner, for the space of three months successively, such slave shall be deemed an outlaw, and, so as an encouragement to apprehend and bring to justice such runaways, any person or persons who shall apprehend any such runaway, EITHER ALIVE OR DEAD, shall be paid out of the public treasury twenty pounds for every slave so apprehended and taken' (Privy Council Report, Part III).
- *St Christopher's (St Kitts)*: 'An Act to prevent the cutting off or depriving any slave in this island of any of their limbs or members, or otherwise disabling them, posed March 11, 1784, "Whereas some persons have of late been guilty of cutting off and depriving slaves of their ears, which practice is contrary to the principles of humanity and dishonourable to society; for prevention whereof in future, be it enacted by the Governor, that if any owner or possessor of any negro or other slave in this island, shall wilfully and wantonly cut or disable, or cause or procure to be cut out or disable the tongue, put out or cause or procure to be put out, an eye, or lip, or cause the same to be done; or break or cause to be broken, the arm, leg or, or any other limb, or member of any negro." The penalty is £500 currency or about £300 sterling, and six months imprisonment' (Privy Council Report, Part III).
- *Barbados*: 'An Act to prevent distempered, maimed, and worn out negroes, from infesting the towns, streets, and highways of this island – posed January 18, 1785. "Whereas it has, for some time past, been the cruel practice of some persons possessing negroes, who, from their old age and infirmities, are incapable of further service to their inhuman owners, to drive them from their plantations to beg, steal, or starve, which said unhappy objects [note the language] are daily

infesting the public street of the several towns in this island." The penalty to such owner is £5 currency, or about £3 12s sterling; and the court orders that these unhappy objects shall be taken home to their masters' (Privy Council Report).

- *Grenada*: 1788: 'Whereas the laws heretofore made for the protection of slaves have been found insufficient; and whereas humanity and the interest of the colony require that salutary and adequate regulations and provision should be adopted for rendering their servitude as easy as possible, and for promoting the increase of their population as the most likely means of reviewing, in the course of time, the necessity of further importations of negroes from Africa, And whereas these desirable ends cannot be so effectively obtained as by prescribing reasonable bounds of the power of masters and after having the charge of slaves, by compelling them sufficiently and prepare to lodge, feed, clothe, and maintain them . . .'

Other reports from the press at the time were also quite revealing, for newspapers are the first drafts of history. From the *Cornwall Chronicle*, a Jamaican paper, on December 1797, an addition to the Consolidated Slave-law was proposed in these terms:

Whereas the extreme cruelties and inhumanity of the managers, overseers, and book-keepers of estates, have frequently driven slaves into the woods, and occasioned rebellions and internal insurrections, to the great prejudice of the proprietors, and the manifest danger of the inhabitant of this island; for prevention whereof, be it enacted . . . And whereas also, it frequently happens, that slave come to their deaths by hefty and severe blows and other improper treatment of overseers and book-keepers in the heat of passion, and when such accident do happen, the violators are entered in the plantation books, as having died of convulsions, fits or other causes not be accounted for, and to conceal the real truth of the cause of death of such slave or slaves, he or they are immediately put underground

A few examples of the advertisement in the papers for runaway slaves will suffice to provide background to the general conditions prevailing.

- In the *Jamaica Gazette* of 8 March 1787 we are informed of 23 runaway slaves (marked) and 44 (unmarked). Among those marked is 'Apollo – WS on his face and breast' – ROBERT RP on each cheek, and KINGSTON marked YORKE on each shoulder and breast'.
- In the *Cornwall Chronicle* of Jamaica, dated 15 December 1787, 84 runaways are advertised, among them 'POMPEY, a Creole negro man, marked on both shoulders and breast MIL, diamond on top', JAMES,

a carpenter 'branded on both cheeks', and BILLY, belonging to the King, marked with a 'broad arrow on one shoulder'.

- In the *Kingston Morning Post* of 8 April 1789, seven runaways from one owner are advertised – namely 'a fisherman, a taylor, a shipwright, a seamstress, and three other wenches'. In the same paper we find an 'old grey bearded Coromanten man, a runaway'; also another taylor 'marked on both shoulders IT, and right should R.G.'. In the *Cornwall Chronicle* of 10 October 1789 a runaway is advertised named Prince, branded 'a black', with a cattle mark 'TH'.

- In the *Kingston Morning Post* of 5 November 1789 we find once again seven runaways from one proprietor, viz. 'an old woman with her two sons and two daughters, one of them very big with child', 'also a field negro and a carpenter'. In the supplement to the *Cornwall Chronicle* of 7 November 1789 there are 135 runaways advertised, viz. 48 with and 87 without brands. Of the former some have two, three, and four brands on the face, breasts and shoulders. One in particular is 'marked DE on both cheeks' and 'left shoulder'. Among those not branded is 'a woman with a wooden leg'. One man is distinguished by having 'both ears cropt' and another by 'his nose and ears being cut off'.

- In the *Jamaica Daily Advertiser* of 11 February 1791 we find six runaways advertised by one owner, viz. two men and four women, besides a girl child. Both the men and two of the women are one family, being an old woman, her brother, her son, and her grand-nephew (marked 'RDC') and who absented themselves at different times.

- An advertisement in the *Jamaica Daily Advertiser* of 24 February 1791 begins thus: 'February, 22, 1791, Escaped on Sunday last with a chain and collar round his neck, a negro man of the Mandingo country, numbered T44 on top'.

- In the *Barbados Gazette* of 14 January 1784 an advertisement reads thus: 'absented herself from the service of the subscriber, a yellow skin negro wench, named Sarah Deborah, whose person and surmised place of concealment, being very particularly described'. The advertisement ends with these words, 'whoever will apprehend the said wench ALIVE OR DEAD, shall receive two Moidolors reward from JOSEPH CHARLES HOWARD'.

The road to abolition – the debate in the Houses of Parliament

When the *Zong* case came to public notice the outrage began to build up to such an extent that parliament could ignore it no longer. The evidence provided by the inquiry meant that efforts by Granville Sharp, Olauda

Equiano, Thomas Clarkson and William Wilberforce to put the question before the House could not be postponed any longer.

The question that was put before the House of Commons on 10 June 1806, and to the House of Lords on 24 June 1806 – following a Resolution moved in both Houses of Parliament by Mr Charles Fox and Lord Granville – was the following: 'That conceiving the African slave trade to be contrary to the principles of justice, humanity, and sound policy, this house will, with all practicable expedition, take measures to abolish it, in such manner, and at such time, as shall be thought advisable.'

In the preface of the report on the parliamentary debate, the slave trade was described as 'a gigantic evil'. A Bill was brought into Parliament in the previous session with three objectives:

- To give effect to the Order of Council which had been issued to prohibit the importation of slaves into the colonies conquered by British arms.
- To prohibit British subjects from being engaged in importing slaves into the colonies of any foreign power, whether hostile or neutral.
- To prohibit British capital and British ships from being engaged in carrying on, or assisting to carry on, a slave trade in foreign ships; and also to prevent the outfit of foreign slave ships from British ports.

Secretary Fox moving the motion argued, 'the time, it is to be hoped, is now not far distant, when Africa will be relieved from the oppression, degradation, and misery of this impious commerce; when arresting the progress of that system of fraud, treachery and violence, which converts a large part of the habitable globe into a field of warfare and desolation, this nation shall begin to atone to the negro race for the accumulated wrongs . . .' He concluded that 'to deal and traffic, not in the labour of men, but in men themselves, was to devour the root, instead of enjoying the fruit of human diligence, and was therefore not only contrary to justice and humanity, but also contrary to sound policy'.[17]

General Tarleton (the MP for Liverpool) naturally opposed the motion:

> We can but ill afford, he argued, 'to adopt any measure that will occasion a diminution . . . in revenue. I have no difficulty in saying that the prosperity of Liverpool is intimately connected with the African Slave Trade. It is difficult for me to assent to any measure which appears to be injurious to the interests of my constituents, closely connected as they are with the general interest of this country. As to the situation in Liverpool, I have this to say, it was once a mere fishing hamlet, but it has risen into prosperity in exact proportion to the extent of the African slave trade, so as to become the second place in wealth and population in the British empire, renowned for its commercial

enterprise. This measure [i.e., the abolition of the slave trade] is one which will cut up, by the roots, the source of our wealth.

He continued,

- Those who are to suffer by the abolition of the Slave Trade, will come to Parliament for compensation for their losses. There will be no pretence for refusing such compensation, because whatever may be the injustice or inhumanity of this trade, it is not to be denied that it is a trade which has been carried on under the auspices of this House, and agreeable to law and therefore, if this trade is now to be abolished, all those who have carried it the most must have their losses made up, particularly those who have been concerned in building up ships for this trade which, from their peculiar construction, are unfit for any other, and this consideration will be very considerable in its amount.[18]

The Honourable Member of Parliament for Liverpool had no doubt whatsoever in his mind that 'much evil will result to this country at large, from the abolition of the Slave Trade, should this measure be adopted; but with regard to Liverpool, I am confident that great distress, public and private will be the result; that bankruptcies will follow . . .' Of course, after the trade was abolished, the merchants were duly compensated, the churches were paid, the shipbuilders, etc. But what about the slaves and the negro race, the unoffending negro race who clearly suffered the most and are still suffering from the effects of this? Perhaps I run ahead of myself. Lord Castlereagh, one of the great statesmen of his age and one of the architects of this modern world, in his contribution noted as follows:

- as to the general principle on which the resolution is founded, I agree to it, and I do not know who can entertain a contrary opinion in this House. I think it is a proposition on which no human being can entertain a doubt, namely, that *the slave trade is a great evil in itself, and I think that as little doubt can be entertained upon another proposition namely that it is the duty of parliament to abrogate that evil and to extirpate it, if that be practicable, it being a stain upon the national character*[19] [original emphasis].

Also contributing to the debate was the Solicitor-General Sir Samuel Romilly. He spoke as a lawyer, indeed the government's chief lawyer: 'I, an individual of this country who feels most seriously the reproachful situation in which we stand at this moment, with respect to the slave trade. I can well understand that nations as well as individuals, may be guilty of the most unusual act, from their not having the courage to enquire into all their nature and consequences.' He was talking about crimes of omission, as well as commission.

He continued:

> Before the year 1789 this nation had not the courage to enquire into
> all the circumstances of this trade. But in that year, this House had the
> courage to investigate the complaints which were preferred against it.
> This committee sat, and after a painful and anxious investigation, they
> reported to this house, a great body of evidence, by which was
> established beyond the possibility of dispute that *the African trade is*
> *carried on by rapine, robbery and murder*; by encouraging and
> fomenting wars; by false accusations and imaginary crimes. Thus were
> these unhappy beings, and in order to supply this traffic in human
> blood, torn from their families relatives and homes not only in war,
> but profound peace, and after being sold in their native land, they are
> carried across the Atlantic, in the most deplorable state in which it is
> possible to convey them alive, and under circumstances of too much
> horror to bear reflection. Now, Sir, after all this have been proved;
> after it has been ascertained by indisputable evidence, that this trade
> cannot be carried on without the most iniquitous practices; *that rapine*
> *and murder are the foundations of it*; ['rapine' in the *Collins English*
> *Dictionary* states: 'rapine (noun – the seizure of property by force;
> pillage from the Latin *rapina* – plundering, also from *rapere* –
> to snatch.] That men are falsely accused, and on these false accusations,
> condemned, in order to supply its victims; that wars are fomented to
> support this traffic; that most disgusting cruelties attend it, in the
> passage of this unhappy part of our species from their native home to
> the place of slavery; that they are subjected to a cruel and perpetual
> bondage; I do say that these ought not to be suffered to continue for
> an hour; it is a stain on our national reputation , and ought to be wiped
> away.
>   The inhumanity of this traffic is most enormous and such as we
> cannot look at without shuddering. Since the period at which we
> resolved to abolish this trade in 1796, no less than 300,000 individuals
> have been torn by us from the coast of Africa to supply this trade. Such
> is the accumulation of guilt that hangs on the English nation at this
> moment. I cannot therefore, suffer this subject to pass, without
> expressing my most anxious wish to concur in the immediate abolition
> of a traffic that has brought upon this nation such indelible disgrace
> . . .[20]

That was the opinion of the Solicitor-General of England.
  The Lord Chancellor (Lord Erskine) added:

> My Lords, I have not been in the internal parts of Africa, but I believe
> what is related of them by men whom I know to be impartial, and

diligent in their enquiries. From them, I find that parents are torn from their children, children torn from their parents, husbands torn from their wives; wives from their husbands; all ties of blood and affection (for negroes have affections, as well as ourselves), torn up by their roots. My Lords I have myself seen these unhappy creatures put together in heaps in the hold of a ship which with every possible attention to their accommodation, must still be intolerable; and I have heard proved in courts of justice, facts still more dreadful, if possible than those which I have seen.

Cases have occurred in which the victims of misery have been made frantic and have fought death by violence, rising up in rebellion and endeavouring to break the chains by which they were fastened to one another; and then have ensued scenes the mere statement of which is a disgrace to a British court of Justice; not to those who administer justice according to the rules of law, but to those who ought to prevent a repetition of the misery, by putting an end to the practice by which it is produced. I allude to a case well known to my noble and learned friend [Lord Ellenborough] upon a policy of insurance in which it became necessary to defend the underwriter from the effects of his insurance; for he had undertaken, by his policy, only to indemnify the assured in the usual way against the perils of the sea. The negroes on board the ship, the cargo of which was thus insured, rose up in a mass to destroy the captain and his crew in order to liberate themselves; and having advanced in pursuit of their objects, it became necessary to repel them by force as well as to save their own lives, as well as the lives of the crew. Some of them yielded; some of them were killed in the scuffle. But many of them actually jumped into the sea and were drowned thus preferring death to the misery they felt on board; while others hang unto the ropes of the ship repenting of their rashness, bewailing with frightful noises, their horrid fate. Thus the whole ship exhibited nothing but one hideous scene of wretchedness.

Those who were subdued into obedience, and secured in chains, were seized with flux (dysentery) which carried off many. These things were proved on trial by a British jury which had to consider whether this was a loss which fell within the policy of insurance, the negroes being regarded as if they are a cargo of dead matter. My Lords, many instances might also be given of mortality on board ships in this traffic. Where, the voyage having been unusually protracted, famine has visited the ship; and death has kept pretty even pace with the short allowance. My Lords these are things only too shocking to describe: and I ask your Lordships, is it possible that you should voluntarily assent to the continuance of so much misery, which you have the power of preventing; or that you should deem this practice consistent with humanity or justice? No, My Lords, it is impossible.[21]

Questions of law and jurisprudence

Issues concerning the morality as well as the legality of slavery have remained, as it were, under lock and key for over two hundred years. All attempts to raise these questions were seriously undermined by the powers that benefited from slavery, i.e., the British Establishment. Why rake up the past? Let sleeping dogs lie, they say. Or, they continue, your ancestors were partners in this so shut up. Indeed quite often the victims have been made to apologise. But with the celebration of the 200th anniversary of the abolition, these uncomfortable truths are beginning to intrude vividly on our public consciousness. Has the 'national disgrace' been wiped away? Does murder cease to be murder because the murderers have decided to stop their murderous ways by abolishing the slave trade in which they were the chief perpetrators? Great Britain, as poacher-in-chief, overnight became gamekeeper-in-chief. But did these crimes then cease to be crimes? These questions must have haunted the British government, and their successors have since agonised over them. So it was not too surprising that on the 27 November 2006 The Rt. Hon. Tony Blair, Prime Minister, issued a statement of regret, which was in many ways a non-apology. He admitted that 'Britain's rise to pre-eminence was partially dependent on the system of colonial slave labour and, as we record its abolition we should recall our place in its practice'. He went on: 'It is hard to believe that what would now be a crime against humanity was legal at the time.' Here we may pause to ask – when was it ever legal to commit murder, to foment murder, or to kidnap? When was rapine ever legal? Does the fact that the British government authorised, sanctioned, and profited from an action make it legal? And when is something legal and something merely moral? Were the actions of Nazi Germany legal because they were sanctioned by the authority of the Third Reich? These are indeed troubling questions.[22]

Africa has waited over two hundred years for the truth. How much longer should Africa wait for justice? Does the Great Britain of today possess the moral courage of her ancestors to seize the opportunity to begin to wipe away this stain on her national character? Perhaps I should conclude as I began. A people will only be able to obtain what they negotiate and ask for. The Lord Jesus Christ admonished us to ask and to be given; to knock and have the door opened; to seek and then find. Secretary Fox in moving the motion for the abolition was truly eloquent and lofty when he said: 'The time it is hoped, is not far distant, when Africa will be relieved from the oppression, degradation, and misery of this impious commerce; when arresting the progress of that system of fraud, treachery and violence, which converts a large part of the habitable globe into a field a warfare and desolation ... then this nation shall begin to atone to the negro race for its accumulated wrongs.'[23]

Will Great Britain be able to mobilise sufficient moral courage to take the lead in this struggle for truth and justice, or will it continue to dissemble and prevaricate, and hope to remain in its current state of selective national amnesia. I conclude here with a parting reminder from William Faulkner: 'The past is never dead; is not even past'.[24]

Notes

1 Debrunner (1967).
2 Williams (1944).
3 Williams (1944).
4 From oral history – Tourist Guide, Elimina Castle, Ghana.
5 *The Dutch and the Guinea Coast* (1674–1742) – A Collection of Documents from the General State Archives, The Hague.
6 Donnan (1969).
7 Donnan (1969).
8 Williams (1944).
9 Williams (1944).
10 Williams (1944).
11 See House of Commons Record – abstract of guidance (1790).
12 See *The Dutch and the Guinea Coast archives of the Dutch West Indian Company* – translated by Van Danzig.
13 See *The Dutch and the Guinea Coast archives of the Dutch West Indian Company* – translated by Van Danzig.
14 Williams (1944).
15 Falconbridge (1788).
16 Falconbridge (1788).
17 Parliamentary Debate – House of Commons (1790).
18 House of Commons (1790).
19 House of Lords (1790).
20 House of Lords (1790).
25 House of Lords (1790).
22 Lloyd (1959). See also Fuller (1964).
23 House of Lords (1790).
24 Faulkner (1951).

Bibliography

Debrunner, Dr H. (1967) *History of Christianity in Ghana*. Accra: Waterville.
Donnan, E. (1969) *Documents Illustrative of the Slave Trade in America vol. 1 (1441–1700)*. London: Octagon.
Falconbridge, A. (1788) *Account of the Slave Trade to West Africa*. London: J. Phillips.
Faulkner, W. (1951) *Requiem for a Nun*. New York: Random House.
Fuller, L. (1964) *The Morality of Law*. New Haven: Yale University Press.
House of Commons (1790) Parliamentary Debate.
House of Commons Record (1790) Abstract of Guidance.
House of Lords (1790) Parliamentary Debate.
Lloyd, D. (1959) *Introduction to Jurisprudence*. London: Stevens & Sons.

Oral history – Tourist Guide, Elimina Castle, Ghana.

Van Danzig, A. (ed.) (1978) *The Dutch and the Guinea Coast (1674–1742): A Collection of Documents from the General State Archive at The Hague.* Accra: Ghana Academy of Arts & Sciences.

Williams, E. (1944) *Capitalism and Slavery.* Richmond: University of North Carolina Press.

Chapter 8

Restitution after slavery

Kate Bracegirdle

The question of whether or not reparations should be paid for the harm caused by the transatlantic slave trade is not a new one. In the United States of America, there have been several attempts to provide or secure reparations ever since the end of the Civil War in 1865 and the consequent liberation of the slaves in the southern states. The intensity of the campaigns for reparations has ebbed and flowed over the years, with the end of the twentieth and the beginning of the twenty-first centuries witnessing a renewed vigour in these demands. 1987 saw the founding of the National Coalition of Blacks for Reparations in America (N'COBRA) to press for reparations specifically for African descendants living in the United States (N'COBRA) and in 2000 another organisation with similar aims, the Reparations Co-ordinating Committee was formed by Harvard Law Professor Charles Ogletree and Randall Robinson, author of the influential book *The Debt*, on the subject of reparations. Most significantly, for the purposes of this chapter, in 2002 a number of class action claims for damages were brought in the American courts (hereafter referred to as the 'US Litigation'), with Judge Norgle handing down a judgment in the consolidated proceedings in July 2005.[1] The US Litigation comprised, in part, claims for restitution with the causes of action being, *inter alia*, various torts[2] and unjust enrichment. This followed successful action in the 1990s against Swiss banks, German industry and European insurers by survivors, and the families of victims, of the Holocaust.

On the world stage, in 1999 the African World Reparations and Repatriation Truth Commission met in Accra and issued a declaration seeking the payment by Western states and institutions of $777 thousand billion in reparations. Similarly, at the UN organised World Conference Against Racism in Durban 2001 requests were made by some African representatives for apologies and reparations from Western states in respect of their roles in the Atlantic slave trade.[3] The Durban Declaration and Programme of Action adopted by the conference acknowledged slavery as a crime against humanity and said that it should always have been so. It expressed regret at the contribution that the slave trade made to lasting social and economic inequalities and referred to the provision of effective remedies. The Durban Review Conference in 2009 called on member states that had not already done so to adopt three UN resolutions[4] relating to commemorating the abolition of the slave trade and to remembering its horrors and legacy.

In the UK, although £20 million compensation was paid to the planters who lost their right to own slaves following the Slavery Abolition Act 1833, no provision was made for compensation to be paid to the freed slaves themselves. In 2007, the Archbishop of Canterbury, Dr Rowan Williams, said that the Church of England, having received compensation in 1833 in respect of the loss of its slaves, should in turn consider making reparation (Oliver 2007). The purpose of this chapter is to consider to what extent the English law of restitution may assist in securing reparations for slavery.

The case for reparations

Demands for reparations are not uncontroversial and are not even wholly supported by all descendants of slaves, just as calls for reparations in respect of the Nazi Holocaust were not supported by all survivors or families of the victims.[5] Clearly the considerable length of time which has elapsed since the Atlantic slave trade was brought to an end during the nineteenth century is one factor which causes many to have misgivings about the validity of paying reparations now. Both those individuals who were enslaved and those who immediately and directly profited have now passed away. There are likely to be evidential difficulties, as much documentary evidence will have been destroyed and witnesses will have died.[6] However, statistics from the USA show that the African-American population does appear to be significantly disadvantaged relative to the White population in several respects.[7] In 1993, for example, the average White household had assets worth $45,740 whereas the corresponding figure for the average Black household was $4,418. In 1999 the average annual salary of a Black male working full-time was approximately $10,000 lower than that of a white male (Loury 2002: 178, 175). Sociologist Dalton Conley reports figures that show the mortality rate of Black infants is more than twice that of White and Hispanic infants (Conley 1999). The reasons for such disadvantage are a matter of some debate, however it does not seem unreasonable to suppose that this is attributable, at least in part, to the fact that the ancestors of many, or most, of today's African-Americans were brought to the continent and held there in slavery, unable to accumulate wealth as a result of their endeavours. When slavery was finally abolished without an accompanying proper scheme of reparation or compensation,[8] they were freed into a life of poverty. This, in turn, resulted in an inevitable lack of inherited wealth for subsequent generations. Similarly, UK statistics show that the infant mortality rate of babies of Caribbean ethnic origin is twice that of infants of White British origin (Office for National Statistics 2008). It would appear that in the UK there is also evidence of inequality in educational, employment and income attainment between white British and black Caribbean people (Li et al. 2008).

Even amongst those who support requests for reparations, the US Litigation did not receive wholehearted support because the US government was not made a defendant and so it seemed to critics that the state was being absolved of its responsibility to deal with the aftermath of slavery (Torpey 2006: 108). The debate over reparations in the USA became increasingly bitter when the commentator and author David Horowitz attempted to place an advertisement entitled 'Ten Reasons Why Reparations for Slavery Is a Bad Idea – and Racist Too' in college newspapers. The editors of many of these rejected it and, inevitably, this led to accusations of censorship. Horowitz also faced counterclaims of racism and protests ensued on campuses where the advertisement was published.[9]

The push for reparations in the USA continues, although since the judgment in the US Litigation the focus has been more on achieving this via a political rather than a judicial route. N'COBRA continues with its campaigning and Democrat Congressman John Conyers makes annual attempts to have a commission set up to look at the continuing effects of slavery and the payment of reparations.[10] Although these have so far been unsuccessful, the House of Representatives did recently make an apology for slavery.[11] As Paul McHugh explained at the conference, public apologies by the State for past wrongs have an important part to play in the healing process of these lasting wounds (Dodge and Sommerville 2009: 4). The sort of commission proposed by Congressman Conyers would be of greater practical benefit, however, as incontrovertible evidence of the effects of slavery on African-Americans' life chances today may persuade government and private companies to make reparation.

The law of restitution

Restitution is a specific legal response which requires a defendant to give up his gain to a successful claimant (Birks 1985: 11). It is different from the damages more usually awarded in civil law claims, as these tend to be compensatory and therefore based on the loss suffered by the claimant. It is possible that a claim for restitution may be preferable to claimants seeking reparations for historic slavery, as it might be easier to establish an identifiable gain made by the defendant than a loss suffered by the claimant who will inevitably not be the person actually enslaved. The primary cause of action resulting in an award of restitution in English law is unjust enrichment.[12] This is not such a nebulous concept as it may at first sound. In this context it has a well-defined meaning and rules governing its application, just as negligence does in the torts sphere. In order to establish a successful claim for unjust enrichment, and thus be entitled to restitution, the claimant must be able to prove that the defendant was enriched at his, the claimant's, expense and that such enrichment was unjust.[13] Again, 'unjust' here does not refer to some vague notion of morality or fairness, but is guided by legal precedent.[14] In addition, the claimant's success is dependant on the defendant being unable to establish a defence or bar to the claim. Besides claims of unjust enrichment, restitution may also be awarded in some cases where the claimant has successfully proved that the defendant committed a wrong against him, for example certain torts,[15] a breach of contract in exceptional circumstances[16] or an equitable wrong.[17]

The US Litigation

Claims had previously been made in the US courts by survivors, and the families of victims, of the Nazi Holocaust, seeking restitution of the value of forced and slave labour, looted assets, the balances held in dormant bank accounts and the proceeds of life assurance policies that had never been paid out. Between 1996–7 three class actions were commenced against Swiss banks in respect of dormant accounts, customers' assets that had been handed over to the Nazi regime and the financing of clients who had established and maintained Nazi slave labour camps. In 1999 a $1.25 billion settlement was reached in these class actions and the administration of the settlement was supervised over several years by Judge Korman of the New York District Court. Claims were also made against German companies in respect of the slave and forced labour from which they benefited. In this case a political settlement worth $5.2 billion was negotiated in 1999–2000 by the German and US governments, as well as representatives of German industry and of victims and, as a result, the courts dismissed the pending legal actions (Weiss 2006: 108). In 1997 class action proceedings were launched against several European insurance companies in respect of unpaid life assurance claims, whilst some states introduced regulations designed to assist these claimants, for example as regards disclosure requirements and limitation periods.[18] This resulted in the insurance industry establishing an ad hoc commission to deal with all such claims and distribute the $500 million dollars assigned to them (Neuborne 2006: 60).

One might therefore assume that there was good precedent in American law on which the descendants of former slaves might base their own claims for restitution. However, the US Litigation failed at a preliminary stage when the court granted the defendants' Motion to Dismiss the proceedings on several fundamental grounds. These were that the claimants lacked sufficient standing to make the claim; that the issues raised were of a political nature and that therefore the executive branch of the state apparatus, namely Congress, was the appropriate forum in which to resolve them; that the proceedings failed to disclose an actionable claim; and that the claims were time-barred. An appeal resulted in the decision being upheld on the grounds of the claimants' lack of standing and the claims being time-barred.[19] As the action was dismissed at this stage, what the court did not do was consider the substantive issues of the claim. This chapter seeks to undertake a consideration of the merits of hypothetical cases under the English law of restitution and to consider the prospects for success of any similar claims if these were brought before the English courts.

Restitution for unjust enrichment

As previously stated, in English law restitution may be awarded when the claimant has successfully proved that the defendant has been unjustly enriched at his expense or, in certain circumstances, has committed a wrong against him. The claim for restitution based on unjust enrichment will be considered first, as this is the primary basis for recovery. We need to consider four separate questions: (1) is the defendant enriched? (2) was the enrichment obtained at the expense of the claimant? (3) is the enrichment unjust? (4) is the defendant able to rely on a bar or defence? However, before examining these issues of substantive law, an important issue of procedure – namely the limitation period – demands our attention. As previously noted, this was one of the reasons for the failure of the US Litigation and it may be presumed to present an inevitable bar to the pursuit of a similar claim in the English courts.

Limitation period

One of the most interesting aspects in formulating a hypothetical case for restitution for historic slavery under English law is that the seemingly obvious barrier of the limitation period is less clearly defined than one might expect. The Limitation Act 1980 does not set a specific limitation period for claims of unjust enrichment or restitution. This is not surprising in view of the very late recognition of unjust enrichment as an autonomous basis of claims for restitution.[20] In *Nelson v Rye*[21] Laddie J, when considering the limitation period applicable in respect of breach of trust and breach of fiduciary duty, accepted the premise that where the Limitation Act did not set out a specific period of limitation, then none was applicable.[22] However, in the earlier decision of *Westdeutsche Landesbank*

Girozentrale v Islington LBC[23] Hobhouse J had come to the conclusion[24] that the term 'simple contract,' to which a six-year period of limitation applies,[25] should be read to include 'quasi-contract', which, in effect, would cover the majority of claims in unjust enrichment. This conclusion was the result of a *Pepper v Hart*[26] examination of the recommendations of the Law Revision Committee in 1936 which had resulted in the enactment of the earlier Limitation Act 1939 containing similar provisions to the 1980 Act. The conclusion was also in line with the decision in *Re Diplock's Estate*[27] where the Court of Appeal assumed that 'actions founded on simple contract' included actions for money had and received.[28] However one academic, writing on this subject, has challenged the received wisdom that a period of limitation should always apply, suggesting that perhaps there should be a general postponement of time running, not just in cases of mistake or fraud, but whenever operation of the Limitation Act would result in a defendant retaining an unjust enrichment (McLean 1989: 480). Although it may be likely that, if the House of Lords were called on to determine the limitation period, it would follow the lead set by *Westdeutsche* and *Re Diplock*, there is sufficient ambiguity here that a case could be argued on behalf of the claimants of restitution for historic slavery that no limitation period would be applicable to their claim.

Is the defendant enriched?

Turning to the substantive elements of the claim in unjust enrichment, this first question tends to be relatively uncomplicated as the defendant is usually in receipt of money from the claimant, for example where it has been paid by mistake or on a consideration which has wholly failed. However, the potential slavery claim poses unusual problems. Not only do the questions of identifying and valuing the defendant's enrichment arise,[29] but also there is also the essential and difficult first question of identifying the proper defendants. In the US Litigation, the defendants comprised a number of well-known US companies such as insurance company Aetna Inc., the bank Lehman Brothers, the railway company Union Pacific Railroad, the bank JP Morgan Chase (now Morgan Stanley), the insurer AIG, as well as Lloyd's of London and the Canadian National Railway. It was alleged by the plaintiffs that these corporations profited from the slave trade directly or indirectly by, for example, using slave labour themselves; making loans to slave traders, planters employing slave labour or merchants of commodities produced using slave labour; or underwriting insurance policies against the loss of slaves and/or the boats used to transport them.

There are advantages to making a claim against private companies. Corporate persons do not necessarily have the same relatively short lifespan that natural people do. So, whilst individuals who were slave traders and owners[30] are no longer alive and available to be pursued through the courts, it may be, in theory at least, that present-day companies within the English jurisdiction were already incorporated at the time of the slave trade and were profiting from it. Several banks and insurance companies in particular have very long histories. Alternatively and more likely, companies that profited from the slave trade in the past may have subsequently been subsumed into another company that remains currently trading.[31] It should be possible in many cases to trace this development thorough company and public records. Expert witness evidence from historians could be presented to establish factual links between modern companies and historical slavery.

On a strict application of the law on separate corporate personality this may throw up some difficulties in piercing the corporate veil, but it may nevertheless allow for the application of moral and/or commercial pressure. Part of the claim in the US Litigation centred on the alleged failure of the defendants to provide information to the claimants and to the defendants' customers as to their historical links to slavery and the consequent breach of various states' consumer protection legislation.[32] UK consumer law, being less well developed in this regard, would not require such disclosures and therefore would not assist potential claimants.

Many individuals and families in the UK profited directly or indirectly from the slave trade, whether they were traders, ship owners, merchants of commodities such as sugar, coffee and cotton, or involved in any number of commercial activities related to and reliant on the slave trade.[33] Some families even had slaves working as personal servants in their homes. Several major UK cities, notably London, Bristol, Liverpool and Glasgow,[34] were also largely built on the wealth generated by the Atlantic slave trade and industries employing slave labour.[35] Much of this wealth will no doubt have been passed down through generations of families so that individual descendants who are living today will be benefiting from inherited wealth that can be traced back to the profits of slavery. It could therefore be argued that they have been enriched at the expense of those who were enslaved. Of course it is not possible to sue a family as such, due to its lack of a separate legal personality. In order to make a claim against inherited wealth, the claimants would need to establish a right to a proprietary rather than a merely personal remedy and would also need to be able to follow or trace the wealth to current funds or substitute property. In practical terms this is unlikely to be possible.

Alternative potential defendants would include nation states. As previously noted, some supporters of the campaign for reparations in the USA thought it essential that the government itself should be named as a defendant and thus required to take responsibility for the injustice that the state had permitted for so long. In a similar vein, campaigners have made repeated calls over the years for the British Government to apologise for the state having allowed slavery to continue until the mid-nineteenth century. Whilst in 2007, the then Northern Ireland and Welsh Secretary Peter Hain apologised for the part Northern Ireland and Wales had played in the slave trade (BBC 2007), Prime Minister Tony Blair in the previous year had gone only so far as to express 'deep sorrow' for the role the country as a whole had played (BBC 2006). In terms of a claim that could be made in the English courts, the UK Government would appear to be an obvious choice of defendant. Clearly it was not just individual cities and their inhabitants which prospered as a result of the triangular slave trade – that is to say, manufactured goods shipped from the UK to West Africa to be sold and/or exchanged for slaves, slaves shipped to and sold in the Caribbean and the Americas and then commodities such as sugar and cotton produced using slave labour being shipped to the UK for their onward sale. The country as a whole benefited from the wealth generated which was then used, in part, to fund the Industrial Revolution and the building of important infrastructure such as the railways. As wealth creates wealth, so the UK became an industrialised and wealthy nation and remains so in the twenty-first century.[36] By contrast it can be argued that Africa, or at least part of it, was (and remains) hampered in its efforts to develop and create wealth by what was effectively the theft of a significant proportion of its most physically able and young people. The lack of manpower cannot have failed to take its toll on the economy of the areas affected, particularly as at that time in history agriculture and other industries would inevitably have been labour intensive.[37]

Since 1947, it has been possible to sue the Crown in much the same way as a private person.[38] There are certain limited exceptions to this, but none would appear to be relevant to the type of claim under consideration here. Is the UK government an appropriate body to be required to pay restitution? Perhaps a moral difficulty here is that the bill for restitution would ultimately fall on taxpayers as a whole. Is it possible to say that the country's taxpayers as a whole have been enriched by slavery? Some of them may be descended from slaves themselves. Certainly, many of them will be twentieth and twenty-first century immigrants with no prior connection to the UK or other Western European countries who engaged in slave trading. Many, if not most, will be descended from British people who lived in abject poverty during the period that the Atlantic slave trade was ongoing. However, it could be argued that all current inhabitants of the UK, including these groups, have been enriched because we benefit from the opportunity of living in a modern industrialised nation and without the wealth generated though slavery the UK may not have become such a nation. Nonetheless, there will be many individual taxpayers who, given their situation in life and their origins, will find it difficult to see why they should be considered to be enriched by an historical slave trade. This could be important to the extent that it impacts negatively on public and media support for a claim for restitution.

In the USA the possibility of launching claims against individual states is one that has also been mooted and several state legislatures have made apologies regarding slavery. In principle, it may be possible to make similar claims against the local authorities of individual cities in England and Wales which have their own corporate personality. Although the elected representatives of some cities have indeed apologised or expressed regret for the roles their cities played in the Atlantic slave trade,[39] it is unlikely that this would make it significantly easier to establish liability in any court proceedings. Just as with claims against the national government, there is likely to be considerable unhappiness amongst those upon whom the burden of paying restitution would fall – namely council tax payers. This would no doubt be combined with a feeling of injustice that inhabitants of certain cities were being required to make reparation for something which had brought economic benefits to the whole country.

Besides commercial companies and local authorities there may also be a number of other corporate bodies or organisations who could be investigated for their potential to be named as defendants to a claim for restitution. For example, as already noted the Church of England is known to have owned a plantation in the Caribbean and the slaves who worked it. On 8 February 2006 the General Synod debated and voted in favour of making an apology for its role in slavery (Church of England 2006).

Preparing a case against any potential defendant would require the assistance of experts, such as historians, economists and forensic accountants, in order to piece together the evidence as to who was enriched, by how much, and whether they continue to exist in the present day. It is generally assumed that the slave trade and the industries built on slave labour were lucrative. It seems to go without saying that a business which does not have to pay its workers wages for the work that they do is bound to be very profitable. However, there has been some dispute over the years amongst historians and economists as to the profitability not just of slave trading, but also of businesses reliant on slave labour.[40] Various factors are mooted as mitigating the profitability of slave labour: for example, although slave owners did not have to pay wages, they did have to pay slave traders for the slaves and this was an initial capital outlay rather than a regular payment out of income which could have had attendant cash-flow consequences. In addition people who are forced to work are unlikely to do so to the best of their ability and be as productive as those working for a suitable reward.[41]

Whether or not these were as high as some estimates put them, it is beyond doubt that profits were made from slavery and many people were thereby enriched. If the legal claims were to be made by a slave himself, he should have no difficulty in establishing that the slave trader who sold him was enriched by the net sum received in payment and that the slave owner was enriched by the value of his labours which were not paid for. The insurer who insured the slave ship or the banker who lent money to the slave owner to establish his plantation could be argued to have been enriched by the receipt of premiums less the amount of any claims or the receipt of interest on the money lent. However, it is not likely that any former slaves will still be alive and able to make claims for themselves so it is important to consider the second question of whether or not the defendant's enrichment was obtained at the expense of the claimant.

At the expense of the claimant

The enrichment of the slave traders and slave owners can clearly be seen to have been at the expense of those people who were transported from Africa and enslaved. The situation in respect of the merchants, insurers and bankers is less clear. The merchant would say that he was enriched by buying and selling commodities. The insurer would argue that he was enriched by a contract in which he accepted a risk and the banker would similarly argue that he was enriched by a contract to supply money. These contracts would not directly involve the slave. Indirectly, the insurer and the banker are enriched at the expense of the slave because without his enslavement there would not be that voyage to insure, or perhaps that plantation in which to invest. The merchant would be able to make purchases at a lower price because of the reduced labour costs incurred in producing goods. He would therefore be able to increase either his profit margin by maintaining his onward selling price or his volume of sales by being able to offer a lower selling price. However it would not be straightforward even for the slave himself to claim against such defendants because of the indirect nature of this enrichment. Although in moral and economic terms one could argue that these parties profited at the expense of the slaves, this would be difficult to establish in strictly legal terms. An initial problem that would arise wherever the benefit was conferred under a contract would be the requirement to show that the contract was no longer operative, for example because it was void, frustrated, discharged by breach, etc. This requirement has the potential to make recovery even from an actual slave trader or owner impossible. Due to the primacy of contract in English law, restitution is not available where a contract was in operation regulating the parties' relationship. One reason the contract might be unenforceable would be if it were illegal, but until 1807 slave trading was not illegal so related contracts would not be either. The passing of the Abolition of the Slave Trade Act 1807 would also not have had any effect on contracts retrospectively. In fact slave trading did not simply cease overnight and British nationals found ways of continuing their business activity. Ownership of slaves in the British colonies remained legal until the passing of the Slavery Abolition Act 1833[42] and the *de facto* expiration of its transitional provisions in 1838. If evidence could be identified at this stage of particular slave trading or purchase contracts post-1807 or 1833 respectively, then such contracts in themselves would be no bar to a claim in unjust enrichment due to their illegality. However the vast majority of potential claims are likely to arise from events that occurred prior to the change in the law.

Having considered the hypothetical question of the slaves themselves being able to claim, it is necessary to consider the identity of more likely claimants. The slaves involved are now of course dead and unable to claim restitution for themselves. Is it then possible to say that potential defendants have been enriched at the expense of people who are still now living and who could make a claim, or for the descendants of deceased slaves to claim on behalf of their ancestors' estates? Generally, it is not possible to say that a defendant has been enriched at the claimant's expense by the conferral of a benefit on the defendant by a third party – that is, the slave who provided the labour. In the US Litigation, the claimants comprised people who either claimed to have been slaves themselves; to be the descendants of slaves generally; to be the descendants of named slaves; or to be the estates of slaves or their descendants. Some of the family relationships between the claimants and the ancestor who was alleged to have been a slave were as close as parent and child. Slavery continued in America for some time after its abolition in Great Britain and indeed one of the claimants was the estate of someone who was alleged to have been a slave in Louisiana between 1927 and 1934, long after the official date of the abolition of slavery, but during the time that the Jim Crow laws enforcing segregation of the races were particularly prevalent in the Southern states.[43] Therefore while the claims are undoubtedly historic, the direct victims may not necessarily be as remote in time and by generation as might be supposed.

It should still be possible to identify British people today who are descended from slaves who could be named as claimants. There is also no reason why people of other nationalities, perhaps the descendants of slaves still residing in the Caribbean or in America, should not also claim against British defendants in the English courts. Although they were not brought to the UK, their ancestors may well have been transported from Africa by British slave traders on boats insured by British insurers and they may also have been enslaved by British citizens in various colonies.[44] This does however raise the question of to whom morally should restitution be made? Even if one could identify, say, 100 or 1000 living descendants of slaves who could make a claim for restitution, the defendants were enriched at the expense of millions of slaves.[45] Practically it would seem impossible to identify all their descendants now let alone prompt them all to make legal claims for restitution. On the other hand, it does not seem appropriate that just a few motivated descendants should receive a windfall in the form of the entire enrichment made at the expense of a much larger group of victims. The claimants in the US Litigation dealt with this not just by claiming on behalf of themselves as descendants, but also by framing their claim as a class action so that they claimed '*on behalf of all "formerly enslaved Africans and their descendants" and all living "former enslaved African-Americans and their descendants . . ."*'[46] The Claimants said that the damages (if awarded) would be applied to improving health care, educational opportunities and housing for Black Americans generally (Torpey 2006: 107).

The same problem had been faced in the post-Holocaust litigation against the Swiss banks in respect of the part of the settlement that had been attributed to looted assets. The class of people involved was so large and the evidence so scarce that the $100 million was distributed to social services agencies worldwide who dealt with the poorest Holocaust survivors, with the majority of the money going to Jews in the former Soviet Union, but about 10 per cent of it also going to Sinti-Roma (Bazyler and Alford 2006: 66). In the case of reparations a very practical, although perhaps imprecise, solution would be for the amount of any unjust enrichment found by the court to be paid to charitable or non-profit making organisations who represent those whose ancestors may have been forced into slavery, but without their having to prove that this did indeed happen. One could make the case that the African people as a whole were placed at a disadvantage in the Caribbean, the Americas and Western Europe because of the existence of the slave trade and the ensuing economic hardship and arguable stigmatisation that it caused (Salzberger and Turck 2004: 52). So, for example, trusts could be established to administer educational scholarships for British people of African descent. Schemes such as these would not necessarily ensure that all the restitution paid was directed towards the descendants of slaves, as many of those claiming the assistance may come from families which had come directly from Africa to settle in Britain long after the end of slavery. However it may still be considered preferable to distribute any restitution to a wider cohort than confine it to a small number of nominal claimants. This is particularly so if one accepts that the economic development of Africa as a continent was stalled due to the consequences of the transatlantic slave trade. In terms of whether such a claim could be made procedurally (although there is now a system of Group Litigation Orders provided for in the Civil Procedure Rules 1999) this does not equate to the Rule 23[47] class action procedure in the USA and this could present obstacles to representative groups making claims in this way on behalf of a general class of people in English courts.

A further suggested alternative therefore would be for African nation states to make claims. Modern-day West African countries could argue that the defendants had been enriched at their expense by the removal of their citizens from their place working in the claimant's economy. Two principal problems with this option can be envisaged. Firstly, there is evidence that some African rulers and officials were involved in supplying people to the Western slave traders, whether they be members of neighbouring societies captured in war or members of their own society who were sacrificed for financial or other reasons.[48] Defendants could use this fact to argue that any benefit received by them from the claimant was conferred under a valid contract, in which case the law of unjust enrichment would not intervene. Morally, it could also seem wrong that some of those who would benefit from the restitution may have already benefited from the inherited wealth, power and status acquired by their ancestors as a result of the part they played in selling slaves to the West. The second potential difficulty is that some African states may be wary of making claims against the UK government for fear of jeopardising future aid and development donations.

Is the enrichment unjust?

The next consideration is whether or not any enrichment which the defendant is found to have received is unjust. The mere fact that the defendant was enriched at the claimant's expense, although by no means easy to establish in these cases, does not by itself found liability to make restitution. The traditional English law approach to this question has been to consider whether one of a number of unjust factors can be proved to have been involved in the transfer of the benefit to the defendant, for example that the claimant transferred the benefit to the defendant by mistake.[49] The most obviously relevant unjust factor for the type of claim under consideration here would appear to be duress. In order to establish duress the claimant must show that the defendant has made illegitimate threats to the claimant or applied actual pressure and that this, at least in part, caused the claimant to transfer the benefit to the defendant.[50] Duress vitiates a claimant's intention to transfer a benefit to the defendant because the claimant cannot be said to have truly consented to the transfer.

It is clear from the historical evidence that extreme violence and threats were used to force people into slavery, so that they had no choice but to provide their labour for free and certainly did not intend to confer any such benefit on those who enslaved them. This factor may then be invoked in respect of claims against slave traders or owners. However, one problem with this part of the case may be that such violence and threats would not be deemed *illegitimate* under the English law then in force. However, Lord Anthony Gifford argues forcefully that this is not the same as saying that slavery was not a crime under international law (Gifford 2007: 247). Effectively what is required here is for the claimant to show that the threats or pressure were illegal. Prior to the Acts of 1807 and 1833 it is therefore likely that the threats and violence employed to subjugate the slaves would have been deemed perfectly legal. As previously observed it may be that specific incidences of illegal slave trading post-1807 or ownership after the end of the transitional provisions in 1838 may be identified and a claim of duress here may then be successful. However, such claims are unlikely to result in mass restitution. The bulk of any restitution that the claimants will wish to seek is likely to relate to fact situations that arose prior to abolition.

A further problem in any case brought on behalf of living descendants of slaves alleging that the defendant had been enriched at their expense would be that the duress was not applied to them directly. Could it really be argued that the defendants have been enriched at the expense of the claimants as a result of the duress applied to third parties (by fourth parties?) The duress factor is also unlikely to be relevant to claims against the indirectly enriched, such as merchants, insurers or banks.

An argument could alternatively be made that the relevant unjust factor here is ignorance. This has not yet been judicially accepted but is supported by some academics (Burrows 2002: 182). The essence of this factor is that a benefit has been received by the defendant from the claimant in circumstances in which the claimant is ignorant of such receipt.[51] One could argue the case that a benefit in the form of wealth that should have been inherited by the claimants as descendants of slaves was transferred to the defendants without the knowledge of the claimants. This is however a highly theoretical argument, particularly as the unjust factor itself is not formally recognised in law.

Defences

The principal defence to a claim of unjust enrichment is change of position, which was recognised as forming part of English law in *Lipkin Gorman v Karpnale*.[52] The essence of this defence is that the defendant is no longer enriched and because he has changed his position in good faith on receipt of the enrichment it would be inequitable to require him to make restitution.[53] This begs the question of whether such a defence would ever be open to a defendant where the relevant unjust factor was duress. In *Lipkin Gorman* Lord Goff said that 'it is commonly accepted that the defence should not be open to a wrongdoer'.[54] This all-encompassing bar seems questionable in light of the fact that in cases of restitution for wrongdoing (see below) the defendant may have committed a strict liability tort such as conversion. In such situations it is arguable that the defendant should be able to avail himself of the defence as he is not morally blameworthy, although technically at fault in law. It would still be necessary for the defendant to show that he had acted in good faith in changing his position. The fact that he was unjustly enriched at the claimant's expense as a result of strict liability wrongdoing should not prevent him from establishing this.

Another question resulting from Lord Goff's statement is whether he was referring to wrongdoers in the sense of only those defendants who are defending a claim of restitution for wrongdoing. Alternatively, would proof of certain unjust factors, that may connote an element of fault on the part of the defendant, preclude a defendant from relying on the defence against an unjust enrichment claim? In the recent first instance decision of *FII Group Litigation v HMRC*[55] Henderson J appears to have assumed that the latter was intended, when he held that the government could rely on change of position as against a claim of mistake, but not in relation to a claim based on the alternative unjust factor of *ultra vires* tax demand, because proof of the latter led to the conclusion that the government was a wrongdoer in respect of that part of the claim.[56] It seems unlikely that a defendant who obtained an enrichment through duress could ever rely on the defence of change of position as he would inevitably be on notice that the enrichment had been received in circumstances of injustice and was not therefore his to retain. He could not therefore change his position in good faith. In terms of any proprietary claim that might be possible although unlikely, the defence of bona fide purchase for value without notice rather than change of position may be employed to defeat the claim.[57]

Restitution for wrongs – tort

The usual remedy when a claimant successfully proves a claim in tort is, of course, compensatory damages, which focus on the loss suffered by the claimant. However, in a limited number of cases, the claimant has been able to obtain damages assessed by reference to the gain that the defendant has made as a result of committing the tort. These cases have tended to be in relation to torts which interfere with the claimant's property rights, such as trespass to land or goods or conversion. For example, in *Chesworth v Farrar*[58] the claimant's landlord had wrongfully converted his property by selling it and the claimant was able to recover the sale proceeds without any need to prove the value of the property lost. One of the interesting aspects of the US Litigation was that the claimants included a claim in conversion. Prior to abolition, slaves had the legal status of chattels,[59] so presumably if one man had taken another's slaves without permission and set them to work on his own land he could have been sued by the original slave owner for damages in conversion. The conversion claim in the US Litigation rested on the premise that the slaves owned property in themselves which was unlawfully interfered with. This seems an ingenious argument but there is a certain incongruity to it when the moral principle behind seeking redress is that it is wrong to treat human beings as chattels. In any case, it is unlikely that any such argument would be successful in the English courts. Either something is property and can be converted, in which case it has no right of standing in the courts, or he is a person in whom there are no rights of property.

Rather, the category of torts which seem most obviously relevant to this type of case is trespass to the person. Claimants could seek to argue that the assault, battery and false imprisonment perpetrated against slaves resulted in the defendants being enriched. This would be a novel cause of action in a claim for restitution, as these torts are not ones which have resulted in a restitutionary award thus far. Again the principal problem with such causes of action would be that the physical contact in question, or threat of the same, was not unlawful at that time. Similarly, slave traders and owners were acting lawfully under the English law of the day in restricting the slaves' freedom of movement.

Any tort that has been committed was done so historically by the ancestor(s) who made their wealth from slavery. Tort liability does survive death in respect of any tortfeasor who dies after 25 July 1934[60] so that the estate may be sued through the deceased's personal representatives. However in view of the time-frame for the abolition of slavery under English law, it is unlikely that many people who were sufficiently directly involved in slavery to be considered a potential tortfeasor will have died so late as this. The rules on post mortem tort liability prior to 1934 were much stricter and more complicated. The deceased's estate could be sued only in respect of a tort that he had committed within the six months prior to his death, in relation to the plaintiff's property and provided the proceedings were commenced within six months of the personal representative being formally appointed.[61]

In terms of the relevant period of limitation for a tort claim, it was recently held by the House of Lords in *A v Iorworth Hoare*[62] that the applicable time limit for claims arising from intentional assaults is three years, subject to extension at the court's discretion.[63] The court has in the words of Coulson J 'a wide and unfettered discretion' to extend the prescribed limitation period.[64] Once again it appears that, although one might have assumed that the rules on limitation of actions would have proved the most difficult hurdle for the claimants to jump, they do at least have a possibility to argue in court that their claims are not time barred. Unfortunately, the other difficulties referred to above mean that even if a tortfeasor's estate could be identified at this stage, which is unlikely as it would ordinarily have been subsumed into various inheritors' estates over the years, it would not be possible to sue that estate under the rules in place at the time of death.

Conclusion

One might have expected that the expiration of the limitation period would be the most significant problem resulting from the passage of time since the events which would form the basis of a claim of restitution for historic slavery. However, it appears that the claimants may have at least an arguable case on this issue. More significant problems arise in trying to manipulate the apparent harm caused to slave descendants as a general class and the disparity of wealth between Black and White people in the West (which may have resulted at least in part from the existence of the transatlantic slave trade) into very precise legal concepts such as unjust enrichment and various torts. The American political scientist Jennifer Hochschild observed that *'using the court system to debate a deeply political and moral issue distorts the case for reparations by framing it in "legalese . . ."'* (Torpey 2006: 131).

A claim for restitution in respect of slavery is likely to be unsuccessful in the English courts. However, the possibility of making a claim could be explored as a means of applying pressure on private entities and government to negotiate a settlement in respect of reparations and to make apologies. At the recent conference Dinah Shelton observed the wider role that litigation can play in galvanising support behind a particular cause (Dodge and Sommerville 2009: 7). Although the UK government, in response to questions about reparations, makes the point that it gives large amounts of overseas development aid to Africa, it appears that for some survivors and heirs money alone is not enough. What is often sought is a recognition of the harm done and an acceptance of responsibility. For this reason money that is given specifically as reparations may be more welcome to its recipients, seeming to be more like an entitlement to seek to make amends for the damage done to them, their ancestors, their country and less like charity.

Considering the largely successful outcomes achieved on behalf of Holocaust survivors and the families of victims following the instigation of litigation in the USA, one might conclude that considerable pressure can be brought to bear by issuing court proceedings even when these look likely to be beset by problems. However, one of the lead counsel for the claimants in the Swiss banks litigation, Burt Neuborne, disputed the view that the settlements obtained were a triumph for the American legal system, commenting that *'The truth is that, with the important exception of Judge Korman and his colleagues . . . the Holocaust settlements were attained despite American judges, not because of them'* (Neuborne 2006: 74). It must also be borne in mind how much damage an adverse judicial consideration of a claim may do to ancillary negotiations. During negotiations for the German Foundation settlement, two adverse court decisions were rendered which, whilst they were subsequently subject to widespread criticism, were estimated by Burt Neuborne to have cost the claimants $5–10 million in the eventual settlement figure (Neuborne 2006: 76). The obvious point must also be made that, whilst the post-Holocaust claims were in respect of historic events, they were from a much more recent past than any transatlantic slavery claims would be.

The claim of unjust enrichment is, in theory, one which should be available to victims of slavery. The problems which arise in pursuing these particular claims are due to the historical nature of said claims. Unfortunately slavery is not only a thing of the past. The myriad difficulties encountered in pursuing claims for restitution in respect of historic slavery should not prevent the present-day victims of slavery from pursuing such claims if they can be emancipated. However, it is unlikely that many such claims would arise in the English jurisdiction and it may also be that jurisdictions in which slavery is prevalent do not have similar rules on restitution.

Notes

1　*Re African-American Slave Descendants Litigation* 375 F. Supp. 2d 721 (United States District Court, ND Illinois, Eastern Division, Norgle J).
2　Such as conversion, replevin, intentional and negligent infliction of emotional distress.
3　This was followed by a meeting of an expert group on slavery in The Gambia in 2008.
4　General Assembly Resolutions 61/19, 62/122 and 63/5.
5　One of the lead counsel in the litigation against the Swiss banks, Melvyn Weiss, recounts some of the criticism encountered from a minority of survivors and heirs who saw 'economic compensation as unseemly and morally denigrating' (Weiss 2006: 109).
6　This was also a problem during the Swiss banks litigation settlement as many bank records had been destroyed.
7　Even the current financial and economic crisis, although a worldwide problem, is likely to disproportionately affect African-Americans due to the high proportion who have sub-prime mortgages. Mike Calhoon of the Center for Responsible Lending, after stating that close to 50 per cent of African-American family mortgages are sub-prime, estimated that between one fifth and one third of African-Americans will lose their homes in the current crisis. He described this as 'the largest loss of African-American wealth ever seen'.
8　It was declared by General Sherman at the end of the Civil War that each freed slave should be given 40 acres of land from property confiscated from defeated Confederate landowners, but this decision was soon revoked by President Andrew Johnson in the interests of promoting reconciliation between the victorious Northern states and defeated Southern ones.
9　Effectively the same text had been published as an article the previous year in an online magazine 'Salon.com' (30th May 2000), but had received relatively little attention (Horowitz 2000).
10　The Swiss bank litigation was preceded by Senate Banking Committee hearings on the subject of dormant accounts held by Swiss banks.
11　29th July 2008 in a bill proposed by Democrat Congressman Steve Cohen.

12 *Lipkin Gorman v Karpnale* [1991] 2 AC 548 (HL). The recognition of unjust
   enrichment as the basis for claims in restitution came relatively late in English
   law, it having previously been stated to be implied contract, see e.g. *Sinclair v
   Brougham* [1914] AC 398. The unjust enrichment theory is not without its
   deniers e.g. (Hedley 2001).
13 *Banque Financière de la Cité v Parc (Battersea) Ltd* [1998] 2 WLR 475.
14 *CTN Cash and Carry Ltd v Gallagher* [1994] 4 All ER 714.
15 Principally in cases of what might be described as proprietary torts e.g. trespass
   (*Penarth Dock Engineering Co Ltd v Pounds* [1963] 1 Lloyd's Rep 359) and
   breaches of intellectual property rights.
16 *A-G v Blake* [2001] 1 AC 268.
17 E.g. breach of fiduciary duty, *A-G for Hong Kong v Reid* [1994] 1 AC 324.
18 However, the US Supreme Court held in 2003 in the case of *American Insurance
   Association v Garamendi* 123 S. Ct 2374 that California's *Holocaust Victim
   Insurance Relief Act* passed in 1999 to require the disclosure of all Holocaust-
   era policies by any insurer doing business in the state was unconstitutional
   (Ratner and Becker 2006: 347).
19 471 F 3d 754, United States Court of Appeals, Seventh Circuit.
20 *Lipkin Gorman v Karpnale* [1991] 2 AC 548.
21 [1996] 1 WLR 1378.
22 At p. 1390.
23 [1994] 4 All ER 890.
24 At p. 943.
25 Limitation Act 1980, s. 5.
26 [1993] 1 All ER 42.
27 [1948] Ch 465.
28 At p. 514.
29 Professor Catherine Hall of University College London is currently being funded
   to work on tracing assets in this regard.
30 Although a chartered company, the Royal African Company, was established in
   1672 to carry on the trade, it was not very successful and generally independent
   traders proliferated (Anstey 1975: 4).
31 Such was the case when in the United States in 2005 JP Morgan Chase, as it
   then was, confirmed that a bank it had purchased the previous year had been
   formed on the basis of assets of two failed banks which had previously accepted
   slaves as security for loans. These banks had ended up as slave owners when
   debtors defaulted. JP Morgan Chase at the same time announced its establishment of a $5million university scholarship scheme for African-American
   students in Louisiana where the two banks had been based (BBC 2005).
   Interestingly, the webpage outlining the scholarship scheme does not make any
   reference to the historical links to slavery: <http://www.jpmorgan.com/pages/
   smartstart/louisiana> (accessed 22 October 2008).
32 Covering 'deceptive trade practices' and 'consumer fraud' for example.
33 Kenneth Morgan gives some examples of individual wealth generated (Morgan
   2000: 37). The website of the International Slavery Museum in Liverpool also
   lists some of the prominent local individuals, families and organisations who
   profited from slavery: <www.liverpoolmuseums.org.uk/ism>, and an article by
   Judy Vickers highlights some of those in Glasgow and Edinburgh who also
   benefited financially from slavery (Vickers 2006).
34 But also including many others which were not ports and so may have profited
   more indirectly, for example Manchester. Anstey doubts that profits from the
   slave trade contributed quite as significantly to the financing of the Industrial

Revolution as some have claimed, but acknowledges the likelihood of 'some meaningful contribution to capital development in the Liverpool hinterland, where, of course, the rapid expansion of the cotton industry was concentrated' (Anstey 1975: 403).

35 There is considerable disagreement over the levels of profits generated. Morgan estimates that normal profit rates were 5–10 per cent in the later years of the trade (Morgan 2000: 44), whereas Anstey notes a Liverpool observer quoted in *Liverpool and Slavery* (1884) as writing in 1797 that in the previous decade profits were running at a rate of 30 per cent (Anstey 1975: 40).

36 There is some debate as to the extent to which this is true. Morgan (2000: 38) quotes leading Caribbean scholar Eric Williams as stating that profits from the slave trade 'provided one of the main streams of accumulation of capital in England which financed the Industrial Revolution' (Williams 1944: 52). However, Anstey concludes that to have made a significant contribution to the supply of capital for the Industrial Revolution the slave trade would have needed to generate profits at a far higher rate (Anstey 1975: 403).

37 Again there is debate as to the extent of the harm caused and there are difficulties in finding sufficient evidence to assess it, particularly as regards the population of West Africa at the time. Anstey concludes that the slave trade was probably an important cause of population decline in Congo and Angola, but not the Bight of Biafra (Anstey 1975: 82). Van Dantzig observed that the rise in demand for slaves from 1700 must have led to considerable changes in economic, political and social structures as there was not a 'service class' of people just waiting to be transported to the Americas (Van Dantzig 1982: 190). He further describes the effects of repeated slave raids, eventually leading to a depopulation of targeted areas and a subsequent over-population of those areas to which victims fled (Van Dantzig 1982: 199).

38 Crown Proceedings Act 1947.

39 Notably Liverpool in 1999, and Bristol and London in 2006–7.

40 Morgan summarises this debate in his Chapter 3 and concludes that most of the higher calculations are now accepted as wrong and that normal profits in the later years of the trade were 5–10 per cent (Morgan 2000: 44).

41 These issues and others relating to the effect of slavery on retarding the economic development of Southern American states are discussed in Woodman (1971: 3–25).

42 And beyond in some colonies, such as India, which were excluded from the Act.

43 In view of the date of the proceedings, other claimants who claimed to have been enslaved themselves must similarly have been claiming in respect of post-abolition slavery.

44 About half of all slaves shipped from Africa to America were taken by British ships (Morgan 1975: 36).

45 It has been estimated that between 8–10 million slaves were imported into the Americas, although some estimates have been considerably higher. Due to the high mortality rate on slave ships, a significantly higher number would have been exported (Anstey 1975: 38–9).

46 *Re African-American Slave Descendants Litigation* 375 F. Supp. 2d 721 per Norgle J, at p. 737 quoting from the Second Consolidated and Amended Complaint.

47 Rule 23, Federal Rules of Civil Procedure.

48 Van Dantzig above, n 48 observes that in Whydah, many misdemeanours, including adultery, were punishable by sale into slavery (Van Dantzig 1982: 193) although 'chattel slavery' as practised by the British took the inhumanity of the slave trade to a new level (Sherwood 2007).

49 *Kelly v Solari* (1841) 9 M & W 54.

50 *Barton v Armstrong* [1976] AC 104.
51 E.g. where it has been stolen.
52 [1991] 2 AC 548.
53 Ibid at p. 580.
54 Ibid.
55 [2008] EWHC 2893.
56 Ibid at paragraph 339.
57 *Foskett v McKeown* [2001] 1 AC 102.
58 [1967] 1 QB 407.
59 During the hearing of an insurance law case relating to an infamous incident on the slave ship *The Zong*, Lord Mansfield likened the throwing overboard of 130 slaves on the orders of the ship's captain to the loss of horses by the same means, *Gregson v Gilbert* (1783) 99 ER 629, Krikler (2007: 29).
60 s. 1(1) Law Reform (Miscellaneous Provisions) Act 1934.
61 Administration of Estates Act 1925, s 26(5) and prior to that Civil Procedure Act 1833, s 2.
62 [2008] UKHL 6.
63 Limitation Act 1980, ss 11 and 33.
64 *A v Iorworth Hoare* [2008] EWHC 1573, at paragraph 20. Having decided the point of law, the House of Lords remitted the case to the High Court to decide whether the discretion should be exercised.

Bibliography

Anstey, R. (1975) *The Atlantic Slave Trade and British Abolition 1760–1810*. London: Macmillan

Bazyler, M. and Alford, R.P. (eds) (2006) *Holocaust Restitution – Perspectives on the Litigation and Its Legacy*. New York: New York University Press.

BBC (2005) 'JP Morgan admits US slavery links' Online. Available HTTP: <http://news.bbc.co.uk/1/hi/business/4193797.stm> (accessed 22 October 2008).

BBC (2006) 'Blair 'sorrow' over slave trade' Online. Available HTTP: <http://news.bbc.co.uk/1/hi/uk_politics/6185176.stm> (accessed 18 June 2008).

BBC (2007) 'British minister's slavery apology' Online. Available HTTP: <http://www.bbc.co.uk/caribbean/news/story/2007/02/070215_hainslaveryapology.shtml> (accessed 18 June 2008).

Birks, P.B.H. (1985) *An Introduction to the Law of Restitution*. Oxford: Clarendon.

Burrows, A. (2002) *The Law of Restitution*. London: Butterworths.

Church of England (2006) Online. Available HTTP: <http://www.cofe.anglican.org/news/gspm0802.html> (accessed 22 October 2008).

Conley, D. (1999) 'Wealth Matters'. *Being Black, Living in the Red*. Berkeley: University of California Press (cited in Salzberger and Turck (eds) (2004) *Reparations for Slavery*. Lanham, MD: Rowman & Littlefield).

Dodge, B. and Sommervile, J. (2009) 'Conference Report: Colonialism, Slavery, Reparations and Trade: Remedying the Past?'

Gifford, A. (2007) *The Passionate Advocate*. London: Wildy, Simmonds & Hill.

Hedley, S. (2001) *A Critical Introduction to the Law of Restitution*. London: Butterworths.

Horowitz, D. (2000) *Ten Reasons Why Reparations for Slavery Is a Bad Idea – and Racist Too*. Online. Available HTTP: <http://archive.salon.com/news/col/horo/2000/05/30/repar ations/index.html> (accessed 22 October 2008).

Krikler, J. (2007) 'The Zong and the Lord Chief Justice'. *History Journal Workshop*, 64(1): 29.

Li, Y., Devine, F. and Heath, A. (2008) 'Equality group inequalities in education, employment and earnings: A research review and analysis of trends over time,' Equality and Human Rights Commission Research Report No 10.

Loury, G. C. (2002) 'The Anatomy of Racial Inequality'. Cambridge, MA: Harvard University Press (cited in Salzberger and Turck (eds) (2004) *Reparations for Slavery*. Lanham, MD: Rowman & Littlefield).

McLean, H.M. (1989) 'Limitation of Actions in Restitution', *Cambridge Law Journal*, 48: 472.

Morgan, K. (2000) *Slavery, Atlantic Trade and the British Economy, 1660–1800*. Cambridge: Cambridge University Press.

N'COBRA (n.d.) *What is N'COBRA?* Online. Available HTTP: <http://www.ncobra.org/aboutus/index.html> (accessed 1 December 2010).

Neuborne, B. (2006) 'A Tale of Two Cities', in M. Bazyler and R.P. Alford (eds), *Holocaust Restitution – Perspectives on the Litigation and Its Legacy*. New York: New York University Press.

Office for National Statistics (2008) News Release 'Large differences in infant mortality by ethnic group'.

Oliver, M. (2007) 'Archbishop urges church to consider slavery reparations'. *Guardian Online*. Available HTTP: <http://www.guardian.co.uk/world/2007/mar/26/religion.race> (accessed 22 October 2008).

Ratner, M. and Becker, C. (2006) 'The Legacy of Holocaust Class Action', in M. Bazyler and R.P. Alford (eds), *Holocaust Restitution – Perspectives on the Litigation and Its Legacy*. New York: New York University Press.

Robinson, R. (2001) *The Debt*. New York: Plume.

Salzberger, R.P. and Turck, M.C. (eds) (2004) *Reparations for Slavery*. Lanham, MD: Rowman & Littlefield.

Sherwood, M. (2007) *Britain, Slavery and the Trade in Enslaved Africans*. Online. Available HTTP: <http://www.history.ac.uk/ihr/Focus/Slavery/articles/sherwood.html> (accessed 10 November 2010).

Torpey, J. (2006) *Making Whole What Has Been Smashed: On Reparations Politics*. Cambridge, MA: Harvard University Press.

Van Dantzig, A. (1982) Chapter 7 in J.E. Inikori (ed.), *Forced Migration*. London: Hutchinson University Library.

Vickers, J. (2006) 'Shame of city's slavery profits' Online. Available HTTP: <http://news.scotsman.com/abolitionofslavery/Shame-of-citys-slavery-profits.2831715.jp> (accessed 22 October 2008).

Webb, J. (2007) 'Sub-Prime Crisis Sours US Dream' Online. Available HTTP: <http://news.bbc.co.uk/1/hi/business/6528387.stm> (accessed 1 October 2008)

Weiss, M. (2006) 'A Litigator's Postscript to the Swiss Banks and Holocaust Litigation Settlements', in M. Bazyler and R.P. Alford (eds), *Holocaust Restitution – Perspectives on the Litigation and Its Legacy*. New York: New York University Press.

Williams, E. (1944) *Capitalism and Slavery*. Chapel Hill: University of North Carolina Press.

Woodman, H.D. (1971) 'The Profitability of Slavery: A Historical Perenial', in H. Aitken (ed.), *Did Slavery Pay?* Boston, MA: Houghton Mifflin.

Chapter 9

Judge, jurisprudence and slavery in England 1729–1807

Sheila Dziobon

It is now over two hundred years since the passing of the 1807 Act for the Abolition of the Slave Trade in England. Today we are familiar with the judicial protection of human rights in our courts, but, as will be discussed in this chapter, such considerations were unusual in the eighteenth century. During that time the judiciary witnessed the enormous growth in commerce that was associated with the use of slaves and the slave trade in England and heard cases involving contracts for the purchase of slaves, bequests including slaves, estate sales including slaves, insurance claims for the loss of slaves at sea, and acts of trespass upon slaves. Throughout all of this, according to the case reports and other bibliographical and historical sources, there would appear to have been no judge who spoke out freely to protect the slave as a human being with inalienable rights. Where slaves and slavery formed the foreground, or background, of the legal action the judges applied legal precedent and principles (then in their developmental infancy), statutory interpretation, the legal scope of the case, and other legal tools to directly or indirectly condone and support the institution of slavery. This chapter reviews some of those cases in an attempt to understand why the eighteenth-century judiciary did not appear to treat slaves as human beings to whom were attached what we would recognise today as legally enforceable human rights.

The first part of the chapter presents a brief historic background to the condition of slavery from an English perspective. Following this I present a chronological account of the significant legal events, detailing cases and other matters which brought their influence to bear on the outcomes and consequences. It is hoped that the structure of the chapter will demonstrate the overwhelming impact of two powerful men and the awakening of a greater respect for slaves as human beings.

Background

The seizure of slaves, as opposed to their purchase, was a usual practice as long ago as the Middle Ages in both Europe and Africa. Thomas recounts the landing on 8 August 1444 of 235 African slaves in the Algarve, Portugal, and notes that the capture and enslavement of people saw a shift away from the belief that they were a reward for victory towards their being a valuable commercial commodity during the sixteenth and, more dramatically in England, during the eighteenth century (Thomas 1997: 20–23).

This commercialisation was exacerbated by the discovery of gold and other precious metals in the New World which required strong, dispensable, labour in order to be mined. In addition the fashionable taste in Britain and other European countries for tobacco, sugar, tea, bananas, coffee, and other 'exotic' products expanded with the growth of plantations and settlements in the colonies. The motivation here was the exploitation of natural resources and the cultivation of crops to meet a new and rapidly expanding market elsewhere – and, of course, the entrepreneurial opportunity of greater wealth through trade and commerce.

This increasingly lucrative trade experienced an upturn for the British after the Treaty of Utrecht in 1715 (which followed the British defeat of the Spanish) when they were granted the 'contract', or 'Asiento' by the Spanish crown to trade slaves into all Spanish-controlled islands and the Spanish territories of mainland South America. This 'contract' was sold almost immediately by the British Crown to the recently formed South Sea Company for a staggering £7,500,000 – a good indication of the future profit expected from the trade. It is estimated that between 1715 and 1731 the South Sea Company alone traded approximately 64,000 slaves (Thomas 1997: 23).

In 1720 nearly 150 ships were engaged in the transatlantic slave trade, mostly from Bristol and London, but also from Liverpool, Whitehaven and lesser ports such as Lancaster, Chester, and Glasgow (Thomas 1997: 243). This total continued to rise and in the 1730s a total of 170,000 slaves were transported. By 1740 the city of Liverpool alone had sent 33 ships that year to Africa. Between 1761 and 1770 the British carried approximately 250,000 slaves across the Atlantic and in the 1780s, when public opinion was galvanising itself against the inhumanity of the slave trade, this volume reached its peak. It is estimated that one slave ship left England every day during this decade. The toll on human life was considerable and the Privy Council (during later discussions prior to abolition) estimated that half of the slaves transported across the Atlantic died in transit or in the initial period after their arrival (called 'the seasoning'). Set against this human misery there is no doubt that the impact on the social landscape of England, and especially the ports of Liverpool and Bristol, was huge, generating employment and consequent economic benefits (Davis 1999: 343).[1]

There was, however, increasing public disquiet about the slave trade in Britain during the late eighteenth century and in 1787 Granville Sharp and Thomas Clarkson founded the Society for the Abolition of the Slave Trade. After considerable lobbying, 519 petitions were presented to Parliament in

1789 seeking its abolition.[2] The engagement of parliamentarians, campaigners and a ground swell in public opinion against the trade led to the passing of the Abolition of the Slave Trade Act in 1807. This Act prevented British traders from removing Africans from the west coast and selling them into slavery in the New World. It would be naïve to believe that the Act did, in fact, have that effect and indeed many slavers continued to trade under the flags of other nations or as pirates, but it was still a hugely important legislative step (Thomas 1997: 570–1).[3] The 1807 Act did not free all slaves under British rule as this was not felt at the time to be politically expedient. That legislation had to wait a further twenty-six years to enter the statute book.

The Abolition of Slavery Act was passed in Great Britain in 1833. This was to take a gradual effect in all British colonies and slave owners (not the slaves) received £20 million in compensation.[4] The emancipation of the slaves in the British colonies was finally achieved in 1834.

Against this background this chapter looks at some of the judicial decisions and the developing jurisprudence concerning slaves and the slave trade. Two significant events – the Yorke/Talbot Opinion 1729 and the passing of the 1807 Act – provide the framework for this discussion.

The Yorke/Talbot Opinion 1729

One of the earliest and most influential statements on the status of slaves in England, and the legal relationship between master and slave, was the Yorke/Talbot Opinion of 1729. The English courts had delivered several decisions concerning property rights in slaves and the master/slave relationship, but at this time there was no clear legal precedent (Wiecek 1974: 88–93). Disputes revolved around the question of ownership, with the slave as the subject matter of the dispute in much the same way as any other chattel. The earliest cases were common law actions in trover. Trover (from the French for 'to find') was an action by the plaintiff to recover a chattel and any loss in value of that chattel because of use by the defendant. In *Butts v Penny* (1677) 2 Levinz 201; 83 E.R. 518, the Court of King's Bench decided that '[T]here being evidence that the blacks were infidels, and usually bought and sold as merchandise, there might be property in a black sufficient to maintain the action'. In *Gelly v Cleve* (1694) 1 L. Raym.147,[5] the Court of Common Pleas decided 'that trover would lie for a black boy because he was a heathen'. In *Chamberlain v Harvey* (1679) 5 Mod.182 K.B., counsel for the plaintiff argued before Chief Justice Sir John Holt, that 'though the word "slave" has but a very harsh sound in a free and Christian country', it could nonetheless exist there, legitimated by a quasi-contract under which the master derived power over the slave in return for providing him with food and clothing (Wiecek 1974: 91).

However, Holt C J, before a jury, decided that '[T]respass will not lie for "taking and carrying away one *negro slave* . . . for by the laws of England one man cannot have an *absolute property* in *the person* of another man; but, as under certain circumstances a man may have a *qualified property* in another, in the character of *servant* . . .'. *Chamberlain v Harvey* (on the facts) also raised the possibility that a Christian baptism could lead to freedom for a slave. Subsequently, in *Smith v Gould* (1706) 2 Salk.666, Holt is recorded as saying that Blacks are no different from other men and that an action for trover could not lie, and later, in *Smith v Brown & Cooper*, he is reported to have said: '[A]s soon as a negro comes into England, he becomes free; one may be a villein in England, but not a slave.' Holt's opinion was supported by his colleague, Justice Powell, who said 'the law took no notice of a negro' (Shyllon 1974: 25). As shown these cases were inconclusive and this made slave owners feel insecure, even though none of the decisions had extended the jurisdiction of the English court to the islands of the West Indies. The court would uphold a contract for the sale and purchase of a slave (an action between buyer and seller), but remained uncertain as to the extent of the legal rights that the purchaser had over the purchased, being of the opinion that the sale could not deny completely all the rights attached to the status of being human.

This idea – that conversion to Christianity was a passport to freedom for a slave once in Britain – spread by word of mouth during the first half of the eighteenth century and slaves attempted to take advantage of this opportunity. The inequality in the power and knowledge of slave and master was such, however, that this opportunity for freedom was not effective in practice and was obstructed, perhaps predictably, by the slave owners (Shyllon 1974: 10–11).

The English judiciary in the early eighteenth century were therefore challenged by this difficult question of slavery and the ownership of humans. As Oldham comments about Lord Mansfield, '[H]e accepted and endorsed the widely assumed mercantile importance of the slave trade, yet he doubted the validity of the theoretical justification of slavery' (Oldham 1992: 1221). Judges were unhappy with the idea of (total) ownership of another human being, but thought that some kind of property rights could exist over a person, even if these rights did not confer an unqualified or absolute property right to the master (Weicek 1974: 93: Oldham 1992: 1224). '[F]or this being a property *ex instituto* only, the owner has only a power according to the instituted right' (*Smith v Gould* at 667).

If an ownership right – limited in some yet undefined legal sense – did exist, it may have been that further cases which might have come before the courts in the early eighteenth century could have clarified the extent of this legal right and the common law would have developed differently. However, the enormous potential from trade and development in the New World, which would follow the mercantile investment to promote this trade, took priority and pushed interested parties to ask for a clarification of the legal status of slaves in England. In order for such clarification prominent plantation owners approached two of the leading lawyers of the day at Lincoln's Inn one evening after dinner.

In January 1729, amidst fears of the likely detriment to commercial interests (national as well as personal) in the West Indies, powerful and wealthy landowners and slave traders approached the Attorney-General, Philip Yorke, and the Solicitor-General, Charles Talbot, for clarification of the status of African slaves when they were brought to England. They also asked these two lawyers whether a conversion to Christianity released slaves from their bonds. This meeting took place at Lincoln's Inn, London, not within a judicial hearing. They made the following clear and unequivocal statement:

> We are of the Opinion, That a Slave by coming from the West-Indies to Great Britain, doth not become free, and that his Master's Property or Right in him is not thereby determined or varied: And that Baptism doth not bestow freedom on him, nor make any Alteration in his Temporal Condition in these kingdoms. We are also of the Opinion, that his Master may legally compel him to return again to the Plantations.
>
> (14 January 1729)

Shyllon describes the Yorke and Talbot opinion as a 'slave-hunter's charter' (1974: 27). He recounts that the repercussions were swift and brutal. Judicial attempts at making incremental legal inroads into this difficult question, as alluded to above, were swept away for all practical purposes.[6]

In 1749, in the case of *Pearne v Lisle* (1749) Ambler 77, presented Yorke, now Lord Chancellor Hardwicke, to reaffirm this Opinion in the Court of Chancery. At the same time he reaffirmed also the earlier decision of *Butts v Penny* that trover was available for a plaintiff when the subject matter was a slave. Hardwicke made the following statement in *Pearne*: 'I have no doubt that trover will lie for a negro slave; it is as much property as any other thing.' Hardwicke continued by criticising Holt's earlier suggestion 'that the moment a slave sets foot in England he becomes free' which he (Hardwicke) said had 'no weight with it'. At this time he raised an issue which was to remain a concern for the English courts for some time: the application of English law in the colonies. He concluded that Holt's statement could have no weight because the slave would enjoy the same freedom wherever he or she travelled if this was the case, 'when they set foot in *Jamaica*, or any other *English* plantation'. He went on to state that a conversion to Christianity and baptism 'did not at all alter their state' (*Pearne* at 77). Hardwicke described clearly his attitude to the slave and slavery later on in the same case:

> The negroes cannot be delivered in the plight in which they were at the time of the demand, for they wear out with labour, as cattle or other things; nor could they be delivered on demand, for they are like stock on a farm, the occupier could not do without them, but would be obliged, in case of a sudden delivery to quit the plantation.

In 1762 Hardwicke's successor, Lord Chancellor Henley, expressed his disapproval of Hardwicke's language about the availability of trover in *Shanley v Harvey* (1762) 2 Eden 125 (Oldham 1992: 1224). Once more the legal uncertainties which had existed pre-1729 were raised.

One could say that the Yorke/Talbot opinion of 1729 had halted the potential evolvement of the common law on this issue for almost fifty years. However, legal certainty had created sufficient space for the enormous growth in the Atlantic slave trade and the increase in social and economic welfare of the towns and cities of England and (some of) their populations.

It is within this post-1762 environment that Lord Mansfield, now Lord Chief Justice, heard a series of slavery cases during a time of increasing public disquiet. Plantation owners looked to Mansfield for legal clarity. Of note here are the apparent differences in attitude by the judiciary to a man standing before him as an individual and a group of slaves suffering hardship as 'commercial cargo'. It is to the first series of cases that we now turn.

Lord Mansfield and cases relating to slaves and slavery

The briefest reading of the events leading up to the 1807 Act would highlight the importance of the anti-slavery campaigner Granville Sharp and his efforts to secure reform (Thomas 1997: 473). Initially, Sharp campaigned on behalf of the slave Jonathan Strong, ignoring the apparent barrier of the Yorke/Talbot opinion, and framing his arguments around the Habeas Corpus Act of 1679.[7]

Strong was a slave purchased in Barbados. He was brought to London by his master Lisle (Fisher 1943: 381). It is pointed out by Shyllon that Strong was subjected to 'brutal outrage' and 'thrown out as a worthless chattel' by Lisle. Sharp saw Strong awaiting medical treatment outside his brother's surgery in London in 1765. The doctor arranged for Strong to be admitted to hospital where he was treated for four months prior to discharge (Shyllon 1974: 17–23). Subsequently, he was found paid employment and continued to thrive until Lisle recognised him, followed him home, and 'seeing that his discarded property had regained its value, he sold Strong to a Jamaican planter, James Kerr' (Shyllon 1974: 20). A term of the sales contract was that the price (£30) would not be paid to

Lisle until Strong was on board ship and ready to sail to Jamaica. With this in mind, and knowing that Strong was not likely to go willingly, Lisle hired two slave-hunters to kidnap him. He was delivered to Lisle and put in the gaol, the Poultry Compter, for onward transportation on a West Indian ship. Strong managed to get word to Sharp of his imprisonment and imminent forced removal from England.

Sharp brought Strong's case before the law, declaring 'that a Jonathan Strong had been confined in prison without any warrant'. The action was heard at the Mansion House on 18 September 1767 and Strong was discharged. However, within days of this success Kerr served a copy of a writ on Sharp claiming £200 damages in a plea of trespass against him for depriving him of his property (Strong). Relying on the Yorke/Talbot opinion Sharp's attorney advised him that in law he had no defence and that he should settle on the best terms he could get (Heward 1979: 142). Sharp did not accept this advice. For two years he studied law, philosophy and religious texts searching for support for his arguments. He found this in the first edition of *Blackstone's Commentaries* which stated:

> And this spirit of liberty is so deeply implanted in our constitution, and rooted even in our very soil, that a slave or a negro, the moment he lands in England, falls under the protection of the laws, and with regard to all natural rights becomes *eo instante* a freeman.
>
> (Shyllon 1974: 59)[8]

Sharp distilled his research on the institution of slavery – which he considered immoral and illegal – into a long Memorandum which he sent to Blackstone (Sharp 1769). Blackstone replied that he 'had no objection to his findings but warned him that "it would be uphill work in the Court of the King's Bench"' (Shyllon 1974: 60).

> In the second edition of the *Commentaries*, published in 1766, and the third edition published in 1768, Blackstone's entry on slavery changed to include 'though the master's right to his service may probably continue'.
>
> (Shyllon 1974: 61)[9]

This qualification may have been influenced by Lord Mansfield (Oldham 1988: 1234) who was one of the editors of the *Commentaries* and, as Shyllon notes, 'the patron and mentor of Blackstone' (1974: 55). Oldham writes, however, that there is no firm evidence to support a claim that Lord Mansfield was in any way influential in the changes made by Blackstone to his first legal definition of slavery. However, Shyllon, in a scathing critique of an article by Fiddes (1934: 499) says that although there is 'no direct evidence . . . to prove that Blackstone added the qualifying phrase in order that it might conform to that "prejudice in the [Mansfield] Court of King's Bench"', he opines that correspondence and public debate 'furnishes us with a most cogent circumstantial evidence' (Shyllon 1974: 70–71). According to Oldham 'the action cannot bear the sinister interpretation given it by Shyllon' (Oldham 1988: 1234). There is no definite conclusion to be reached here.

It could be suggested that Blackstone's first edition definition does not carry the import that Sharp was looking for anyway, as the statement attributes to the slave in England the protection of the laws 'with regard to all natural rights' but it does not say that he is totally free and his liberty unfettered. In England at this time it was legal for a master to have rights in an apprentice, for example, but these rights were limited by law. So what were the natural rights in question?

At a meeting between Sharp, Blackstone and the Solicitor-General, Recorder of London, Sir James Eyre, Blackstone withdrew his earlier support of Sharp on the question of the total freedom of the slave in England and Eyre followed suit. There is no evidence to explain this apparent *volte face* but the success of these two men was linked to the patronage that was necessary at the time if one was to reach any high office. If Mansfield was prepared to read Blackstone's work it might be suggested that it was important to Blackstone to keep the peace, but it might equally be suggested that, at this time, there was no definitive legal answer to the question.

Sharp circulated his memorandum and the lawyers for Lisle and Kerr were sufficiently unsettled to withdraw their action against him. His memorandum was received favourably at the Inns of Court and his campaign was also generating interest amongst a wider public (Davis 1975: 343–385).[10]

One of the legal points that Sharp used as the core to his argument was that in English law the burden of proof, if an individual's freedom was at stake, lay with the person who claimed to restrict that freedom. He also raised a further persuasive point, later exploited by the abolitionists, that the plantation owners, by claiming complete rights over the slave, were claiming rights that were greater than those enjoyed by the Crown over its subjects. Sharp repeated the words of the judges of the late seventeenth and early eighteenth century – that natural rights existed in all human beings and even slavery could not remove a residual right to freedom. It was not sufficient for Smith to leave the limitations in natural freedom to chance though and adding to the master's legal burden he argued that proof of ownership, and its extent, must be in writing and obtained without any compulsion or illegal duress (Davis 1975: 375). These arguments that were based in law would have been attractive to Mansfield as they had as their foundation the long-standing principles of English common law and a respect for the authority of the Crown.

Sharp did not try to gain total emancipation for all slaves and in fact may not have supported such a stance, but he still framed his action narrowly so that established legal principles could be applied to the facts. To start from the position that an individual has his freedom in England unless it is proved that a contract exists limiting this freedom, or that he or she has been legally detained in prison, required the application of existing legal principles. These principles would need extension and development to embrace a total loss of individual freedom in England. Such a deviation from established legal principles would need to be argued and that argument would also need to persuade a court that theories of natural rights and freedoms should be limited in relation to certain individuals with the law developed to meet this new order. If the principles of the common law could not be developed to encompass the status of slave, it was suggested that the alternative would have to be legislation that would uphold the rights demanded by the masters.

Mansfield believed passionately that legal principles could be garnered to apply to new fact situations and judgments carried forward for a further application of 'the common law that works itself pure'. Heward states that 'Lord Mansfield's greatest contribution to the law of England was to establish principle as the mainspring of the common law and as a means of threading through the thickets of particularity' (1979: 170): '[B]ut the law does not consist in particular cases; but in general principles, which run through cases, and govern the decision of them.' So said Lord Mansfield in *Rust v Cooper*, 2 Cowp. 629, at 632 (a fraud case). Mansfield also believed in the principles of equity developed in the Court of Chancery and if he was not bound by a strict rule of law he exercised equitable principles to do justice (as he saw it) in an individual case. At this time there was a divided court system in England and Mansfield's use of equitable principles in his common law court was not approved of by many who considered the two systems separate. The statutory amalgamation of the courts of common law and equity did not happen until 1873.[11] The judge that Sharp and others were testing was a rationalist first and foremost who believed that if he searched hard enough and long enough the law would present a resolution to any case. If that resolution was considered harsh he might mitigate this outcome by applying equitable principles – but only if the common law was not clear. If there was applicable law it may be that Lord Mansfield would interpret it in line with equitable principles if he considered this necessary.

After his victory in supporting Strong, Sharp worked on behalf of the slave Thomas Lewis in *R v Stapylton* (Oldham 1988: 1242). Lewis was in danger of being shipped from England to Jamaica and (re-)sold as a slave against his will after a very colourful life, which saw visits to Santa Cruz, Havana, New York, Carolina, Jamaica and England with Stapleton and others. Lewis is reported in the judgment as stating in his evidence:

When I went to Waterside [there were] 3 men & a Waterman. [Two were] Defendants Moloney & Armstrong. 2 of them seized me directly. [There was] a struggle. They dragged me, put me in a boat, & [put] a cord round my leg. They put a stick cross [my mouth] to gag me. Defendant on the side [of the] shore cried, 'Gag him.' [I was] carried to Gravesend & put aboard the *Captain Seward*, a West Indiaman. The Captain said [he] had a Bill of Sale from Defendant Stapylton. Defendant Stapylton [was] blind and old.

A criminal action for battery and false imprisonment was brought against Stapylton and the case was heard before Mansfield in February 1771. The question of whether the master had established a claim to his property (Lewis) was put to the jury by Mansfield. Sidestepping the difficult issue of the legal scope of ownership of slaves in England, he said that if the jury found that Stapylton's proprietary interest in Lewis was established on the facts he would rule whether such property could exist in England and the extent of the property rights. He put the facts before the jury and in doing so placed considerable emphasis on Lewis's early voyage in Stapylton's ship when they were set upon by Spanish pirates and he was taken to and worked in Havana. With this emphasis he implied that these events, and the break in Stapylton's association with Lewis, were sufficient to deny him ownership of the slave. The jury found that the case was not made out, that Stapylton was not Lewis's owner, and, as a consequence, Mansfield never had to decide on the question of ownership rights. Stapylton was found guilty of assault and false imprisonment applying long-standing principles of English law. This was a victory for Lewis but did not present a legal analysis of the extent of the rights that a master held over his slave whilst in England. Lord Mansfield is quoted by Hoare in *Memoirs of Granville Sharp*, as saying after the discharge of Lewis:

> I hope it never will be finally discussed; for I would have all masters think them free, and all negroes think they were not, because then they would both behave better.
>
> (Hoare, 1820: 60–61)

His hopes were not realised when in the following year the case of *Somerset v. Stewart* came before him.

Somerset v. Stewart

In *Somerset v Stewart* 98 E.R. 499 (1772) Lofft 1, James Somerset was imprisoned on board a ship, the *Ann and Mary*, bound for Jamaica. It was stated in the legal papers that Somerset was a slave and the property of

Charles Stewart from Virginia (although subsequent investigation has shown that he was, in fact, from Boston, and Somerset had travelled with Stewart from Boston (Shyllon 1974: 79)). During his stay in London as Stewart's body-servant he ran away, was recovered, and then delivered on board the ship bound for Jamaica. He did not go voluntarily with his captives and had to be restrained. If Somerset was the property of Stewart (as, for example, a horse might belong to Stewart) the return and imprisonment would have been unquestioned. The case of James Somerset has been investigated thoroughly by many writers and debates still continue based on the validity of the several reports, commentaries and various other papers written about the case itself, as well as other related matters (Oldham 1988: 45–68).[12]

Generally, writers today would agree that Lord Mansfield did not free all slaves in Britain and her colonies in 1772 and it is impossible to argue that this was the practical consequence of the decision. The Atlantic slave trade and the trade from Britain to Africa and from the West Indies back to Britain continued to expand post-*Somerset*. The judgment, as we shall see, injected an element of uncertainty, but writers suggest that the plantation owners merely adjusted existing practices to meet the new legal landscape. If they were planning, for example, on bringing a slave to England they would require that slave to sign a document prior to leaving the West Indies stating that they would voluntarily return at the end of the trip. Whether this would meet with Sharp's evidential requirement that such a document was obtained voluntarily and without duress was not tested in a court (Oldham 1988: 1240).

Following the arguments, presented by Hargrave for Somerset, and by Dunning for Stewart, Lord Mansfield ordered the release of Somerset. The basis of Somerset's claim was against the captain of the ship *Ann and Mary* for false imprisonment and nothing more. There was no doubt that Stewart had purchased Somerset by lawful contract. The actual legal decision and the public perception of the decision were two separate but inseparable issues. How the decision was promulgated by abolitionists, and the effect of the decision on the growing abolitionist movement in England, is a complex question and beyond the scope of this chapter.

The *Somerset* case can be distinguished from *Staplyton* on the facts. There was no doubt about the master's right to the slave (under a contract formed in Jamaica) in *Somerset*. However, what was the legally enforceable extent of the master's rights in the slave, and did these rights exist in England? This was the very question which had been side-stepped by Lord Mansfield in *Staplyton*, and the question he had (apparently) hoped to avoid. Sharp pressed the case forward to the King's Bench. If he could obtain a judgment that a man could not be treated in the manner that Stewart was treating Somerset, and if an action lay against the ship's captain for false imprisonment, the implication would be that a slave was not a chattel and therefore not able to be owned and disposed of at the will of his master.

It is reported that Mansfield tried hard to avoid a trial, pressing for a settlement between the parties, and even suggested that Parliament might introduce a law to secure property rights in slaves, thus resolving the issue by legislation (Thomas 1997: 474, Shyllon 1974: 78–80).

The trial, which lasted for six months, is discussed in detail by Shyllon (and others) and although the delay in the case coming to trial might have been attributed to Mansfield's tactics it is stated by Shyllon, and confirmed by Oldham, that he was not responsible for the delays (Shyllon 1974: Ch. 7, Oldham 1988: 1229). Alternative means of bringing the dispute to a close failed and Stewart (supported by the powerful plantation owners) refused to release Somerset. Heward notes in his biography that Mansfield was keen to adopt the role of negotiator on many occasions and was well respected both legally and politically for this ability. He also notes that in this capacity Mansfield was 'always on the side of caution' (Heward 1979: 78). This cautionary approach and a desire to settle the matter out of court support his reluctance to decide the issue. Why would Mansfield hope for an out-of-court settlement?

In his (1974) book Shyllon offers four reasons for Mansfield's reluctance to give a judgment in the case: his personal weakness; the impact on the slave-owners in Britain; the 'fact' that Blacks were property; and the consequences of his professional standing if he were to reverse the Talbot/Yorke opinion (1974: 119–121).[13] Whilst harsh these reasons do appear to reflect the attitude towards the question of slavery and the slave trade that prevailed amongst the ruling classes in Britain at this time.

Hargrave, representing Somerset and the abolitionists, presented a robust case including a reference to *Cartwright's case*, 11 Eliz. Rushworth 2, 468.[14] According to Rushworth (Heward 1979: 143) it was held in this case, heard during the reign of Elizabeth I, 'that England was too pure an air for a slave to breathe in'. On cross-examination by Mansfield, Hargrave admitted that he could not support this statement with written evidence but it captured the public imagination. Dunning, on the other hand, who had represented Lewis in the earlier case against Stapylton, lacked Hargrave's conviction when acting for the slave owners and seems to have presented a weaker case for the defence. Prior to his judgment Mansfield again remarked that he had hoped that the case could have been 'accommodated by agreement between the parties'.[15]

Mansfield continued:

> Compassion will not, on the one hand, nor inconvenience on the other, be to decide; but the law; in which the difficulty will be principally from the inconvenience on both sides. Contract for sale of a slave is good here; the sale is a matter to which the law properly and

reasonably attaches, and will maintain the price according to the agreement. But here the person of the slave himself is immediately the subject of enquiry; which makes a very material difference. The now question is whether any dominion, authority, or coercion can be experienced in this country, on a slave according to the American laws? The difficulty of adopting the relation without adopting it in all its consequences, is indeed extreme; and yet many of these consequences are absolutely contrary to the municipal law of England. We have no authority to regulate the conditions in which the law will operate.[16]

Mansfield notes the passage of time since the Yorke/Talbot Opinion before considering the possible consequences of freeing Somerset whilst indicating how many slaves were living in England at that time:

The setting 14,000 or 15,000 men at once loose by a solemn opinion is very disagreeable in the effect it threatens.

He also notes the extent of the legal action and the possible economic consequences:

Mr Stewart advances no claim on contract; he rests his whole demand on a right to the negro as a slave, and mentions the purpose of detainure to be the sending of him over to be sold in Jamaica. If the parties will have judgment, fiat justitia, ruat coelum, let justice be done whatever be the consequence. 50l. a head may not be a high price; then a loss to the proprietors of 700,000l. sterling. How would the law stand with respect to their settlement; their wages? How many actions for any slight coercion by the master? We cannot in any of these points direct the law; the law must rule us ... An application to Parliament, if the merchants think the question of great commercial concern, is the best, and perhaps the only method of settling the point for the future.[17]

First and foremost Mansfield was a commercial lawyer and his concerns as expressed in these extracts underline the economic consequences of his judgment.

Bearing in mind the important consequences which flowed from the decision, Lord Mansfield's judgment is brief and lacking in legal references and specificity.[18] An extract is quoted from the judgment:

[T]he only question before us is, whether the cause on the return is sufficient? If it is, the negro must be remanded; if it is not, he must be discharged. Accordingly, the return states, that the slave departed and refused to serve; whereupon he was kept, to be sold abroad. So high an act of dominion must be recognised by the law of the country where it is used. The power of a master over his slave has been extremely different, in different countries. The state of slavery is of such a nature, that it is incapable of being introduced on any reasons, moral or political; but only by positive law, which preserves its force long after the reasons, occasion, and time itself from whence it was created, is erased from memory: it's so odious, that nothing can be suffered to support it, but positive law. Whatever inconveniences, therefore, may follow from a decision, I cannot say this case is allowed or approved by the law of England; and therefore the black must be discharged.[19]

Judgment was given on 22 June 1772. His review of the relevant law and the brevity of the judgment have been criticised subsequently. It is noted, for example, that he failed to refer to the earlier case of *Shanley v Harvey* when Lord Chancellor Northington decreed that 'As soon as a man sets foot on English ground he is free.'[20]

Perhaps Mansfield did not want to articulate the judgment broadly or perhaps he did not want to cite precedents which, as we have already discussed, were handed down at a time of some indecision. Mansfield did not make a general declaration of slave emancipation in England. He concluded only that whilst the master retained (undefined) property rights under the contract for purchase (which was recognised in England) that these rights did not extend to the 'high act of dominion' claimed by the master in this case. The offensive act was the violent detention of the slave and his forced removal from the country. It is difficult to appreciate the logic of this distinction, but perhaps Mansfield was hoping to leave the master/slave relationship unscathed except as to this particular circumstance (Oldham 1988: 1239–40). Lord Mansfield had the opportunity to reaffirm the narrow *ratio* of *Somerset* in 1779 in the following terms:

> There had been no determination that they were free, the judgment went no further than to determine the Master had no right to compel the slave to go into a foreign country.
>
> (Shyllon 1974: 164)[21]

However, the decision was interpreted liberally in published writings as well as in the press. One example is the poems by William Cowper and here the reference by Hargrave to the *Cartwright* case caught the public imagination:

> *Slaves cannot breathe in England; if their lungs*
> *Receive our air, that moment they are free:*
> *They touch our country, and their shackles fall.*
> (*The Task*, Book 11, 1784)

In 1785, in *The King v The Inhabitants of Thames Ditton* 4 Dougl. 299, at 30, Mansfield considered again the position of an impoverished slave. Charlotte Howe was a slave who had been brought to England. After her owner's death she had stayed on in the service of his widow. She had left this position and was now needing financial assistance from the parish in which she lived. Could she seek the protection of the 1662 Act of Settlement which bound workers to the parish and the charity of the parish? Mansfield had no hesitation in deciding that this Act was clear: 'the statute says there must be a hiring, and here there was no hiring at all. She does not therefore come within the description'. Charlotte remained a slave and not a worker during her time in England. Her work for the widow of her owner was that of a slave, not an employee, so there was no statutory obligation to support her.

Mansfield himself must have had doubts about the consequences of the *Somerset* decision. He and his wife had taken care of the illegitimate child of his nephew, a child born of a Black mother. The child, named Dido, was educated and raised by Mansfield as a family member. Oldham notes that in addition to making a legacy in his will for this now grown woman, he also 'confirms to Dido Elizabeth Belle her freedom' (Oldham 1988: 1240).

The case of the slave ship *Zong*

The focus of the action in *Somerset* had been individual liberty and the outcome had secured the captive's release. Subsequently, the case of *Gregson v Gilbert* (1783) 3 Dougl. 233, raised the most serious public criticism of the law's ability to consider the desperate plight of the slave (Rupprecht 2007: 329; Armstrong 2004: 347). The case was decided in 1783, over a decade after *Somerset*, and in front of Lord Mansfield (Willes J and Buller J concurring). This case illustrates the law's ability to distinguish between the condition of slavery (in England) and the slave trade, which had as an objective the continued creation of slavery in the colonies seemingly at any human cost. The case was an insurance dispute and as such the fact of slavery was hidden behind the legal issue (Armstrong 2004: 167, Oldham 2007: 299).[22]

Conditions upon trading ships at this time were poor, but conditions upon those ships involved in the slave trade were appalling. It was in these conditions that the Liverpool slave ship *Zong* operated.[23] The ship left São Tomé, West Africa, in September 1781 with over 450 slaves on board. There was some evidential dispute at the time about the events leading up to the decision by the ship's captain, Luke Collingwood, to throw 130 slaves overboard (Shyllon 1974: 184 and Lewis 2007: 357–70). The insurer questioned whether this was an economic decision – suggesting that as the slaves were in poor condition and the owner would get more revenue from a successful insurance claim than from selling the slaves on arrival in the West Indies.

The captain claimed that the sea conditions had resulted in a much longer voyage than expected and, consequently, a shortage of water. This was disputed by the company as the true reason because of heavy rains and the proximity to port. The way in which the events are described and argued in the case makes for chilling reading. The only issue considered by the court was whether the insurance policy held by the ship owners would cover the loss of the slaves or whether they were lost because of fault by the captain.

When giving permission for the *Gilbert* re-trial (the insurance company appealed the decision of the first instance court in favour of the ship owners requiring them to pay £30 for 130 of the lost slaves), Mansfield is quoted as saying:

> The matter left to the jury was whether it was from necessity [that the slaves were thrown into the sea]; for they had no doubt (though it shocks one very much) that the case of slaves was the same as if horses had been thrown overboard.
>
> (*Gregson v Gilbert* at 233)

It was decided before a jury that this catastrophe was linked to the 'perils of sea' and the insurers were liable. The responsibility of the captain to ensure safe transit seemed to be minimal and there were no effective arguments presented in court from which a criminal action could arise. Sharp's attempt to have the ship's captain tried for murder in the Court of Admiralty was defeated. The Solicitor-General at the time, John Lee, declared that a master could drown slaves without 'a surmise of impropriety' (Thomas 1997: 489). Furthermore the jury did not raise the question of murder, with or without a consideration of the captain's defence of necessity. If the victims were analogous with horses it is unsurprising that there could be no count of murder – or even manslaughter.

Although of no consolation to those who died on the *Zong*, the public were outraged by both the facts and the outcome. It was the failure of the King's Bench Court to send a stronger message to slave ship owners, captains and traders on the Atlantic crossing which caused such public consternation. Again, Sharp and others successfully used the media, influential London debating societies and the distribution of pamphlets to press their cause for the abolition of the slave trade.[24] The notoriety of the case produced much commentary. One of J.M.W. Turner's most famous paintings – *Slave Ship (Slavers Throwing Overboard the Dead and Dying, Typhoon Coming On)*, circa 1840 – was based on the events surrounding the slave ship *Zong* (Boston Museum of Fine Art).[25]

The insurers were surprised at the outcome and put in place additional limitations on the cover offered to the ship owners and increased their premiums. Public anger resulted in parliamentary action and amended insurance legislation was passed in 1788 concerning the insuring of slaves at sea. At this time Sir Lloyd Kenyon was appointed the new Chief Justice following Lord Mansfield's retirement on 23 June 1788.

Commercial cases – post Mansfield

The literal application of the law, as seen in *Gilbert v Gregson* was not an isolated example of how the importance of trade obscured the suffering of the slaves. The eighteenth century had seen the emergence of commercial law and a new set of legal procedures instigated by Mansfield. His rational approach was to seek out the relevant law and apply it logically and methodically to the facts before him. As we have seen from his judgments in *Somerset* and *Gregson* he did not allow himself to be influenced by external factors. He had great confidence in the ability of legal principles to develop incrementally to cover new and emerging areas. He did not believe that it was his role to change the law. That was the role of parliament.

A later commercial case, which may have given an opportunity for *obiter* commentary on the slave trade by the English judiciary, was that of *Tarleton and Others v M'Gawley* (1794) Peake 270.[26] This case is well known when interference with a contract, or potential contract, is contested, but references rarely mention the nature of the trade (in this case the slave trade).

Tarleton was associated with the Liverpool slave trade and was the owner of approximately 20 slave ships. General Bonastre Tarleton, an MP at the turn of the eighteenth century, considered that Liverpool owed its existence as a commercial centre to the slave trade and spoke in its defence during the debates in Parliament in 1806 (Thomas 1997: 509). This legal action arose from an incident off the coast of Calabar, West Africa, involving the *Tarleton*: 'the ship had been fitted out at Liverpool with goods proper for trading with the natives of that coast for slaves and other goods' (*Tarleton v M'Gawley* at 271). A smaller vessel, the *Bannister*, was dispatched from the *Tarleton* and sailed to another part of the coast to trade. It was at this time that a canoe from the coast approached the *Bannister* for the purpose of establishing a trade and then proceeding back to the shore. The defendants, in another English ship the *Othello*, saw this event and fired their cannon at the canoe, killing one of the 'natives' on board. The effect of this was that the planned trade between the *Tarleton*, via the *Bannister*, did not take place as the Africans, unsurprisingly, took cover and left. It was emphasised in the case that the trade did not take place because of the danger to the lives of the crew of the *Bannister*.

The defendant (M'Gawley, owner of the *Othello*) argued that the Africans in question owed him money and that he would not permit them to trade with another party until that debt was paid. Furthermore, during cross-examination Smith, the captain of the *Bannister*, confirmed that Tarleton did not have a licence to trade along this part of the African coast (*Tarleton v M'Gawley* at 272). In view of this the defendant claimed that the *Tarleton* was engaged in an illegal act and could not, therefore, enjoy the protection of the English civil courts in support of 'such illicit commerce'.

Kenyon in *Tarleton* had some opportunity, therefore, to express a judicial comment that might express disapproval of the Atlantic slave trade. An outcome of the incident was a human death, the death of an African. Kenyon gave judgment for the *Tarleton*. He agreed that 'a person engaged in a trade which violated the law of the country cannot support an action against another for hindering him in that illegal traffick'. But, he also said, this did not apply in this case as this was a 'foreign law' requirement. He confirmed that the actions of the *Othello* were an intentional interference with legitimate trade and that the *Bannister*, and therefore the *Tarleton*, were unable to trade because of the unlawful coercive action of the *Othello*. Furthermore, Kenyon is reported as saying that 'the act of trading is not itself immoral'. He made no distinction between trading for goods and trading for slaves and whilst recognising that if the natives did owe M'Gawley money it would be difficult for him to enforce a claim in Africa he saw that as no lawful reason for the disruption.[27] Furthermore, illegality did not bar the action in England.[28]

The inferences to be drawn from the decision could be judicial disapproval of M'Gawley's action to fire on the natives to enforce a debt, or equally these could imply judicial support of unlicensed trading for slaves who were to be regarded as chattels for this purpose. The case of *Tarleton* again saw the issue of slavery concealed by a legal issue which was based in a civil law action for interference with trade.

Tatham v Hodgson[29] – another *Zong*?

In *Tatham v Hodgson* (1796) 6 T.R. 656, the owners of a slave ship claimed that it was 'by tempestuous weather and through the mere perils and dangers of the sea greatly retarded and delayed' (*Tatham* at 656). The initial intake was made up of 168 slaves of whom 128 died 'by hardships in the delay of the voyage'. They died of starvation, and illnesses arising from starvation, and by ingesting rotten food. The voyage, which would normally have taken from six to nine weeks from West Africa to Grenada, took six months and eight days and only made Barbados. Counsel for the ship-owner argued that:

> [T]he misfortune had arisen from no carelessness or inhumanity of the captain in not laying in sufficient provisions for the voyage, but from

the extraordinary and incalculable duration of it, in consequence of which the ordinary and proper food of the slaves had been exhausted, and against which no common precaution could avail.

(*Tatham* at 658)

Kenyon could not accept without comment the terrible human tragedy. It is reported by Shyllon (1974: 208), referring to two contemporaneous newspaper publications, that during the proceedings he asked '[W]hether the Captain of the ship was starved to death? He was answered in the negative'. Acting for the insurance company was the same advocate as in the *Zong* case, Mr Law. The insurance regime was now regulated by two Acts. The first was 30 Geo. 3, c. 33, s.8, which stated that:

It shall not be lawful for any owner of a vessel to insure any cargo of slaves against any loss or damage, except the perils of the sea, piracy, insurrection, or capture by the King's enemies, barratry by the master or crew, and destruction by fire.

The second was 34 Geo. 3, c. 80, s.10, which in addition provided:

[T]hat no loss or damage shall be recoverable on account of the mortality of slaves by natural death or ill treatment or against loss by throwing overboard of slaves on any account whatsoever.

(*Tatham* at 657)

Could the loss that had happened be attributed to the perils of the sea within the meaning of the Act or was this ill-treatment or another fault which could be blamed on the captain and owner? Kenyon discussed the existing and additional legislation and concluded that finding in favour of the ship owner would negate the substance and purpose of the legislative provisions. He is reported as saying:

This Act of Parliament being founded in humanity, we ought not on any account to put such a construction on it as to render it useless even if its expressions are doubtful . . . A captain, who knows the possible length of the voyage, does not discharge his duty, if he takes an insufficient quantity of provisions.

(*Tatham* at 658)

Grose J concurred. He commented that if they allowed recovery it would 'open a door to the very mischiefs that the legislature intended to guard against, because it would encourage captains of slave ships to take an insufficient quantity of food for the sustenance of their slaves'.

Lawrence J. applied a literal interpretation to reach the same outcome, describing the losses as natural deaths and, therefore, not recoverable within the existing legislation. Clearly, his definition of 'natural death' extended to cover death by starvation.

Kenyon was willing to adopt what might now be called a purposive approach to statutory interpretation. The passing of the statute so soon after the case of the *Zong* would have been well-known to him. He was aware of the reasons behind it and was also keen to apply them to the facts before him.

Supported by the legislation, the case marked a shift in judicial attitude to the way in which slaves on the transatlantic crossing were to be treated. Conditions might still be barbaric, but on pain of financial loss captains and owners were obliged to consider the conditions on board ship. In this the justices were not leading but following public opinion. The first attempt to pass legislation to ban the slave trade had been before Parliament by 1796 and had only been defeated by a narrow margin.

The contrast between judicial attitude towards the individual and the group, the victim appearing before the court and the victims enslaved on board ships continued. The legal rights of an individual to approach the court and expect redress equally with other subjects in England emerged incrementally as can be seen in the following case examples. The plight of the slaves travelling across the Atlantic and suffering in the English colonies had to wait for Parliament to act.

An emerging recognition of the legal rights of individuals before the courts

At the end of the eighteenth and the beginning of the nineteenth centuries there were two further cases which also deserve mention and which illustrate an increasing recognition of slavery's horrific conditions by the English judiciary.

Keane v Boycott (1795) 2 H. BL. 511, was heard before Lord Chief Justice Eyre in 1795. Both parties claimed legal ownership of a slave boy, Toney. He had been bought by Keane in the West Indies for a term of five years. On a visit to England Boycott had approached Toney and persuaded the boy to enlist in the army.

The case revolved around the question of the validity of the contract Toney had made with Keane when he was a slave and a child. The court recognised that the boy 'was both an infant and a slave of his master at the time when he entered into the contract: he was very young and entirely in the power of the master'. If the court declared the contract void the consequence would have been freedom for Toney, but this would mean that Boycott could insist that he be taken back to the army. Eyre decided that whether the contract with Keane should subsist was a decision for Toney. The contract was voidable at the boy's request. Would he stay in service with Keane, or would he go into the army?

By 1795 the anti-slavery movement had gained considerable ground and in this decision Eyre shows an understanding of Toney's predicament and also recognises his right to choose – but not the right of Keane or Boycott to dictate his fate.

In 1799 in *Robinson v Smyth* (1799) 1 Bos & Pul 455, the court refused to delay a trial to enable the defence to call a witness who would contend that the plaintiff was a slave to the defendant in order to prove his case.

> This is an odious defence, to which the Court will give no assistance. If the Defendant were to offer to put it on the record, we should not give him a day's time. It is as much a denial of justice as the plea of alien enemy, which is always discouraged by the Court.[30]

By the time the case of *Williams v Brown* (1802) 2 Bos & Pul 71, arrived in court in 1802 jurisprudence had shifted a considerable distance away from the perception of slavery which had existed in 1772. The abolitionist movement was at its most active during the final years of the eighteenth century, although events such as the French Revolution and the American War of Independence were to have a tempering effect on public support.

The difference between the case of Williams and the earlier cases of Strong, Lewis, and Somerset is that Williams was bringing the action himself, for his own financial benefit. It could be argued that in the earlier actions the slaves would certainly have benefited from the outcome. Their benefit was physical freedom and the issue was dominion. In many ways the slaves in the earlier cases were instrumental in the cause of the abolitionist movement. Here Williams was seeking an acknowledgement of his freedom and also confirmation that he had enforceable civil law rights in the English courts.

The facts show that whilst in England Williams entered into an agreement with a ship's captain, Brown, to work as a seaman during a voyage to and from the West Indies for an agreed sum. On arrival in Grenada Williams was claimed as a runaway slave and delivered to his master. Mansfield's narrow interpretation of the *Somerset* decision was reiterated. A slave, whilst free in England, would again become a slave if he or she entered a jurisdiction which recognised slavery. Rooke J noted 'he might enter into a contract to go to any other place but to Grenada, yet he could not engage to go there without danger of being detained' (*Williams* at 72). Furthermore, it is noted that Williams knew this and 'entered into articles which his situation rendered him incapable of performing'. He was captured in Grenada where he faced serious criminal punishment. At this point the captain began negotiations with Williams' master and on the payment of an agreed sum secured the manumission of Williams: in return Williams agreed to serve the captain for three years and at a wage which was less than that agreed at the outset (*Williams* at 73). Williams then brought an action claiming that the Grenada contract was concluded under duress and was therefore void and he claimed wages at the rate agreed under the original contract. In the judgment Lord Alvanley was concerned that to uphold the manumission and later contract might be to allow a form of English slavery 'through the backdoor'(*Williams* at 71). Justices Heath, Rooke and Chambre did not share this view. Heath, for example, considered that '[T]his was an agreement for the advantage of the Plaintiff: he was to be relieved from punishment; he was to become a freeman; and he was to receive a compensation for his service' (*Williams* at 72). Chambre went further:

> In this case an actual manumission took place, the master was a party to the agreement, and nothing occurred in the transaction to impeach the validity of the contract. This is the decision which I think the Court bound by the rules of law to make, and which is most consistent with the dictates of humanity.
>
> (*Williams* at 74)

Conclusion

With modern eyes it is hard not to criticise the English judiciary over this one hundred year period. Can any conclusions be reached however? A most obvious one is that the attitude of the judges in these cases reflected the position of the men in power at this time in English history, the landed gentry. This group, while small in number, vigorously promoted and supported each other in their quest for wealth and power and their desire to hold on to that wealth and power. Lord Hardwicke wielded his power with great confidence. He believed in the values of the class into which he was born. He would have found it difficult to be compassionate towards slaves (or anyone else of lowly status perhaps) and seemed truly to believe that it was his duty to rescue the African from a pitiful heathen existence and save him or her through enslavement. Hardwicke was Mansfield's benefactor and patron. Mansfield did not have the unshakeable personality of Hardwicke but believed passionately that the law offered a solution in a dispute. If the solution was difficult to find, he reasoned, it was because he was not looking hard enough and long enough. He most definitely did not see his role as that of a campaigner in judicial decision making and fervently believed that if the common law could not evolve to meet a new social situation then it was up to the legislator to make the necessary step change and not the judiciary. He was an intellectual legal giant and appears to have considered it a failure of character to deviate from the logical outcome that legal principles presented. His faith was in the law – although as we have seen, it could be tempered with equity. Perhaps these judges could not have been any different as they were products of their day, but they most certainly allowed the law to fall behind a change in public opinion towards the plight of the slave during their time in power. It was not until the retirement of Mansfield and the engagement of Kenyon that a more enlightened attitude began to emerge. Perhaps this too is an exaggeration. The political activity at the end of the eighteenth century was such that it would have been hard for the courts to maintain the respect of the country and ignore the change in attitude towards the slave trade. Times had moved on. Justice Chambre's final sentence in *Williams v Brown* marked, perhaps, an important watershed: a recognition that English law should take into consideration the dictates of common humanity when reasoning an outcome.

Notes

1 The utilitarian argument against the abolition of the slave trade was based on the benefits gained by the country's population as a whole and, in contrast the work of Adam Smith and other free marketers, was in favour of abolition because it distorted the market.

2 See, later, the impact of *Gregson v Gilbert* (1783) 3 Dougl 233.

3 Thomas notes that '[S]ome English captains sailed under United States flags, and later under Swedish, Danish, and even French ones. Many English firms still supplied the "trade goods" for slave voyages of Portuguese and Spanish ships. But most important English firms did drop out. They even abandoned the slave trade between the Caribbean islands.'

4 It was not until 1886 that slavery was abolished in Cuba, and 1888 that it was abolished in Brazil.

5 Trover was a common law action to recover the value of personal property wrongfully taken and used.

6 See, for example, *The Interesting Narrative of the Life of Olaudah Equiano or Gustavus Vass, the African* (1814 edition). Details from the National Archive: available at http://www.nationalarchives.gov.uk/pathways/blackhistory/rights/abolition.htm (August 2008)

7 An Act for the better securing the Liberty of the subject, and for Prevention of Imprisonment beyond the Seas 31 Car.II.c.2.

8 Ch I is entitled 'Of the Absolute Rights of Individuals' and Ch xiv 'Of Master and Servant', both deal with slavery.

9 Bk. I, ch. I, p.127 In the 4th ed. (1770), 5th ed. (1773), 6th ed. (1774), and subsequent editions, *possibly* replace *probably* (italics added). Eight editions appeared in Blackstone's lifetime, and the ninth edition was ready for publication when he died. See Shyllon, op cit 60. Shyllon cites Blackstone's additional comments on slavery taken from the 14th Chapter of the *Commentaries*. Blackstone is later criticised by Edward Christian, first Downing Professor of the Laws of England in the University of Cambridge, in his editorial notes to the 17th edition of the *Commentaries*. Professor Christian is of the opinion that the master's right to the service could not continue because 'such

a contract with a person in a state of slavery would be absolutely null and void.' 1820, Bk. 1, ch. I, p.127n: Bk. I, ch. xiv, p.425n. See Shyllon, *op.cit* p.61. As noted later in *Keane v Boycott* it may be that such a contract is voidable, not void.

10 Davis argues persuasively that the anti-slavery movement gained momentum because it coincided with the formation of the new 'middle class' of English society. This new 'middle class' was not enfranchised, but adopted this platform for a common purpose and to cement its unity. This was also a time of important developments intellectually with the publication of Adam Smith's *The Theory of Moral Sentiments* (1759), and *The Wealth of Nations* (1776) and a time of great upheaval in America and France in particular.

11 Judicature Act 1873, s.24 established the Supreme Court of Judicature and all divisions of that court were directed to apply equitable principles.

12 Some of the most extensive works which look at the original papers of the case include: F.O.Shyllon, *Black Slaves in Britain* (Oxford University Press, 1974), (published 200 years after the decision); James Oldham *The Mansfield Manuscripts and the Growth in English Law in the Eighteenth Century* Vol.2 (University of North Carolina Press, 1992) Ch.21; W.Wiecek, 'Somerset: Lord Mansfield and the Legitimacy of Slavery in the Anglo-American World,' *University of Chicago Law Review* 42 (1974), 86; E. Fiddes, 'Lord Mansfield and the Somerset Case,' *Law Quarterly Review* 50 (1934), 499, Nadelhaft, J. 'The Somerset Case and Slavery: Myth, Reality, and Repercussions,' *Journal of Negro History* 51 (1966), Thomas, H., *op.cit* and Davis, D.B. *op cit* Chapter 10, 'Antislavery and the Conflict of Laws', pp 469–522. Davis, for example, says that although T.B. Howell's *State Trials*, which incorporates a 1772 pamphlet printed by Somerset's lawyer, Francis Hargrave, 'has been thought to provide the only detailed account of the Somerset case, its reliability has been questioned', by Nadelhaft (above), but goes on to say that Howell's report supplemented the report by Capel Lofft which was 'skimpy'. Lofft was the only transcriber in the court at that time. He was also an abolitionist and a noted Whig.

13 It is suggested that Lord Mansfield owed his meteoric rise at the bar to 'the patronage of Talbot and Yorke'.

14 Although cited the writer has not been able to find reference to the particular quote used and made popular by this case.

15 Lofft.1, at 17, 'In five or six cases of this nature, I have known it to be accommodated by agreement between the parties: on its first coming before me, I strongly recommended it here.' per Lord Mansfield. See also, *20 State Trials*, ibid, p.145.

16 Lofft 1, at 17.

17 Lofft 1, at 17–18, per Lord Mansfield. See also *20 State Trials*, ibid, 146.

18 There is continuing discussion about what was actually said in the judgment and Weicek (op cit) reviews the several reports of the case.

19 Lofft 1, at 19 per Lord Mansfield.

20 *The Slave Grace James* (1827) 2 St. Tr. (N.S.) 274, col. 292. For an analysis see: Stephen Waddams, 'The case of Grace James (1827)' (2007) 13 *Texas Wesleyan LR* 783.

21 Lord Mansfield, 29 August 1779. See also his statement in 1785 'The determination goes no further than that the Master cannot by force compel him to go out of the kingdom.' Shyllon (*op cit*) 164.

22 For a more detailed account of insurance and maritime trade (including slaves) see, Armstrong, T. 'Slavery, Insurance, and the Sacrifice in the Black Atlantic',

in Bernhard Klein and Gesa Mackenthun (eds), *Sea Changes: historicizing the ocean.* New York (2004) pp 167–185, Oldham, J. 'Insurance Litigation Involving the *Zong* and Other British Slave Ships', 28 J Leg Hist (2007) 299–318.

23 The ship belonged to a large and influential Liverpool firm of slave-ship owners, Messrs. William, John, and James Gregson, Edward Wilson, and James Aspinall (Shyllon, 187 fn. 1) although Thomas (op cit p.488), says that the ship was owned by William Gregson and George Case.

24 For example, 25 February 1788 Westminster Forum debate 'Can any political or commercial advantages justify a free people in continuing the Slave Trade?': 6 March 1788 Coachmakers' Hall: 'Would it be consistent with the political and commercial interests of Great Britain for the legislature to pass an Act for the total Abolition of the Slave Trade?': 25 September 1788 Coachmakers' Hall: 'Can an Advocate for the Slave Trade be justly deemed a real Friend to the Constitutional Liberties of this Country?', From 'London debates: 1788', London debating societies 1776–1799 (1994), pp. 216–46. http://www.british-history.ac.uk/report.asp?compid = 38852&strquery = slave* (August 2008).

25 The picture is a part of the Art of Europe collection at the Museum of Fine Art, Boston. To see the painting online search the European collection at: http://www.mfa.org/collections/ (accessed August 2008).

26 See Halsbury's Laws of England, para. 694. Inducement, coercion . . .

27 Legal point affirmed in *Carrington v Taylor* (1809) 11 East 571.

28 See *Holman* v *Johnson* (1771) 1 Cowp 341 where Lord Mansfield CJ declared: '[n]o court will lend its aid to a man who founds his cause of action upon an immoral or illegal act'.

29 Oldham, op cit 28 *J Leg Hist* points the reader to the case of *Rohl v Parr* (1796) 1 Esp 445, heard in the same year, as confirming the decision. In the case of *Rohl v Parr* the delay and subsequent loss of life was caused by worm damage to the boat, not the perils of the sea, and the losses were excluded from the insurance cover.

30 *Sed per Curiam* only. No judge named in case report.

Bibliography

Armstrong, T. (2004) 'Slavery, Insurance, and the Sacrifice in the Black Atlantic', in G. Klein and Mackenthun (eds), *Sea Changes: Historicizing the Ocean.* New York: Routledge.

Armstrong, T. (2007) 'Catastrophe and Trauma: A response to Anita Rupprecht', *Journal of Legal History*, 28: 347.

Blackstone's Commentaries on the Law of England (1765), 1st edn (1770), 4th edn (1773), 5th edn (1774), 6th edn, London.

Davis, D.B. (1975) *The Problem of Slavery in the Age of Revolution 1770–1823.* New York: Cornell University Press.

Fiddes, E. (1934) 'Lord Mansfield and the Somerset Case', *Law Quarterly Review*, 50: 499.

Fisher, R.A (1943) 'Granville Sharp and Lord Mansfield', *Journal of Negro History*, 38: 381.

Heward, E. (1979) *Lord Mansfield.* London: Barry Rose.

Hoare, P. (1820) *Memoirs of Granville Sharp, Esq.* London: Henry Colburn & Co. (now available digitally on Google Books).

Lewis, A. (2007) 'Martin Dockray and the *Zong*: A Tribute in the Form of a Chronology', *Journal of Legal History*, 28: 357.

Nadelhaft, J. (1966) 'The Somerset Case and Slavery: Myth, Reality, Repercussions', *Journal of Negro History*, 51.

Oldham, J. (1988) 'New Light on Mansfield and Slavery', *Journal of British Studies*, 45.

Oldham, J. (1992) *The Mansfield Manuscripts and the Growth of the English Law in the Eighteenth Century*, Vol. 2. The University of North Carolina Press.

Oldham, J. (2007) 'Insurance Litigation Involving the *Zong* and Other British Slave Ships', *Journal of Legal History*, 28: 299.

Rupprecht, A. (2007) 'A Very Uncommon Case: Representations of the *Zong* and the British Campaign to Abolish the Slave Trade' *Journal of Legal History*, 28: 329.

Sharp, G. (1769) *A Representation of the Injustice and Dangerous Tendency of Tolerating Slavery in England; or of Admitting the Least Claim of Private Property in the Persons of Men, in England*, London.

Shyllon, F.O. (1974) *Black Slaves in Britain*. Oxford: Oxford University Press.

Thomas, H. (1997) *The History of the Atlantic Slave Trade 1440–1870*. London: Picador.

Waddams, S. (2007) 'The case of Grace James (1827)', *Texas Wesleyan Law Review*, 13: 783.

Wiecek, W.M. (1974) '*Somerset*, Lord Mansfield and the Legitimacy of Slavery in the Anglo-American World', *University of Chicago Law Review*, 42: 86.

Websites

Andrews, Donna T. (1994) British History Online, London debating societies 1776–1799: 'London debates: 1788', available at http://www.british-history.ac.uk/report.asp?compid=38852& strqery=slave* 216 (accessed August 2008).

Liverpool Museums: Petition of Liverpool to the House of Commons, 14 February 1788: available at http://www.liverpoolmuseums.org.ukmaritime/slavery/petition.asp (accessed August 2007).

Museum of Fine Art, Boston, Art of Europe collection: available at http://www.mfa.org/collections/ (accessed June 2010).

National Archive: available at www.nationalarchives.gov.uk/pathways/blackhistory/rights/abolition.htm (accessed August 2008).

The Task, Book 11 (1784) available at http://www.brycchancarey.com/slavery/cowperpoems.htm (accessed June 2010).

Part III

Pluralism

Strategies for reparations

Chapter 10

Slave trade reparations, institutional racism and the law[1]

Fernne Brennan

The reluctance of White Europeans and White Americans to come to terms with the historic injustice of slavery is caused, I believe, by both the depth of the prejudice and the magnitude of the issues to be faced. The notions of White virtue are so ingrained that they cannot admit to barbarities which their ancestors committed. If they respond at all to the claims of Black people for justice, it is by way of 'development aid' or 'anti-discrimination laws', which imply that their generosity is bestowing gifts on the poor suffering Blacks. It is easier to help victims than to pay for past crimes.

(Gifford 2007: 267)

Introduction

At a recent meeting in Geneva with the people in the Human Rights Council Anti-Discrimination Unit[2] responsible for overseeing the Durban process,[3] the one part of the dialogue that stood out for me was the phrase 'the question of reparations will not go away'. This is indeed the case and also my one great passion – slave trade reparations – by which I mean reparations for the legacy of the slave trade. This legacy I consider to be institutional racism, although it adopts many different guises. The aim of this chapter is to pull out some of those disguises, and in the context of a legal framework to assess critically the extent to which the law turns its face against slave trade reparation claims.

There are many non-governmental organisations (NGOs), civil society organisations and individuals working in the field of slave trade reparations. These individuals include academics and advocates[4] who believe that reparations are due for the wrongs shaped by chattel slavery (Blackburn 1998). These voices can be heard on both sides of the Atlantic, in the Caribbean,[5] in America,[6] in Canada, Africa and Brazil. And while we argue about the nature of the harm, or contest whether or not the chattel slavery was legal at the time,[7] whether or not we identify those who profited in the name of chattel slavery or try to identify those who suffered under its ferocious regime, I would argue that morally, politically and legally we should not back away from the challenge that the legacy of slave trade reparations claims produces. It is argued that the real challenge is to look at today's legacy that is sourced in chattel slavery as institutional racism and that until we face this scenario very little progress will be made. As Gifford explains,

> Most White people find it impossible, either at a national or personal level, to say, 'My people did your people a grievous wrong. I apologise, and I want to do what is necessary to remedy the damage which that wrong has caused.' Yet it would be such an easy thing to say. Both Black and White societies are sick from the consequences of slavery. Black societies around the world are economically sick, deprived of land, psychologically made to feel inferior. White societies are spiritually sick, deprived of soul, psychologically infected with racial prejudice. I advocate the cause of reparations because a just society which faces the horrors of its past is a happier society for me as well as for you.
>
> (Gifford 2007: 266)

Background

Blackburn's work is of special relevance to this topic because he argues chattel slavery was a special form of human control that brought a vast accumulation of wealth to the Western Europeans and death or near death to those people who were turned into chattel slaves in order to serve the Europeans (Blackburn 1997). In order to do this the Europeans accorded to Black human beings living in Africa the status of animals without rights. In Blackburn's (1997) book *The Making of New World Slavery* he documents the various phases of slave trading in Africa that concerned Portugese, Spanish, Brazilian, Dutch, French and English colonial slavery (Blackburn 1997: Chapters 2–7). What was interesting about this slave trade, he argues, is that:

> Talks of ideology [were] riddled with bad faith because in practice whilst slaves were perceived as inferior beings, treated as beasts of burden to be driven like cattle, slaves were useful precisely because they had the capacity to deal with complex orders. The most terrifying thing is the similarity between the slave holder and the enslaved.
>
> (Blackburn 1997: 12–20)

Thomas continues this theme in his (1997) book *Slave Trade: History of the Atlantic Slave Trade 1440–1870*, in which he quotes from Diogo

Gomes (c.1460) on the river Gambia: 'Twenty-two people ... were sleeping. I herded them as if they had been cattle towards the boat' (1997: 68). Williams writes that although there was white servitude, such servitude, 'was the historic base upon which Negro slavery was constructed ... the Africans were latecomers fitted into a system already developed' (1994: 19). Indeed chattelisation was so rooted in that nefarious trade that Lord Mansfield likened slaves to horses in the insurance case of *Gregson v Gilbert* (1783) 3 Dougl. 233. In this case several slaves were bound and thrown overboard under the Captain's orders whilst alive. Dziobon (see Chapter 9 this volume) surmises that 'the public were outraged at the facts and the outcome. It was the failure of the King's Bench to send a stronger message to slave ship owners, captains and traders on the Atlantic crossing which caused such public consternation.' Even after the abolition of the slave trade in Britain in 1807[8] Sherwood argues that the enterprise did not cease: she provides documentary evidence that the Acts (of which there were several)[9] were insufficient on their own to end the trade in Africans. And although 'slave trading was declared as piracy, punishable by death, no such prosecutions were ever made'. Sherwood concludes that the reason why many British Acts to abolish the slave trade were not enforced was because the higher echelons in society were not willing to give up this lucrative trade – they had too much invested in it and 'companies profited both from the sale of enslaved Africans and from importation and local sales of the produce of the enslaved such as sugar, coffee and cotton' (Williams 1994: 23).

There have been three world conferences[10] on racism thus far. The modern watershed came with the Durban 2001 conference, the *Durban Declaration and Program of Action* (DDPA),[11] and a global review called the Durban Review Process, held in Geneva in 2009. These conferences were aimed at giving effect to the notion of peace rather than 'war' between people of different nationalities and so on. The 2001 conference was particularly interesting because of its focus on the slave trade and remedies for this and the fact that its outcome document (the DDPA) was unanimously adopted by all member states.[12] A declaration was drawn up, as was a programme of action, and the 2009 Durban Review process aimed at looking into what exactly member states had done since 2001 regarding the issues raised at that time. For our purposes the most important part of the DDPA relates to the sources of contemporary racism. In paragraph 13 on the origins of racism the declaration refers to:

> slavery and the slave trade, including the transatlantic slave trade, [as] appalling tragedies in the history of humanity ... because of their magnitude, organised nature and especially their *negation of the essence of the victims*, and [we] further acknowledge that slavery and the slave trade were crimes against humanity and should always have

been so, especially the transatlantic slave trade, and are among the *major sources and manifestations* of racism, racial discrimination and xenophobia and related intolerance.

The DDPA includes an acknowledgement that Africans and people of African descent suffer from racial discrimination now (paragraphs 4–14) and that such peoples should be afforded remedies, reparations and compensation (paragraph 165). The aim of the Durban Review process was to 'provide an opportunity to assess and accelerate progress on [the] implementation of measures adopted by consensus at the 2001 World Conference against Racism, Racial Discrimination, Xenophobia and related Intolerance, held in Durban, South Africa' (United Nations 2009). Three resolutions of the General Assembly (GA) and two resolutions of the Human Rights Council (HRC)[13] were used to give substance to the Third World conference. The GA resolved that, '[The General Assembly], through its role in policy formulation, the Economic and Social Council, through its role in overall guidance and coordination, in accordance with their respective roles under the Charter of the United Nations and Assembly resolution 50/227 of 24 May 1996, and the Human Rights Council shall constitute a three-tiered intergovernmental process for the comprehensive implementation of and follow-up to the Durban Declaration and Programme of Action.'

Via resolution GA 61/149 the General Assembly 'Acknowledges that no derogation from the prohibition of racial discrimination, genocide, the crime of apartheid or slavery is permitted, as defined in the obligations under the relevant human rights instruments'; moreover, 'States should implement and enforce appropriate and effective legislative, judicial, regulatory and administrative measures to prevent and protect against acts of racism, racial discrimination, xenophobia and related intolerance, thereby contributing to the prevention of human rights violations'. Needless to say the issue of the transatlantic slave trade and reparations does not appear to have come at the top of any of the Western states' agendas.

Jamaica is probably the most active of the slave trade and chattel slavery recipient countries in the Caribbean, convincing the UN General Assembly to adopt a resolution to mark the bicentenary of the abolition of the slave trade.[14] Jamaica has also set up a National Commission on Reparations:[15]

> The National Commission on Reparations has been created by the Government of Jamaica to recommend the form or forms which reparations may take, and to receive testimony from the public and from experts, with the aim of guiding a national approach to reparations. The Commission's work programme will include public meetings, presentations in the media, the showing of films, and maintaining an interactive website.

The big problem here is how to link the legacy of the slave trade with contemporary forms of racism and to look to reparations to resolve the matter. As Professor Barry Chevannes (chair of the National Commission) pronounced:

> Should there be reparation made for slavery? Is it too far gone to worry about that? Are there legacies that we are still suffering from? And if reparation should be made, what form would you like to see it? That's the objective of the thing.
> (Jamaican National Commission on Reparations, 2010)

These are indeed the questions that need to be addressed and the commission's obligation is 'to listen to people's views, consult with professionals, and advise the Government on what approach should be taken'.

Slave trade legacies and contemporary institutional racism

Institutional racism has the potential to cause disruption as well as allowing those who are racist to hide behind an institutional veil whilst they carry out their racist behaviour. There are two related arguments – one that posits that the focus on institutions is superfluous since only individuals and not institutions can be racist; and the second which states that institutional racism is the 'elephant in the room'. The latter cannot easily be seen but almost certainly occupies a large space in institutions. These conceptual frameworks also reveal the critical discourse in human rights as to whether or not the individual is the pinnacle of concern or whether we should be concerned with groups and institutions. In my view this division is a faulty one since what is at stake here is the issue rather than individuals and/or groups. This is often known in the law as 'horses for courses', or what is suitable for one person or situation might be unsuitable for another. The former argument is very much at the centre of human rights in the West, whereas for other nations such as those in the Caribbean and parts of Africa the notion of divisible individuality is a mystery. This is why there is a clash in human rights between the individualist reading and the group/institutional idea. These conceptual frameworks are played out in the reparations arena and no more clearly than when the argument for reparations is based on group harm and the institutional legacy of slavery – namely, institutional racism. Before we go any further we need to see what institutional racism is and consider how it puts a brake on the calls for reparation.

Institutional racism[16] explained

The phenomenon of institutional racism has been defined on a number of occasions and stretches as far back as 1881 (Douglass), moreover Wells suggests that institutional racism is ingrained in the institutional system (Feagin 2000). Seminal work by Carmichael and Hamilton (1967) possessed a captivating narrative that detailed the institutionalised racial discrimination faced by the descendants of emancipated African-Americans. They argued that institutional racism was insidious, that it lurked in the very essence of societal relations. In its overt form this could be hyper-visible in the form of civil disobedience, marches, and the like (Williams 1997). This provides a window through which we may catch a fleeting glance of the real problems faced by the Black community, since covertly the continuum is one of hyper-invisibility in which people are not consciously aware of the difficulties which Black people face. Black people are dying unnecessarily, as in the USA for example they have been incarcerated and executed disproportionately to their numbers. In addition they receive poor medical services and a poor education and are heavily policed in their neighbourhoods and elsewhere.

Bowling and Phillips (2009: 156–7) suggest at least four theories to explain the problem with discriminatory policing and by implication this applies to other institutions. There is also the 'bad apple' thesis which is referred to in Scarman's report as well (see below). A species of this is the 'reflection of society' thesis which suggests that if people are prejudiced in society this will also play out in the police service whose officers are themselves recruited from wider society. Bowling and Phillips also point to the 'canteen culture' thesis. This relates to an organisational culture that is 'marked by specific languages, rituals, values, norms, perspectives and craft rules'. This culture is reinforced by the daily tasks that have to be performed. This includes ways of seeing: the public and Black and Asian people in the context of policing are likely to be seen as 'police property' – according to Reiner this property is seen as 'lower status, powerless groups whom the dominant majority perceive as problematic and distasteful'. The final thesis they suggest is called 'institutional racism' and there have been many comments on this concept. Scarman's (1981) view was that we are not a society that 'knowingly and as a matter of policy, discriminates against Black people'. The Home Secretary of the day said, 'on that definition institutional racism exists ... [in] institutions countrywide' (Bowling and Phillips 2002: 160). Hall remarks that, 'Well-formed prejudices and institutional attitudes are deeply based and emotionally held in place; the culture of organisation is difficult to shift' (1998: 6). Bowling and Phillips finally conclude that the statistics show that Black people are more likely to be stopped by the police per 1000 of the population – 95 times compared to 19 for Whites (2002: 166).[17] That is to say, according to Bowling and Phillips, a Black person is five times more likely to be stopped than a White person.

According to the Equality and Human Rights Commission recent research suggests that Black people are 26 times more likely to be stopped than Whites under Section 60 of the Public Order Act where police have 'maximum discretion'. These stop-and-search tactics put one in mind of similar actions suffered by Black slaves in days gone by. They would have to carry a letter permitting them to go to market, for instance, and could be stopped by any White person and asked to account for their movements. Are we perhaps moving backwards in this regard?

Added to this information is the Scarman Report in which it is concluded, 'If by [institutionally racist] it is meant [1] a society which knowingly, as a matter of policy, discriminates against Black people, I reject the allegation.[18] If, however, the suggestion being made is that [2] practices may be adopted by public bodies as well as private individuals which are unwittingly discriminatory against Black people, then this is an allegation which deserves serious consideration, and, where proved, swift remedy'(Scarman 1981: 28). The terms 'unwittingly' and 'practices' in the context of public service delivery have come to the fore on a number of occasions. Smith argues that 'a hallmark of institutionalised racism is detachment from the intentionality of individual managers and administrators . . . some racist practices must be regarded as the product of uncritical rather than unconscious racism . . . practices with a racist outcome are not engaged in without the actor's knowledge, even if they have failed to consider the consequences of [their] actions for Black or Asian people' (1994: 40). Smith goes on to say that 'institutional racism . . . is . . . a pervasive process sustained across a range of institutions . . . they have procedures which combine to produce a mutually reinforcing pattern of racial inequality' (1994: 41)

The watershed moment came with the Macpherson definition of institutional racism:

> [Institutional Racism is] the collective failure of an organisation to provide an appropriate and professional service to people because of their colour, culture or ethnic origin. It can be seen be seen or detected in processes, attitudes and behaviour which amount to discrimination through unwitting prejudice, ignorance, thoughtlessness and racist stereotyping which disadvantage minority ethnic people.
>
> (Macpherson 1999: 0.34)

This is a very useful working definition that fits well with the idea of 'hyper-invisibility' identified by Williams (1997) in the sense that unwitting racism persists and is unchallenged although Black people as an ethnic minority suffer from its effects. Macpherson's contribution was to suggest we should look at institutions rather than focus on individuals alone and to look at the appropriateness of services delivered and consider whether that service delivery could be racially discriminatory in an unwitting, non-malicious way that, nevertheless, would have negative implications for service users from diverse ethnic minority groups. It is important to see here how Macpherson's view forms a solid ground from which to launch a reparations claim. He stresses 'processes', 'attitudes', 'stereotyping' and 'unwitting prejudice', which are all undetected unless institutions are alert to them. This leads neatly into the idea that institutional racism as the legacy of racism can be seen or detected in the failure to deliver services to Black people in a sensitive and relevant way.

There have been several critiques of Macpherson's definition of institutional racism, for example that of Green (2000). Furthermore the argument that reparations are not due comes from Horowitz and others who argue that it is racist to pursue reparations against White people because this action would in itself be racist. We can presume that Lord Gifford[19] would be likely to argue that Horowitz has got it wrong. When many people write and talk about slavery reparations they are including the European governments who sanctioned chattel slavery and profited from its proceeds.

It is understood that despite the recommendation from the Macpherson Report and the admission by the police that they record the ethnicity of those they stop (as a way of monitoring the potential targeting of ethnic minorities), they will not be required to record that factor any more. 'Black police officers, Lawrence [i.e., the family of Stephen] and a coalition of minority ethnic groups say: the new proposals to widen this area opens the door to racial targeting ... and are a dangerous concession to racism' (Dodd 2010). This was a factor which hitherto has been denied as part of police operational practice (Scarman 1981).

There have been several critics of the notion of institutional racism who would argue that this does not exist. And this view is despite scholarship from the USA which states that institutional racism persists. Randall (2006) argues:

> Institutions can behave in ways that are overtly racist (i.e., specifically excluding people-of-color from services) or inherently racist (i.e., adopting policies that while not specifically directed at excluding people-of-color, nevertheless result in their exclusion). Therefore, institutions can respond to people-of-color and whites differently. Institutional behaviour can injure people-of-color; and, when it does, it is nonetheless racist in outcome if not in intent.

Green (2000) has also argued that focusing on 'race' is the wrong way to build social cohesion between individuals. Quoting from the famous speech delivered by Dr Martin Luther King, Green points out that individuals should 'not be judged by the colour of their skin but by the content of their character'. 'Should' is an apt word here, and if only the sentiment were true we would not have had Scarman, Macpherson, or the deliberate targeting of ethnic minorities by the police based on racial profiling (Dodd 2010). The point of all this is that Black people are not seen as individuals but as a group who have the potential to create disharmony and bring problems to society. Others such as Lea[20] contend that the Macpherson definition does not work because the remedy boils down to training individuals about their statutory duty not to discriminate and is not focused on institutions.

Nevertheless the British government adopted most of the recommendations and amended the Race Relations Act 1976 (RRA), by virtue of the Race Relations (Amendment) Act 2000, in order to extend the reach of the RRA to police and other public bodies. Accordingly, all public institutions listed in the schedule to the amended provision are bound by two central duties. The 'general duty' applies to all institutions listed in the schedule and states that public bodies must have 'due regard to the need to eliminate unlawful racial discrimination, promote equality of opportunity, and promote good relations between people of different racial groups'. The 'specific duty' places a statutory duty on institutions to publish a race equality scheme, to identify all the functions and policies that might relate to racial equality, and to set out how the general duty will be arrived at. In particular, in order to assess and consult widely, monitor policies for adverse impact, publish the results of impact assessments, and so that the public should have access to information and services, staff should be trained on both duties and there should be a review of all functions and policies every three years (Equality and Human Rights Commission 2010). What is clearly missing in this legislation is a definition of institutional racism and how that should be removed from institutions. Given that Macpherson provided the groundwork it is difficult to see why the government of the day did not adopt and work with that definition. It is argued that this failure has been another way in which to avoid the legacy of the slave trade. Creating legislation that applies equally to all without reference to the particular history and legacy suffered by African-Caribbean people is another example of how the legacy works – namely, that the law is created as though the legacy did not exist. This is another example of the refusal to provide an appropriate service to people based on their ethnicity.

The link between institutional racism and reparations

Let us start with the meaning of reparations. It is a myth that reparations equate to hard currency. There may be instances where some form of financial compensation is desirable and a sensible matter to pursue. A useful example might be some financial compensation for Bolivian people of Black African descent. These are direct descendants of the Bonifaz of Africa who were brought as slaves to work the silver mines in Bolivia. There are approximately 35,000 in all who now work as farmers growing cocoa amongst other things. As a group they are extremely poor (Shipani 2009). In a situation like this one could envisage financial compensation making a difference to their livelihood and life outcomes. However, such is not the main or only focus of reparations.

In 2005 Theo Van Boven and Cherif Bassiouni (UN appointed specialists to look at the issue of reparations) gave us *The Basic Principles and Guidelines on the Right to a Remedy and Reparation for Victims of Gross Violations of International Human Rights Law and Serious Violations of International Humanitarian Law*. The substance of their work was based on what reparations looked like across the world. What emerged from their presentation to the United Nations included a number of critical factors such as the right to respect; the adoption of effective legislative and administrative procedures; that perpetrators should be prosecuted; that statutory limitations should be lifted in the context of a right to bring a complaint, where the violation was one of human rights; that priority should be given to the voices of the victims of human rights abuses; and that reparations should also be targeted at physical as well as mental harm. There should also be something put back into the fold for the loss of opportunities which could include employment, education and social benefits; material damages and a loss of earnings, including the loss of earning potential; moral damage; costs required for legal or expert assistance, medicine and medical services, and psychological and social services (in terms of *rehabilitation* this should include medical and psychological care as well as legal and social services); and lastly, *satisfaction* – such as an apology, commemoration, accurate accounting of the atrocities and a non-repetition, all of which could be part of the reparations package (Bassiouni and Van Boven 2005: paras 20–22).

It is not the case that 'victims of historical injustices' (Posner and Vermeule 2003: 689) have not been able to claim reparations. As Posner and Vermeule tell us there have been reparations programmes for interned Japanese Americans and reparations for Holocaust victims. However, when it comes to support for reparations for the legacy of the transatlantic slave trade there are few takers. So why is this? Horowitz (2001) provides ten reasons: that no single group was responsible for slavery and there was no single group that benefited; Americans today have no connection with slavery; there are no precedents for such a claim and the claim is based on race not injury; the claim suggests all African-Americans suffer economically and that they are all victims; reparations have already been paid to African-Americans and they owe America; and finally reparations are a separatist idea that sets Blacks apart from American society. There is not sufficient space here to pick up on Horowitz's ideas but it is interesting to note that he does not see 'race' as injury.

Race/racism/institutional racism as injury is precisely what those who engage in the slave trade legacy and reparations discourse focus on. Torpey (2003) argues that the reduced status of Black people has evolved through a particular form of enslavement which is the 'historical crucible out of which the diminished status of blacks ... is generally said to have developed' (2003: 17). And the law has not addressed this system of oppression by providing for legal reparations (Feagin 2000). Litigation, it is argued, makes racial harms visible and provides a catalyst for public education and empathy in an area that remains under-represented in national and international history, and under-researched and isolated from its contemporary and continuing consequences. Some of the legal discourse raised by Corlett, Feagin and Thompson brings into focus the institutional barriers that are raised against contemporary claims that are sourced in a history that has not taken seriously the continuing problems of institutional racism and the need to deal with this through reparations such as relief and apologies. And reparations could provide a form of relief – to relieve is to deliver from pain, distress, anxiety. Relief can exorcise demons and reorder political relations, argue Gibney et al. (2008). And it can also reconcile, heal and be forward looking, suggests Thompson (2002). But those who apologise and those to whom apologies are made need to 'talk' to each other in case what is ignored is also what is at stake, states Brophy (2006). 'Talk' enables 'the living to keep promises and contracts [with] the dead ... [as] inseparable in the value we assign to self realisation', suggests Long (2007: 6).

Law (in Europe) should allow the dead and those who suffer from the legacy of the slave trade to 'talk'. It does not. Law puts up bars depending on whether or not the claimant has *locus standi* (standing), and also depending on when and where a claim is brought and the type of remedy. Law as an institution has collectively failed (in the Macpherson sense) to provide justice to those who still suffer from the legacy of the slave trade. The anti-discrimination laws that deal with race are not adequate enough to do justice to this particular area because they are not fit for this purpose. Such laws are inadequate because they have evolved jurisprudentially to treat all people the same and they are a-historical as well – taking scant notice of the historical context within which Black people must fight on a daily basis.

More and more people, however, are interested in the arguments, including those like Horowitz who would like to see the whole enterprise abandoned. Four hundred years of slavery and two hundred years of advocacy cannot simply be blown away like grains of sand because the reason for that sand still remains. To tackle the underlying cause of racial discrimination we must locate it in institutional racism, a racism whose bed was first made by the slave trade and slavery. As more and more people write about these problems the more it can be prophesied that the pen, being mightier than the sword, will make a dent in the all too familiar refusal to believe, accept responsibility, apologise and make restitution for a tragedy that we have *all* lived through and continue so to do.

Conclusion

More and more people are asking the question as to why reparations for the slave trade and its legacies have not been made. This failure to attend to reparations in the widest Van Boven / Bassiouni sense of the concept, whilst realising that Britain gave away the equivalent of 40 per cent of her gross domestic product to slavers, leaves an unpalatable taste in the mouth. It has become increasingly clear that the fight to obtain reparations is also part of the legacy of institutional racism, thus far more work needs to be done to address these issues. We have only just begun. As an American NGO remarked at the Durban II conference, the National Coalition of Blacks for Reparations in America (N'Cobra) has argued, 'We need to flip the script'.

Notes

1 Special thanks to Chris Burnett and others who have helped in this area. All mistakes remain mine alone.
2 The unit's remit is to provide the infrastructure or capacity so that racism can be challenged at a national level; see http://www.ohchr.org/EN/ABOUTUS/Pages/RacialDiscrimination.aspx
3 The 2009 Durban Review Conference checked the global progress made in overcoming racism and concluded that much remained to be achieved. Undoubtedly, the greatest accomplishment of the conference was the renewed international commitment to the anti-racism agenda.
4 See, for example, Gifford (2007).
5 For example, B. Chevanns, the Chairperson for the National Reparations Commission Jamaica. The Commission was set up to consult with the Jamaican public and others in the Diaspra in order to make recommendations regarding reparations claims; see http://www.jis.gov.jm/special_sections/reparations/index.htm (accessed 10 February 2011).
6 See, for example, Awagboe: The author argues that '(1) the broader scholarship on the slave trade, especially African-American intellectual history; (2) the present state and utilisation of available data on the slave trade; and (3) the need to clarify our theoretical formulations and find more powerful explanations for why we see the patterns in the slave trade that we do, and even why it emerged in the first place are areas that are under-researched.'
7 Nora Wittmann writes that slavery was contrary to international law in her thesis entitled 'The International Responsibility of Western/European States for Slavery and the Slave Trade'. This point has also been raised by the National Commission on Reparations, Jamaica.
8 The Abolition of the Slave Trade Act 1807 which was not effectively put to rest until 1811. See http://www.nationalarchives.gov.uk/pathways/blackhistory/rights/abolition.htm

9 Countries included in the abolition of the trade in Africans included Denmark in 1803; for some it took longer with regard to the USA and other European countries. Spain haggled with Britain over financial inducements at the former's request but there was no real change until the abolition of slavery itself. See Sherwood, Chapter 2 this volume.

10 The 1978 World Conference on Racism focused in the main on apartheid in South Africa. There was a similar conference in 1983 and then a relatively recent conference held in South Africa in 2001.

11 The full title of the conference was 'World Conference against Racism, Racial Discrimination, Xenophobia and Related Intolerance, Durban 2001'.

12 According to the United Nations 'the outcome document of the 2001 World Conference ... the (DDPA)'.

13 See the full list at <http://www.un.org/durbanreview2009/resolutions.shtml> (accessed 7 December 2010).

14 UN Resolution on the Bicentennial Commemoration of the Abolition of the Slave Trade: http://portal.unesco.org/culture/en/ev.php-URL_ID=32897&URL _DO=DO_TOPIC&URL_SECTION=201.html (accessed on 8 December 2010).

15 The National Commission on Reparations website is available at http://jis.gov.jm/ special_sections/reparations/index.htm (accessed on 8 December 2010).

16 Racism has been identified as 'a well developed ideology of race, which dominates the thinking of a sizeable number of extremists and affects a wider proportion of society' (Bowling and Phillips 2009). It is also 'a vocabulary with which to examine the social construction of 'race' as a cultural, historical and political phenomenon ... and to unearth the effects of racism on groups defined by reference to their "race"' (Bowling and Phillips 2009: 23).

17 The figures given are 37 times for Asians and 13 times for people from other ethnic minority communities.

18 It is likely that Scarman had in mind apartheid-era South Africa at the time.

19 Op. cit.

20 Lea, J. (2000) 'The MacPherson Report and its consequences', *The Howard Journal of Criminal Justice*, 29(8).

Bibliography

Bassiouni, C. and Van Boven, T. (2005) *The Basic Principles and Guidelines on the Right to a Remedy and Reparation for Victims of Gross Violations of International Human Rights Law and Serious Violations of International Humanitarian Law*. New York: United Nations. Available at: <http://www2.ohchr.org/english/law/remedy.htm> (accessed 10 December 2010).

Blackburn, R. (1997) *The Making of New World Slavery: From the Baroque to the Modern 1492–1800*. London: Verso.

Bowling, B. and Phillips, C. (2002) *Racism, Crime and Justice*. Essex: Longman.

Brophy, A.L. (2006) *Reparations: Pros and Cons*. Oxford: OUP.

Carmichael, S. and Hamilton, C.V. (1967) *Black Power: The Politics of Liberation*. New York: Vintage Books.

Corlett, J.A. (2003) *Race, Racism and Reparations*. Ithaca: Cornell University Press.

Dodd, V. (2010) *The Guardian*, 15 November.

Equality and Human Rights Commission *Race Equality Duty*. Available at <http://www.equalityhumanrights.com/advice-and-guidance/public-sector-duties/

what-are-the-public-sector-duties/race-equality-duty/> (accessed 13 December 2010).

Feagin, J. (2000) *Racist America: Roots, Current Realities and Future Reparations.* New York: Routledge.

Feagin, J.R. (2006) *A Theory of Oppression.* New York: Routledge.

Gibney, M. et al. (2008) *The Age of Apology.* Philadelphia: University of Pennsylvania Press.

Gifford, A. (2007) *The Passionate Advocate.* Kingston: Arawak.

Green D. (ed.) (2000) *Institutional Racism and the Police: Fact or Fiction.* London: Institute for the Study of Civil Society.

Horowitz, D. (2001) 'Ten Reasons Why Reparations for Blacks is a Bad Idea for Blacks and Racist Too', *Frontpagemag.com.* Available at <http://archive.frontpagemag.com/readArticle.aspx?ARTID=24317> (accessed 15 December 2010).

Long, C.P. (2007) *Long Overdue: The Politics of Racial Reparations.* New York: New York University Press.

King, M.L. (1963) '*I have a dream*', speech delivered in Washington, DC. Available at < http://www.civitas.org.uk/pdf/cs06.pdf> (accessed 11 December 2010).

Macpherson, W. (1999) *The Stephen Lawrence Inquiry.* London: CM4262-I.

Posner, E.A. and Vermeule, A. (2003) Reparations for Slavery and other Historical Injustices: *Columbia Law Review* 689 (2003).

Randall, V. (2006) *Race, Racism and the Law: Speaking Truth to Power: Institutional Racism.* Available at http://academic.udayton.edu/race/intro.htm (accessed 11 December 2010).

Scarman, L.G. (1981) *The Scarman Report.* London: The Home Office.

Shipani, A. (2009) *Hidden Kingdom of the Afro-Bolivians*, BBC World News. Available at <http://news.bbc.co.uk/1/hi/world/americas/7958783.stm> (accessed 14 December 2010).

Smith, S. (1994) *Racialised Barriers: The Black Experience in the United States and England in the 1980s.* New York: Routledge.

Thomas, H. (1997) *Slave Trade: History of the Atlantic Slave Trade 1440–1870.* Basingstoke: Picador.

Thompson, J. (2002) *Taking Responsibility for the Past: Reparations and Historical Injustice.* Cambridge: Polity.

Torpey, J. (ed.) (2003) *Politics and the Past: On Repairing Historical Injustices.* Lanham, MD: Rowman and Littlefield.

United Nations (2009) *The Durban Review Conference Information Note 4.* Available at <http://www.un.org/durbanreview2009/pdf/InfoNote_04_BasicFacts_En.pdf> (accessed 7 December 2010).

Williams, E. (1994) *Capitalism and Slavery.* London: University of California Press.

Williams, P. (1997) *Seeing a Color-Blind Future: The Paradox of Race.* New York: The Noonday Press.

Websites

Jamaican National Commission on Reparations, http://jis.gov.jm/special_sections/reparations/index.htm (accessed 8 December 2010).

Chapter 11

The value of experience

What post World War II settlements teach us about reparations

Clemens Nathan

I was deeply honoured to have been invited to such a distinguished academic conference. Let me at the outset say that I have been on the Board of Human Rights organisations for over thirty years, dealing with the making of policy decisions. I am not a professor, researcher or academic as many of the people there were. They had played an important role in drafting legislation at a national and international level. My function, on the other hand, has been to see what can be done to try and implement much of that work and to create new legislation through lawyers where necessary.

My contribution to the conference was on a limited and clearly-defined scale, focusing as it did on practical experiences in a narrow field – the Holocaust survivors, albeit that they encompassed over 600,000 refugees in 1945 who remained alive throughout a web of complex social and welfare agreements in 36 countries. The lessons we have learned from our experiences over this uninterrupted period of sixty years, we hope will benefit those people dealing with genocides elsewhere.

I would remind the reader that six million Jews, amongst many other people, were murdered in the vast extermination policies organised by the Third Reich all over Europe in the concentration camps and elsewhere. Among these were 1.5 million Jewish children who were gassed and burnt in the most ruthless and efficient way. I will briefly highlight later a conference we recently held for genocide victims, together with the Claims Conference which deals with Holocaust survivors only, at the International Criminal Court Peace Palace in The Hague. Additionally, the Clemens Nathan Research Centre held a conference this year in Chester at the International Society for Prosthetics Annual Meeting, in order to see what can be done for victims today to quickly obtain and manage artificial limbs and plastic surgery for those brutally maimed in national warfare, primarily on the African Continent.

To begin with, I have tried to distil eight general questions from our experiences since 1945 which still concern me personally and for which I am not sure there are any straightforward solutions:

1   Can compensation really be meaningful? What are the main practicalities versus the idealism which many of us have for this?

2   Is it not extremely dangerous to raise the emotional high hopes of survivors which can never be fulfilled? Modest lifetime pensions are a limited measure of justice.

3   Should we consider compensation for descendants of survivors for personal suffering or injury?

4   Where do we draw the lines between relief, welfare and compensation? If one looks at the major concentration camps all over the world which were liberated after the Second World War, thousands of people died in the first few days in each one because of the inappropriate food supplied or because there was no food at all. How should this be dealt with? Are funds from relief organisations really sufficient and sufficiently well-organised?

5   How can a political priority be given nationally and internationally to fund reparations between states for economic damages and property restitution, and compensation for the individual for personal suffering or injury? And how does one promote this concept to different countries? Is it not a low priority when compared, for example, with climate change or armaments for most countries? Is it possible to change attitudes and therefore ultimately governments in democratic states to help with this on a large scale in addition to the various UN Resolutions already in place which have also been accepted into their domestic law? All NGOs, such as Human Rights Watch, need to continue to promote this internationally and nationally.

6   What is the impact of an invasion on liberalising a genocidal regime? How can it become accountable and responsible, if this is possible at all, in dealing with victims? And can this be done on an international basis?

7   Who should be responsible for transferring victims to new countries where they can settle peacefully with the support of other people who are already there, perhaps of the same ethnic or religious background? The High Commissioner for Human Rights and The International Organisation for Migration play an important role here but for some reason are not yet acknowledged by everyone as an integral part of a liberating force. Stateless refugees remain a problem.

8   Legal agreements can only function if they can be implemented. To what extent have we failed to implement our legal skills in those countries where genocide takes place and is there any way in which the world community can strengthen its possibilities? Economic sanctions do not seem to work and often make life worse for the victims. War is usually a catastrophe. What else can be done to stop brutal, cruel fanatics from destroying the lives of innocent people or maiming them? The UN protocols on the prevention and punishment of the crimes of genocide and definitions have not stopped them.

I had the privilege of working for a short while with the late René Cassin. His work was the foundation for many remarkable attempts to try and stop what had happened to the survivors of the First and Second World Wars. He firstly became well known after the First World War for his major contribution in insisting that war widows in France should receive compensation. This had not even been considered by the French government. He succeeded in this endeavour. During the Second World War, Cassin joined General de Gaulle in London where he was his legal adviser. When the war ended and he saw how horrific the suffering had been in Europe he felt very deeply that something needed to be done to avoid this happening again in the future.

Cassin was chairman of the Human Rights Commission of the United Nations in 1946. As such he was able to push through the Declaration of Human Rights. Forty-eight member states were in favour of it: there were eight abstentions in all and no-one disagreed. There was opposition at first and the Declaration had to be fine-tuned to meet the wishes of the majority of the United Nations. Most international declarations, covenants and acts are only workable by compromise and this often weakens their value. While it was only a declaration, it has remained as a useful benchmark to highlight what must not be done towards our fellow human beings. Much of the Declaration has been expanded into covenants and human rights Acts as well as into the work of the UN Human Rights Commission and recently the work of the International Criminal Court in different parts of the world. However, the right to remedy and reparation for the victims of gross violations of international human rights law and serious violations of international humanitarian law was only established as a principle in October 2005. It seems to me an absolute scandal that it has taken so long for this recommendation to be able to come to the Third Committee of the UN on its 60th Session for approval. This Declaration is slightly ambiguous but at least it is an attempt to underpin what many have been fighting for generations. Cassin would have been horrified if he had known just how long this would take to be adopted by the UN and especially so as he was a French Jew.

If the world Jewish community had not, for example, taken it into its own hands to care for those victims left alive in the camps after the Holocaust, they would have continued to rot in the stench-infested displaced persons camps and would have found no safe haven elsewhere to survive, grow and develop.

So how did the Jewish community manage alone, without the help of the UN, to achieve negotiations? Property restitution was a concept which the Western Allies had already agreed to in 1947. This assisted later arguments by the World Jewish community, especially through the four major international Jewish organisations based in the United States. The military government of the Soviet Union was, however, never interested in this or in any other concept of the need for help. You will perhaps recall that until 1949 there was a vacuum in the former Third Reich which was then controlled by the four Allied powers. The Western Allies supported the concepts which the Jewish community presented to them based on their own views of the previous agreements. The Jewish community then set up a Conference on Jewish Material Claims Against Germany, with the leading personality of that time, Nahum Goldman, who had been educated at Heidelberg. He understood Konrad Adenaeur who had befriended him when he was Mayor of Cologne and before he became Chancellor of the Federal Republic of Germany. They both agreed that the new Germany could never be accepted by other nations as an equal partner unless it did something to atone for the monstrous, horrific bestialities deliberately perpetrated by the Third Reich. Adenaeur was a deeply sincere Catholic who felt strongly that this had to be dealt with from a moral point of view first and foremost, but he was also mindful of course of the agreement of the Western Allies with whom he had to negotiate on many other matters.

He persuaded the newly-formed Federal Republic of Germany that there was an obligation and it must be dealt with. The voluntary agreements for compensation of the three parties in Luxemburg that culminated from these discussions in 1952 between the Claims Conference and the Federal Republic of Germany, and the newly-formed state of Israel in 1948, were a remarkable achievement. We should remember that none of the countries or the Claims Conference, who were all gathered round the table, had existed during the Third Reich period.

The legislation which was enacted covers many volumes. The complex agreements were divided into two groups – those concerned with the state of Israel that had been newly-created by the UN and those that were outside Israel. The two Protocols alone for those outside Israel covered 20 pages and were made together with the Claims Conference to help with the reconstruction of the Jewish community which had been almost entirely destroyed. The agreements with the state of Israel were more complex. Funds were given over a twelve-year period for infrastructure building and goods, with all of this to come from Germany, and to help Israel absorb the refugees from the policies of the Third Reich. Israel's plea for this in 1951 was ignored by the Soviet Union and only the Americans, the UK and France supported it once again. Since then there have been additional agreements with the FRG, plus further ones after the ultimate collapse of the German Democratic Republic. These highly complex individual agreements cover healthcare, compensation for slave workers, and compensation for a loss of assets including art, insurance and many other items which gradually evolved from the initial agreements. These were later extended to Austria, with endless problems until the Austrians accepted their own responsibility for the Holocaust. As the reader will know, many Austrians claimed for a long time that they had been occupied like other countries in

Europe and therefore had no responsibilities. They slowly accepted the reality that they had been 'raped with love' and this was finally understood. Several of their more outstanding politicians were also able to persuade others to pay compensation.

I cannot possibly highlight all of the work which covered these difficult and complex negotiations but four of the principal categories might give the reader some idea.

Firstly, there were the international bilateral treaties and agreements. Subsequently, there were specially-funded German programmes for people who had suffered by living in the West. Later on an agreement was signed which dealt with the former German Democratic Republic after its collapse. This was a remarkable step, one that was supported by the Federal Republic of Germany. There were also various pacts with the Austrian government as well as with other countries and the Claims Conference.

Secondly, there were multilateral agreements between governments, industry and various parties representing victims and heirs. Among these governments were the German, Polish and Russian as well as those from other parts of Europe. 'The German Foundation' was created in 2000 to compensate former slave and forced labourers, not only from Germany but also from all parts of Europe that had been occupied by the Third Reich on a 50/50 basis between industry and government. Both parties had been responsible for collecting and using these labourers, many of whom had come from Eastern Europe.

Thirdly, there were the 1998 Collective Bank Settlements with Switzerland. These were extremely complex agreements which have now been settled.

The fourth category covered specialist parties dealing with insurance and similar matters. Many victims had life insurances in different European countries and it was felt strongly that the insurance companies needed to honour their liabilities for both the insured and their descendants, mostly the children and grandchildren of those exterminated. The five major insurance companies of Europe were deeply involved with these agreements.

Attitude to settlements

Perceptions of what was being created with the Federal Republic of Germany were slightly different for both parties. The Germans liked to call the payment to Holocaust survivors '*Wiedergutmachung*', which can be translated as 'to make whole', but the Claims Conference could never accept this wording. No matter how much money was given, it could only be symbolic in its attempt to compensate those victims left alive and for heirless property. No human being can ever receive compensation that has been based on their suffering. All the money given is only a *token* towards the nightmares experienced by those people who suffered.

Complexity of settlements

The complex work of the Claims Conference since its inception is difficult to visualise. Over its many years, $60 billion has ultimately been paid out for personal injury and suffering and personal pensions for all requests received by 1969 when these agreements were closed. Payments for individuals who had lived, or were living, in the German Democratic Republic, were negotiated after its collapse. These included property belonging to Jewish families which was then restituted or, where heirless, was given to the Claims Conference for its welfare and educational work worldwide – this has amounted to approximately $1.8 billion dollars so far but negotiations are still continuing. To illustrate the difficulty, in order to find out where properties existed which belonged to Jews who had been exterminated, 60 surveyors in the former GDR had to work for several years looking through documents. Court cases then had to be made for each individual property to certify that it had belonged to members of the Jewish community. Only after that did the German government accept that this should go to the Claims Conference if the properties had not been claimed by the descendants of the people who had originally owned them. Numerous descendants were found in almost 40 countries. The endless court cases and lawyers appointed to work with these problems alone belie imagination. Through the German indemnification laws, 278,000 survivors in total have received lifetime pensions and tens of thousands of survivors still receive their pensions. Hundreds of thousands also received one-off payments under the various German compensation laws.

In the 1970s, after the Helsinki Agreements, the Soviets finally allowed Jews to emigrate. Among these were some who had been in concentration camps in the USSR, or had gone eastwards at the end of the war. The Federal Republic finally agreed in 1980 to create a new Hardship Fund for these refugees but on this occasion the funds were to be administered as one-time payments by the Claims Conference for the first time. Until then the Conference had only acted as facilitators and negotiators. It started with 25,000. Today, 74,000 have been paid and an additional 6,000 will probably receive pensions by the end of the year. The Nazis also persecuted people in North Africa as well. There are still ongoing discussions about these.

The former Slave and Forced Labour Funds Compensation Agreements included many people who were not Jewish. The amounts they received were extremely small but nevertheless appreciated as an acknowledgement of their suffering. The German Government Foundation was specially created for some of the forced and slave labourers. The reader may not know that the difference between a slave worker and a forced labourer was that a slave worker was to be worked to death within six months whereas a forced labourer was able to continue working wherever they had been sent during the period of the Third Reich. Forced labourers came from all the various occupied countries. The Agreements covered not only Jews but also slave workers like the Roma and Sinti.

Processing of claims

I could go on at length about many of the other compensation funds but the reader would perhaps be interested to hear something about the complexity of running these funds. Highly sophisticated data-processing equipment exists for this. Conversations with victims are monitored. They will often enquire if they are entitled to claim in one way or another. All of this information is then fed into computers and quite often relatives, for the first time since the war, will suddenly appear in other countries and movingly the Claims Conference can help link these people together again who have hitherto been lost to one another. Claims have to be co-ordinated with all their potential recipients, especially for property. There are many groups of young people who carry out this wonderful work in the United States, Israel and Germany, helping to telephone victims in their different languages. This can be very complicated. Many of the victims will speak unclearly and sometimes, for example, how the name of a concentration camp is spelt can be done in completely different ways. The word 'Auschwitz', amazingly enough, has been spelt in 700 different ways. Today the computer can recognise these and the different spellings will be dealt with automatically. The database of victims is also extremely valuable and the analysis of this has helped enormously in negotiating new claims for many. In addition it helps the German and Austrian Governments to analyse what they need to do. The New York computers recently processed over one year 280,000 claims in eight languages. An average of 8,500 telephone calls, 1,200 letters and 1,000 e-mails from survivors and families were sent and received every week for a year. The Claims Conference also has 500 Holocaust-related archives today, scattered in 29 countries around the world, which needed to be documented for settlements.

All the German funds created had to be negotiated in great detail to show the specific requirements for victims to be eligible. The criteria for these settlements were often narrow and restrictive, but the Claims Conference was not in a position to deviate from the agreements made with Germany or other countries. They desperately needed to agree to settle claims whilst beneficiaries were still alive, even if these were not ideal. In some cases, the

Germans have changed agreements after many years of negotiation in order to make them fairer. For example, a person had to have been in a concentration camp for six months minimum in order to be eligible for compensation for being in a camp. However, the majority of people in this situation were dead after six months. Indeed it was a miracle that any of them survived. Other funds were later created for those in ghettos and for several other categories of suffering.

I think the reader can see from my description how important it is to have a government or a public agency that is able to create and organise settlements for genocides.

How has the Claims Conference coped with all these complex problems for all the different funds? Four key areas would probably give a simplified explanation:

1   They had to identify those survivors who could be eligible.
2   They had to mail applications to those who have received previous compensation and who might be eligible for additional funds in respect of, for example, slave labour.
3   Using massive international media advertising campaigns, they drew attention to when a new fund was available.
4   A total of 350 social service agencies, as well as survivor organisations around the world, assisted claimants with these complicated applications. To illustrate this task, in Israel alone, Homes for the Elderly were asked to inform their residents of nine help-lines that had been established for survivors wishing to contact the Slave Workers Fund. Over 50 per cent of all survivors lived in their homes.

Every new application is digitally scanned with linkages to with offices in New York, Tel Aviv, Frankfurt and Budapest. The database permits unlimited information input, storage and retrieval whilst allowing staff to trace the progress of claims. These are further electronically sorted and analysed to identify and group them for streamlining procedures. This sophisticated computerisation system has been the key to this most pressing and imperative challenge faced by the Claims Conference. All this computerisation has revealed much of the history of persecution which was previously unknown. It has led not only to the restitution of a little money for each victim but also to the restitution of history.

Importance of historical information

In the case of medical experiments on women, there were 195 procedures in the 32 different camps dealing with medical experiments. It was only after painful efforts by elderly survivors reluctantly submitting applications that this was really known about. Nothing can express the torments endured by these victims when, in filling in these forms, they were reminded of their previous horrific experiences. The experiments that were performed were beyond human imagination and their victims then had to endure the most terrible traumas once again. This was one of the many complex conflicts dealt with by the Claims Conference.

Other settlements

There are many other claims which needed to be sorted out, such as those concerning the Hungarians. In their case, bank settlements, insurance settlements and complex gold compensation – like the agreement for the misappropriation by the Americans of assets belonging to the Hungarian Jewish community at the end of the war which was settled by $25 million which had to be paid out to Hungarian Jews. There was also an agreement with Hungary about looted art treasures. The Hungarian government has not been easy to deal with but today it has formed joint committees with the international community. It has had to deal with the problems of private and communal property and heirless property, all of which was stolen, as well as the loss of life and political persecution. They have still not allowed public access to the database which was developed regarding looted artworks. Neither have they allowed a national policy for state-operated museums and art institutions in their country to be required to provenance research on their holdings, many of which were stolen from Jewish families. In addition they have still not retrieved from Russia, or negotiated with Russia, to bring back cultural objects to Hungary. These are just a few examples of the highly complex and separate negotiations which are still ongoing in countries like Bulgaria, Poland and Romania.

Implications of the work of the claims conference elsewhere

In March last year we held a conference at the International Criminal Court in the Peace Palace in The Hague, with over 80 genocide victims organisations from different countries participating. The objective of this conference was to highlight what had been done by the Claims Conference and how their experiences could be of benefit to victims elsewhere. It was a deeply moving experience and many of the genocide-victims' countries' leaders were encouraged that people outside their territories cared deeply about their problems. It was very moving for us to see that some of our experiences could be applied elsewhere. I could go into many details about this conference but what it highlighted above all was the urgent need to create a database in each area of conflict, which could be used later for negotiations. In addition each country should decide on suitable neighbours or trading partners who could be induced to help and support them. It was also essential to avoid any form of corruption. To highlight this, the Executive Director of the Trust Fund for Victims at the Criminal Court stressed how in some villages he had organised a donation of chickens, with the condition that each year the newly-hatched chicks should be moved to another area when the original villages had sufficient numbers for themselves. They also had an incentive scheme in parts of Africa where people could build new roads which had been destroyed. In exchange for their efforts they would be given seed for growing crops. This is an experiment which may or may not work but it is now starting to take place. The director of the trust fund came with me to New York where together we studied the databases we have at the Claims Conference, with the objective of transposing some of these ideas to help the victims of gross violations of human rights. We also held meetings with the lawyers who dealt with the Swiss bank settlements and the director was given all the documentation we had previously created for victims. These are very complex documents which, in turn, must fit into the data processing. Finally, we were able to introduce him to several major charitable foundations in America who we hoped would finance some of the work which has yet to be done for genocide victims.

The conference we held recently in Chester was created as we saw an urgent initial need for new limbs and plastic surgery for victims of the most horrific bestiality in countries such as Sierra Leone and North Uganda. Some of the trusts were very helpful to the director of the trust fund in backing the ideas of the Criminal Court to obtain voluntary young surgeons (about 30 for North Uganda) and plastic surgeons to operate with funding from these foundations. This work is now in progress. The main problem is not only creating new limbs for victims but also ensuring that their families and communities know how to care for them, including after-care. There are already some very good schools in Tanzania and Iraq, amongst others, dealing with this but an enormous amount of work still needs to be done towards establishing training centres throughout geno-cidal areas of the world to make sure that there is support for these victims who have lost a limb, a nose or an ear. I hope that much more will emanate from our work. Huge amounts of funding are needed. We were impressed by the work already undertaken by the International Red Cross in developing new polypropylene artificial limbs and seeing to the pressing needs of all of these victims for a very long time. They have enormous experience.

It is a tragedy that despite the Declaration of Human Rights (which this month celebrates its sixtieth year in existence) in many countries we still have an enormous deprivation in rights for so many people, let alone the horrific victims of whom we have spoken. This year especially it would perhaps be better not to celebrate this birthday. The world community has failed to implement the genocide conventions and the punishments for crimes of genocide have not worked since the conventions of 1949 in a way which will reduce the horrors appearing all over the place. Leaders of certain countries flagrantly disregard any of the legal agreements they have entered into with the United Nations or other parties. All nations are responsible for trying to stop the initiation of genocides and where these do occur they also remain responsible for stopping them.

Chapter 12

An interview with Clemens Nathan

Chris Burnett

Do you think that the pursuance of reparations for the legacy of the transatlantic slave trade is a fruitful idea?

It all depends on how the reparations are going to be formed. I'm not so sure about paying reparations to individuals generations after something has happened. There must be a statute of limitations to every form of human activity – but this limit is in relation to the extent of what was done before. To blame later generations for what happened in the past could be interpreted as an intrusion into their human rights, although some would argue that the sins of the father are the sins of the son. However this is surely not about persecuting individuals, it is about those who exploited another group – which was legal at the time. Reparations were never paid to the victims of the slave trade or their descendants, and some Europeans and Americans subsequently benefited from this.

There were many people involved in the slave trade. In parts of Africa indigenous Africans collected individuals and sold them into slavery. Although there were already slaves in West Africa, they were more like servants and were mostly not exposed to the appalling brutality seen elsewhere.

The organisations involved in the shipping of human cargo across the Atlantic (the middle passage) should also be held responsible in one way or another. I am ashamed to say that some of those involved in the shipping process were also Jews, but we all must recognise our own people's involvement in this atrocity if we are to move forwards.

In my experience of reparations, the greatest comfort is to give people respect and dignity. By that I have in mind museums in particular – we have a series of Holocaust museums, in Washington, at the Imperial War Museum, Yad Vashem – and these give dignity and also document what happened in an objective way without making anyone a hero or a martyr. Although I would acknowledge that it is not for me to decide, I believe that this sort of approach could be one way forward to make reparations for the slave trade. There could be museums created in Europe and America showing what happened, documenting and demonstrating the horrors that slaves experienced. There could also be educational courses alongside these museums explaining, for example, how some of the early African-Americans fought against the net of slavery, how the Declaration of Independence was partly unbalanced as it did not include women and African-Americans at that time, etc. This could also be encompassed in an educational system, giving the descendants of the slave trade the dignity they are entitled to, while at the same time also giving all children education on this important subject.

This might have the added benefit of teaching and following the remarkable success stories of these ancestors given their debilitating history, as well as documenting the extreme hardships that the African-Americans continued to experience after the slave trade had supposedly been abolished. If this was done with a budget from the US, European and Middle Eastern governments, I think it would be a major contribution to reparations. Ken Livingstone, the former Mayor of London, initiated an annual Black History Month each October here in the UK which I think was an excellent idea in order to acknowledge both Black people's contribution to the Western world and also their history prior to the slave trade. I've seen the consequences of educational programmes with victims of the Holocaust – the emotional path that people have gone through at Yad Vashem, at Auschwitz, Bergen and Belsen – and for some of them at least this is much more important than money. I think that's one way I would highlight this challenge.

Is it possible to restore history such that it is understood by all without there being a recognition of the disproportionate financial gains made by one side over the other?

The history of history has often shown how biased this can be. How would you go about allocating who would get money and who should not? And who is really responsible today? In my experience with reparations, someone will always feel the allocation of funds is unfair. I think all new and old social organisations set up to help the impoverished should play an active part there. Racism is of course a serious matter affecting this and this needs to be tackled, not only for itself but also for the well-being of all.

If you give grants to museums, educational institutions and to more general welfare structures, to help, I consider it essential for affluent African-Americans to be partners who are involved in allocating and giving. From my experience, the Jewish community worldwide has given enormous sums of money to help refugees from the concentration camps and elsewhere. Only later did they receive, to a certain extent, from the Claims Conference, money from Germany – but the real support was that the world's Jewish community mobilised people to provide aid in fundraising, practical help, and in educational training, for those who had lived their formative lives in the camps or were refugees – and they continue fundraising and helping to this day.

At the Claims Conference Headquarters in New York even now we have 8,000 phone calls a week coming in, from people who may or may not get pensions, or have other problems, all of which we monitor in New York. Many of them are therapeutic calls for help – these people just want to know they can talk to someone. In some cases they have not received what they were due to receive.

We have also found that the work of reparations in the Claims Conference, in spite of all we have negotiated for the victims and the victims' families, causes conflicts to arise – why did we give money to A and not to B, and why is the other person getting more? So you say, well look, one lives in Florida, and another victim lives in Belarus or Moldova and is dying of hunger, has no heating in the winter, and they get food parcels, a soup kitchen and a small pension from us which keeps them warm.

The person in Florida might have worked most of his adult life in America, he may have welfare from America and a personal pension scheme, and so on. Is it fair to give them as much money as the person who has never had these opportunities? You can see how complex these debates quickly become. With the slave trade, you are going back generations and dealing with global migrations. These complications mean endless committees, endless discussions, and not much financial help for many more people. This is why I believe that education and memorials, to restore dignity, together with an international exchange of information, could be more constructive and meaningful.

Since the demise of the British Empire, many countries have involved themselves in international development, seeing the provision of aid to African nations as part of their foreign policy. As with anything, whilst there are mixed motives involved in this, it is not the case that nothing has been done in the intervening years to assist those nations which suffered from the slave trade. For example, the European Development Fund (EDF) develops a programme every six years and the 2008–2013 fund has a budget of £22.7 billion; British aid to Africa under Tony Blair's premiership was also tripled to £1 billion in 2006. Again, as I have repeatedly said, money can never make reparations, but equally, such activity cannot be discounted when considering this issue.

What sort of obstacles do you envisage such a claim might meet?

The principal obstacle would be how to get governments to agree. This includes the US government as well as those in European and Middle Eastern countries – will all of these establish museums which show the dignity of the people who suffered? Will all of these correctly investigate and document a balanced history of what actually happened, so that everyone around the globe can see the role of their ancestors not personally but collectively – Americans, Europeans, those from the Middle East, and of course Africans. Everyone must be involved in this.

Agreements by non-governmental organisations who were responsible to acknowledge this might also be difficult to achieve – for example, the various churches; these are known to have played a part. Were they introduced in order to pacify the slaves and remove their native identity? The churches involved may argue that their religion gave hope to many slaves – most Africans were obliged to adopt Christianity, despite their attitudes during the slave trade. Many individual ministers of religion, however, may have worked in all sincerity, but others perhaps did not? The hope delivered through Christianity was something which the slaves clung to, giving them the hope of a better life.

Should such claims be pursued legally, diplomatically or both?

Such claims, if they are to be meaningful, should be done diplomatically – otherwise it is a reinforcement of one side over another and will create more conflicts. In the Claims Conference we have tried to do everything diplomatically, persuading the Germans or the Austrians to pay reparations. This took a lot of pressure, but once the agreements had been settled then of course they had to be legally underwritten. Nevertheless, the wish to settle, the wish for something to be done, must be done voluntarily. If it's not done voluntarily it will never leave the courthouse. There will be teams of lawyers who will find loopholes and they will make a fortune out of these loopholes. In the Claims Conference we found that there were lawyers who made a great deal of money by representing individual claims for people and by taking 50 per cent of whatever they received. In some cases it is quite shocking how people will happily profit from anything more than the reasonable expenses incurred. So I would say diplomacy first, underpinned by the law.

After the Second World War the Federal Chancellor, Konrad Adenauer, was probably aware that he had to do something morally. However, politically he knew that the United States, which was occupying one part of Germany, had insisted on some form of reparations from the very beginning.
Therefore Adenauer was very conscious that to remain on good terms with America, which was very powerful and important, he had to do something morally and politically which was acceptable to the Americans. By and large the British, French and Russians were not interested in reparations.

Returning to the slave trade – I think one possibility might be to have another conference in which the subject of the slave trade was discussed again. You would have to hear from all sides, so there could be an open exchange. That was the remarkable achievement of Bishop Tutu in South Africa with the concept of the Truth Commission there, which some people believe has worked.

If we take the example of the Nuremburg and Adolf Eichmann trials, we can see their significance today more clearly. It was not just about punishing Eichmann – it also opened up the history of this period. Throughout these trials, hundreds of people had to submit documents to show what had happened. No-one knew how the Nazis had planned to exterminate every Jew in Europe. No-one knew how the transport had been organised and all the other activities that came with it. That was crucial in our work later on in the Claims Conference. We were able to look at the statistics and then negotiate with Germany for restitution. Accountability here was a key concept in all the talk about reparations.

What is sufficient reparation? Can reparations ever be sufficient?

If you take the example of the thalidomide babies, how do you compensate for the fact that a person does not have full use of their arms and legs at birth? You simply cannot. In a court of law you would probably give the person enough money to live without working – but that was unthinkable with Germany and Austria, because there wasn't that sort of money available for 600,000 people. So reparations could only be a token amount, to show that you respected the person's needs and perhaps a modest compensation for injuries.

It is difficult for me to draw parallels between the Holocaust and the slave trade in order to relate to both of them. The crimes are not comparable. There are differences in the numbers of deaths, the period over which they occurred, the intention and result of the atrocity, etc. The Claims Conference may help us think about the debate over reparations to descendants of the slave trade but there are no simple equations or calculations to be made for both of these together.

However, in all cases it is important to remember that it's always material reparations, never spiritual. You can never give back something spiritual. You can give people dignity and reduce their trauma by increasing education and recognising their suffering. Recognition is the most important thing rather than money, although in some cases financial assistance to reduce poverty does help.

Chapter 13

Reparations for slavery and the transatlantic slave trade

The case for special measures

Marcus Goffe

Introduction

By declaring slavery a crime against humanity, the World Conference Against Racism (WCAR) made it patently clear in 2001 that, contrary to the sentiment in some quarters, the move for reparations for slavery is not only an African and African-descendant struggle, but also a world struggle. It is not just another historical wrong – it is one of if not the most horrific, shameful, widespread and enduring wrongs of recorded global history and a continuing contemporary wrong, with its effects and manifestations still existing to this day.

The pattern of European slavery and the colonisation of Africans was very similar to that of American indigenous peoples around the world who were subject to the dispossession of traditional lands and genocide. However, in degree and length of time, slavery and the trade in Africans were unprecedented and have never again been replicated. Whereas there were over 20 million indigenous people subject to genocide, in contrast to the more than 15 million Africans who were shipped to the New World, it must be borne in mind that in addition to that 15 million,over 30 million Africans were displaced, while over 5 million Africans died in captivity on land and sea (Beckles 2008).[1] This was over the space of four hundred years, much longer than the European extraction of forced labour from indigenous peoples which preceded it. The transatlantic slave trade in Africans has thus been labelled as the 'largest forced movement of humans in history' (Beckles 2008).

Over those four hundred years, it wreaked untold mental, spiritual, social, psychological and economic trauma on the Africans and Africa, while yielding unprecedented profits for Western European countries, economies and societies. What further distinguishes this 'New World' chattel slavery of Africans from other previous forms of slavery was that, unlike any previous form of slavery, it denied human status to the enslaved. Africans were considered sub-human property, not just by individual members of society but also by society as a whole, including governments and the Christian churches. As Beckles (2008) describes it, it was a 'unique project invented for a specific race'.

However, the argument that is oft repeated and relied upon is that slavery, while illegal now, was not illegal at the time it was committed against Africans from the fifteenth to the nineteenth centuries. This argument has been used at the national and international levels of debate. Some have argued for a moral but not a legal obligation to repair the damage wrought. Some would also argue that an apology is good enough. Still others are of the view that more must be done financially and otherwise to even begin to make meaningful reparations.

This chapter analyses the strengths and weaknesses of the current debates and attempted litigation experiences and argues that chattel slavery of this sort and on the scale conducted by the major European nations states over four centuries was not legal at the time, despite it not being expressly illegal according to the West European Westphalian conceptualisation of international law. However, even if it was not illegal, that does not remove the obligation to repair. Just as international and national laws have had to respond to repair the injustice and damage done to indigenous peoples around the world, in similar circumstances where what was done was obviously immoral but not expressly illegal at the time, so too must international and national laws respond to create the mechanisms and strategies that will repair the injustice and damage done to Africans and the descendants of Africans as a result of slavery and the transatlantic slave trade.

Existing legal obstacles nationally and internationally

At the national level it has been found in litigation in the United States, for example, that slavery does not give rise to any legally actionable claim against the state for reparations. In one of the earliest and thus landmark cases in the United States, *Cato v United States*, the plaintiffs sued the state for one hundred million dollars for the kidnapping of ancestors from Africa, their forced ancestral indoctrination into a foreign society, forced labour, destruction of families and traditional values, deprivation of liberty, imposition of oppression, discrimination, intimidation, mis-education and lack of information about various aspects of their indigenous character (du Plessis 2007: 303).

Both the trial and appellate courts dismissed the claim on the cumulative grounds that the plaintiffs lacked *locus standii* in that they also lacked a tangible, personal injury that was traceable to the defendant's conduct (causation), and that the US government had sovereign immunity from such claims (this was in the specific context of the US Federal system). The Appellate Court's advice to the plaintiffs was that the appropriate forum for such complaints would be the legislature, as such claims were non-justiciable by the judiciary (du Plessis 2007: 303).

Litigation has also been used to make reparations claims against private companies and the various entities that profited from slavery. Again, these have been most prominent in the United States. These included a federal class-action lawsuit filed on Tuesday 18 March 2002 by a group of US lawyers in New York on behalf of all African-American descendants of slaves, seeking compensation from FleetBoston, Aetna, and CSX for the profits earned through slave labour and the slave trade (Ogletree 2002). Often statutes of limitations and a lack of evidence of personal injury will prevent the success of actions grounded in tort.

At the international level, the Chorzow factory (Jurisdiction Case) affirmed that a breach of international obligation triggers a state obligation to make reparation in an adequate form. According to the 2005 United Nations' Basic Principles and Guidelines on the Right to a Remedy and Reparation for Victims of Gross Violations of International Human Rights Law and Serious Violations of International Humanitarian Law, 'statutes of limitations shall not apply to gross violations of international human rights law and serious violations of international humanitarian law which constitute crimes under international law'. Such arguments of non-retroactivity and statute of limitations have been equally made and countered in respect of indigenous peoples (Francioni 2008: 42).

However it has also been said that '[a]ny attempt to pin responsibility on today's governments for the slavery committed by their predecessors runs into obvious difficulties involving complex questions of State succession, continuity and identity' (du Plessis 2007: 152). Additionally, only actions that are directly attributable to a state via its organs of government, or those who have acted under the direction, instigation or control of those organs, are subject to state responsibility (du Plessis 2007: 152).

At an international level, however, the greatest hurdle is the inter-temporal rule by which acts which are to be judged as potential wrongs, the subject of state responsibility to repair, must be judged within the context of the international law as it existed at the time of the act or acts. Similarly in national laws, whether for tort (common law) or akin civil law concepts of non-criminal wrongs, the retroactivity of a law unless expressly enacted to be so by the legislature, is not permissible.

Arguments agaomse inter-temporal law

Slavery was never lawful. Western European law does not equal international law.

By this doctrine is meant that the legality of state action is to be judged by the norms of international law as they existed at the time of the state action. However, 'international law as we know it today is the development of the practice of the European Christian states' (Green and Dickason 1993: 4). It is their conceptualisation of international law which has been used to interpret the inter-temporal law.

The argument that slavery was not a crime at the time and that therefore it is not right to hold the 'Great Powers' accountable for reparations for slavery has been rightly criticised as 'legal fiction' and a 'remarkable disjunction between international law and justice in regard to slavery' (Pete and du Plessis 2007: 21), perpetrated by a 'legal vanishing trick' in which an obvious and unprecedented crime against humanity is 'banished from the realm of law and relegated to the field of morality, as if it were no more than an offence to our sensibilities, a sin perhaps, but not serious enough to deserve the label "crime"' (Pete and du Plessis 2007: 22).

The reason for this is not difficult to see, as it was the very same Great Powers who at the time largely defined the international law which they used to pillage and pilfer from weaker countries and peoples, and which they do not wish to see any substantial contemporary wealth diverted back to their many victims of the past and present in the developing world. Thus it has been said that the intertemporal law has been often used as a 'handmaiden for political interests' (Castellino and Allen 2003: 88): 'To hold that we must now judge the successors of the "great powers" in terms of their own mutually agreed rules of domination is ludicrous' (Irvine 1970: 24).

Pre-existence and validity of African (customary) law

It has been said that 'scholarship about African laws remains heavily influenced by a brand of deficiency in plurality-consciousness which denies the existence of law in social contexts' (Menski 2006: 380). This positivist bias has led many to claim erroneously that there was no proper law in traditional ancient Africa, in an attempt to deny a place to Africans at the global table. This was done by 'culture-blind European legal observers [who] ignored massive evidence of mainly oral African laws and brushed it aside as "culture"' (Menski 2006: 381). Despite being the first historically, 'Africa was the last of the inhabited continents to have its history included in the curricula of European and American universities' (Curtin 1998: 29). This was probably due to the racist premise that Africans are primitive, sub-human, uneducated, uncivilised and incapable of governance.

It is well documented that in pre-colonial Africa, European missionaries, adventurers and traders found systems of family law, land law, criminal law, tax law and compensatory justice (Okupa 1998: 1). Irrefutably, several African states were well established long before some of the European states claiming predominance. That this denial of the facts continues in the face of voluminous evidence to the contrary that was well known to Europeans, is an injustice that in and of itself is worthy of reparations. Therefore, such a wilful self-intoxication of the truth cannot operate in any just system of law as a defence to deny the immorality and illegality of slavery throughout the entire sordid period of its existence and the concomitant moral and legal liability to repair, restore and compensate.

By the process of slavery and colonisation especially, Europeans intended not only to deny, but also to exterminate the African traditions and customs and to supplant these with Eurocentric laws and ideals. This was the false justification for what was often termed a 'civilising mission' – namely, to civilise the African 'barbarians' on the 'dark' continent: 'Such undercurrents of racist thought have severely affected much of the international scholarship on African laws' (Menski 2006: 385).

In fact, the roots of much of the 'civilised' law today can be traced to the Greeks and subsequently the Romans. However, as part and parcel of the racist and white supremacist ideologies in the West which prevailed at the time, the source of that ancient knowledge – Egypt – is often not attributed. The recognised godfathers of jurisprudence, Plato and Aristotle, gained much of their knowledge and learning from Egyptians (Menski 2006: 386). Egypt has been called the most ancient civilisation of mankind, older than any other major civilisation of the old world, and successor only to the Ethiopians (Irvine 1970: 11–12).

'[T]here were no equivalents to full plantation-based chattel slavery among Amerindian or African cultures at the time of the Columbian contact' (Eltis 2000: 18). That dehumanising mode of slavery, that magnitude of human trafficking, and that cruel and inhuman treatment and torture of humans, was never lawful according to African law, was never seen as acceptable conduct and contact between nations, was never treated as such by the Great Powers between themselves, and was never imposed on any other race of people than the African race.

The slaving nations of Europe knew that slavery was immoral

Thus it was the influential and powerful few in the Western world, comprising philosophers, royals, the church, wealthy businessmen, merchants, bankers, etc., who propagated this racist ideology of white supremacy and non-white inferiority, in an attempt to justify to themselves that what they were doing in enslaving Africans and subjugating indigenous peoples was both moral and lawful. And it is their successors and descendants today who continue to hide behind such a racist diatribe while they cautiously issue legally crafted 'apologies' in an attempt to appease their guilty consciences. Thus it should be readily seen that international law was interpreted specifically to ensure the disempowerment and disenfranchisement of conquered, colonised peoples (Anghie 2005: 31).

As one writer puts it, in order to justify European expansionism while wrestling with how to apply European social and political concepts to territories and peoples new to them, 'a consensus' developed that New World peoples did not possess full sovereignty in relation to their persons or their territories (Green and Dickason 1993: 143). Thus developed the unjust laws and policies that would facilitate the enslavement and denial of basic natural and human rights to millions of humans: 'This challenged and even contradicted concepts in legal thinking that had been evolving since the twelfth century' (Green and Dickason 1993: 143). History clearly shows that 'the weight of canonical opinion, both before and after Columbus' voyages, upheld the rights of non-Christians to property and to their own governments' (Green and Dickason 1993: 144).

Contrary to the prevailing views human rights did exist at the time, even though these were not formally recognised by treaties, declarations and conventions as they are today. From as early as 1594, Fray Alonso de Espinosa declared that '[i]t is an acknowledged fact, both as regards divine and human right, that the wars waged by the Spaniards against the natives ... as well as against the Indians ... were unjust and without any reason to support them' (Green and Dickason 1993: 243).

Further arguments that the slaving nations of Europe knew that it was immoral and unjust to enslave humans can be seen in the fact that during the seventeenth and eighteenth centuries, periods of the greatest traffic in Africans, many of these European nations had moved away from subjecting their own citizens to overtly forced labour on the basis of personal liberty and freedom. Slavery had been abolished among the Christians of Western Europe in the twelfth century, three hundred years before Europe revived it with Africans (Irvine 1970: 61). This contrast and contradiction – a double standard – between Europe's social institutions and values at home, and the evil they wrought in their colonies, must have been apparent to the Europeans of the day: 'A theory however elegant and economical must be rejected or revised if it is untrue; likewise laws and institutions no matter how efficient and well-arranged must be reformed or abolished if they are unjust' (Rawls 1972: 3–4).

A comparison of the rights of indigenous peoples with the rights of Africans and Afro-descendants

One of the fundamental bases of acquisition of territory prior to the Peace of Westphalia was that territory could be lawfully applied by conquest, cessation, or settlement. Also fundamental to the international law system was the concept of *terra nullius*, whereby lands that were not occupied or inhabited by other Europeans were treated as nobody's land and thus liable to be 'discovered', occupied, claimed and appropriated by the invading European state.

This fictional and fundamentally unjust legal doctrine was used during the period of European expansionism to justify the enslavement, exploitation and decimation of indigenous peoples and the theft and rape of their lands and resources. This rationale for plundering indigenous peoples and their lands was used by all the European powers in the 'race for space' from the fifteenth to eighteenth centuries, which included Portugal, Spain, England, France, the Netherlands and Belgium among others. However, the doctrine has come to be severely criticised and rejected in more recent times, especially in relation to the rights of indigenous peoples.

The first recognised landmark common law court case to not only criticise but also overrule the *terra nullius* principle was the Australian case of *Mabo v Queensland* (No. 2) (1992) 175 CLR 1. The High Court of Australia held that aboriginal native title did exist in Australia and that the Murray islands, part of the Torres Strait Islands, were not *terra nullius* when they were settled by the colonists.

Specifically rejecting the 'fiction' of *terra nullius* in relation to indigenous peoples, Justice Brennan said that 'it is imperative in today's world that the common law should neither be nor be seen to be frozen in an age of racial discrimination'. 'Whatever the justification advanced in earlier days for refusing to recognise the rights and interests in land of the indigenous inhabitants of settled colonies, an unjust and discriminatory doctrine of that kind can no longer be accepted.' It is clear therefore that the law can be and has been interpreted, both at the national and international levels, to redress historical injustices and, in doing so, can overrule and/or avoid the application of archaic, fundamentally unjust principles, rules and laws. The *Mabo* decision has been followed in South Africa (2003),[2] Botswana (2006)[3] and Belize (2007).[4]

As Justice Brennan put it, a contemporary law ought not to apply legal rules, principles or doctrines which do not accord with 'our present knowledge and appreciation of the facts'. Therefore, even if it was ever believed that slavery was not immoral and unlawful, that principle or belief cannot be applicable today in light of our present knowledge and appreciation of the facts that slavery was one of if not the most morally reprehensible crimes of the last four hundred years. Just as the legal doctrine of *terra nullius* has been unjustly applied and used for centuries to deny land reparations claims by indigenous peoples, so too is the legal doctrine of inter-temporal law used to unjustly preclude any successful reparations claims against the Great Powers for slavery.

The similarity in historical injustice suffered by indigenous peoples and Africans is striking, including forced labour/slavery, the dispossession of lands and culture and cruel, inhuman and degrading treatment, and the denial of the fundamental right to life. But the rights that have been recognised and to a large extent restored to indigenous peoples, as well as the reparative remedies and special measures which have been required of states in respect of indigenous peoples as a means of reparations for historical injustices, are not the same or even similar in relation to Africans.

Ways and means have been found to achieve restorative and reparative justice while also not overturning the entire international legal system. The question then begs itself, why can't similar strategies be used to repair the historical injustices meted out to Africans and African-descendants today?[5]

'Special measures' for indigenous peoples under international law

The International Labour Convention No. 169 was one of the first designed to specially protect indigenous peoples. It recognised that indigenous peoples in many parts of the world 'are unable to enjoy their fundamental human rights to the same degree as the rest of the population of the States within which they live, and that their laws, values, customs and perspectives have often been eroded'. The Convention provided that 'due account shall be taken of the nature of the problems which face them both as groups and as individuals' and it imposed an obligation on states to 'establish means for the full development of these peoples' own institutions and initiatives, and in appropriate cases provide the resources necessary for this purpose'.

The United Nations Declaration on the Rights of Indigenous Peoples 2007 (UNDRIP) in its preamble affirms that 'all doctrines, policies and practices based on or advocating superiority of peoples or individuals on the basis of national origin or racial, religious, ethnic or cultural differences are racist, scientifically false, legally invalid, morally condemnable and socially unjust', and that 'indigenous peoples, in the exercise of their rights, should be free from discrimination of any kind'. Importantly for the purposes of this present analysis, the Declaration recognises that 'indigenous peoples have suffered from historic injustices as a result of, *inter alia*, their colonisation and dispossession of their lands, territories and resources, thus preventing them from exercising, in particular, their right to development in accordance with their own needs and interests'.

The Declaration also commits states to 'take effective measures, in consultation and cooperation with the indigenous peoples concerned, to combat prejudice and eliminate discrimination and to promote tolerance, understanding and good relations among indigenous peoples and all other segments of society'. It gives indigenous peoples the right to access financial and technical assistance from states, in co-operation with the entire United Nations system, in order to realise their rights. Nowhere are the rights of

Africans and African-descendants so delineated and protected. Neither is there any regime or forum established that is capable of providing substantial relief and redress to Africans and African-descendants for the atrocities of slavery, the slave trade and colonialism.

In *Cato v. the US* the court distinguished between Native Americans and African-Americans on the basis that the former had treaties with the US government (Fortson 2004: 117). However, this distinction is inapplicable in the current international context where special measures are not only applicable to indigenous peoples with treaty rights but also to all indigenous peoples. In fact, the Inter-American Court of Human Rights (IACtHR) has recognised the indigenous-like land rights of non-indigenous African-descendant Maroon communities in Suriname, on the basis of their ancestral relationship to their lands (Torres 2007: 128–137). In the context of descendant diasporic communities, this relationship to land will have to be negotiated, as done by the IACtHR and as stoutly advocated for by the Ras Tafari community.[6]

Also arguable here is that it is as a result of contemporary consequences of historical wrongs, including racial discrimination and a lack of equal opportunities, that indigenous rights have been asserted and affirmed. This criterion is also equally applicable to the African slavery context as, without a doubt, slavery and the slave trade continue to have deleterious effects on Africans and African-descendants today.

Causation and countinuing consequences

For several centuries prior to the fifteenth, the Western economies were less developed than most of the economies of the Near and Far East (Inikori 2002: 473). It is as a result of the transatlantic slave trade and slavery that many of the Western economies and societies flourished and developed at the expense of African economies and societies (Gowok 2007: 5–6). The wealth that the colonies comprising of African labour made for Western economies was largely responsible for the growth and development of those economies in the eighteenth century, which led to those economies today being considered 'developed' and most of the economies of the African and Caribbean ex-colonies considered 'developing' or 'least developed' countries.

The Industrial Revolution in England was the first example in the world of trade-led economic development which laid the way for economic developments of the seventeenth and eighteenth centuries (Williams 1944: 52; see also Rodney 1972: 95). That revolution was due mainly to the Atlantic trade (Inikori 2002: 156) and to the first successful case of import substitution industrialisation (ISI) in world history (Inikori 2002: 10).

The several colonising nations subjugated Africans as the most expedient labour supply to meet the demands of mining and agriculture (Davis 1975:

41). The competitive advantage in production was as a direct result of the coerced African labour rather than the free or waged non-African labour (Eltis 2000: 18). Therefore, 'there can be little doubt that the labour of Africans and their descendants was what made possible the growth of Atlantic commerce during the [Industrial Revolution]' (Inikori 2002: 486).

'From the sixteenth century onward, as a result of the slave trade, African society was subjected to a continual drain of its manpower, to the dissipation of its energies in internal conflicts, and to the disruption of normal commercial development' (Inikori 2002: 59). By imposing foreign laws and customs, most African states suffered severe problems in state building and organisation (Sandbrook and Barker 1985: 42). In addition, by creating artificial national boundaries in Africa, irrespective of cultural and linguistic affinities, this has caused a multiplicity of ethnic tensions which, as we have seen in Rwanda and elsewhere, have had great social, political and economic consequences upon generations of Africans.

The imposition of a capitalist market trading system in which the majority of Africans have been marginally included has left many African and Caribbean states unable to compete effectively with developed manufacturing countries. This is largely due to the fact that the Africans were for the most part still exploited after slavery for cheap labour, with most of the land, capital, and means of production still in the hands of foreign individuals or corporations (Inikori 2002: 54).

Although many African and Caribbean states were very productive as a result of African labour, the education and skills training of local Africans was not encouraged or planned in a large scale to foster self-sufficiency as a nation after colonialism (Inikori 2002: 53). The result has been continued dependence on debt finance from former colonial masters, a spiral which most ex-colonies still find themselves in today. This spiral is ongoing largely because most ex-colonies inherited the least diversified economies from the colonial era and still rely heavily on non-oil primary commodities for their export earnings (Mengisteab and Logan 1995: 5).

Racism and discrimination still continue against Africans at the international level and against Africans in the diaspora where they are minorities in their countries of residence: 'African diaspora communities, for the most part, are confronted with problems of marginalisation and exclusion in their respective countries ... [t]his also applies to those in the Caribbean in possession of state power who, like the African continent, are marginalised and excluded at the global level' (Maloka 2009).

Piracy, biopiracy and biocolonialism

'Piracy' may be defined as (1) 'robbery on the seas', or (2) 'a felony, such as robbery or hijacking, committed aboard a ship or aircraft', or (3) 'the unauthorised use or appropriation of patented or copyrighted material, ideas, etc' (Collins 2009). All of these are relevant for analysis in relation to reparations for slavery.

In 1820 the US Congress, not surprisingly, defined the slave trade as piracy (Davis 1975: 34). During the slavery centuries, many of the European governments used privateers to do their slave bidding for them. For example, the British used Sir Francis Drake and Sir John Hawkins. However, privateers were little more than state-endorsed pirates.

In the post-Columbus era, the global search for precious metals, flora and related methodologies became systematic and purposeful (Eltis 2000: 36). Bioprospecting, plant identification and transportation often went hand-in-hand with European colonial expansion (Schiebinger 2004: 7). Many crops, such as sesame seed, were first domesticated in Africa and that knowledge was then transported to the countries of the North (Curtin 1998: 30). There was not only a transfer of goods but also a transfer of plants between Europe and its colonies (Schiebinger 2004: 3). After 2500 BC, Egypt and northwest Africa began to associate much more, as new technologies and discoveries from the South passed to the North (Curtin 1998: 31).

Schiebinger describes three ways in which colonial botanists, as agents of empire, extended the imperial power of the European nations: (1) by identifying and collecting precious plants in new territories in order to provide a cheap supply of drugs, food and luxury items in Europe; (2) by identifying substitutes for luxury import products such as tea and coffee; and (3) by building up stocks of valuable plants in collections in Europe. Names and taxonomies of plants, almost as badges of origin, will often signify their attribution to one or other European power. Numbering about 1,600 by the end of the eighteenth century, these collections were established by Europeans from specimens collected throughout Africa and the Americas but not merely for aesthetic value in beautifully ornamental gardens – these were in actuality 'experimental stations for agriculture and stations for plant acclimatisation for domestic and global trade, rare medicaments, and cash crops' (Schiebinger 2004: 11).

At the same time, the many unique and novel artistic expressions 'discovered' by Europeans in Africa, were often captured, mimicked and appropriated as exotic. The term 'folklore' was used to describe such literary, artistic, dramatic, or artistic works and performances, referred to in 1846 as the 'knowledge of the people' (Dommann 2008: 5). From the latter part of the nineteenth century onwards the study of folklore was increasingly undertaken by western researchers who were evolving new academic disciplines in folklore studies which sought to collect, record, interpret and classify the 'folk' traditions of oral cultures and communities: 'Historically, the appropriation of that knowledge was "justified" as legitimate spoils of colonial, scientific and anthropological endeavour, where the knowledge (like any other aspect of the environment discovered through colonial exploration) was itself deemed "natural", part of human-ity's global heritage, and for the benefit of all' (Dommann 2008: 5).

The European intellectual property regime therefore subjugated the knowledge and cultures of colonised people to the 'superior' knowledge of the coloniser (Dommann 2008: 5). By virtue of the idea/expression dichotomy in copyright law, whereby the underlying idea or style is not copyrightable, only the expression or fixation of that idea, many Europeans were able to acquire rights over the folklore, traditional stories, music, art and dance of indigenous American and African peoples. The idea/express-ion dichotomy is also largely responsible for certain styles of popular music that were developed by Africans and African-descendants being misappro-priated by non-Africans. By way of an example, in the United States, 'African-American innovators historically created the genres which defined popular music in America: blues, jazz, rock and roll, soul, and more recently, rap and hip-hop' (Greene 1999: 364).

Furthermore, during the early formative years of the entertainment industry, African artists were generally unacceptable in the racist western societies, and many of the songs and styles created by African-Americans were copied or 'covered' by white artists in order to be marketable. This proved very profitable to the White music producers, White artistes, and the growth of the entertainment industry globally. Many of the White artistes who performed covers of songs and styles of Black musicians became very popular and wealthy as a result, while many of the African authors died penniless (Greene 1999: 369–73; see also Greene 2008: 1198). This was also true for several genres usually attributed to Europeans. The discriminatory societal structures that many Africans and African-descendants produced as fine works denied the African value in such works of music, art and culture, by the promotion of stereotypes, exclusion, segregation and discrimination, facilitated by copyright and contract law (Greene 2008: 1189).

Today, it is the World Intellectual Property Organisation (WIPO), through its Intergovernmental Committee on Intellectual Property and Genetic Resources, Traditional Knowledge and Folklore (IGC), that is the United Nations specialised agency which is tasked generally with address-ing issues of the legal protection of folklore, traditional knowledge (TK), traditional cultural expressions (TCEs) and the genetic resources (GR) of 'indigenous, local, traditional and other cultural communities' from misappropriation. In the environmental law context, the Convention on Biological Diversity (CBD) is the international body that is also seriously advancing laws, policies and procedures to protect the 'knowledge, innovations and practices' of 'indigenous and local communities' that are relevant for the conservation and sustainable use of biodiversity. The CBD does this by requiring the prior informed consent of all contracting state parties and indigenous and local communities, as well as the equitable sharing of benefits from the utilisation of these.

These developments therefore represent a progressive development of laws to repair the historical injustices meted out to 'indigenous, local, traditional and other cultural communities'. This will benefit not only African states, but also African indigenous, local, traditional and cultural communities, as well as African diaspora communities which it is recognised 'constitute a significant African presence in their respective countries in, for example, their music, dance, dishes, mannerisms, and religion' (Maloka 2007).

The UNDRIP clearly recognises the right of indigenous peoples to maintain, control, protect and develop their cultural heritage, traditional knowledge and traditional cultural expressions, and the manifestations of their sciences, technologies and cultures. Such special measures would serve African populations well in halting and redressing the piracy and biopiracy that both historically and currently plague the products of African knowledge systems. There seems to be no justifiable reason why this approach to push internationally for special measures to be implemented at the level of international law, cannot be part and parcel of a bundle of remedies, either negotiated or litigated, that are aimed at providing substantial repair to Africans and the descendants of Africans for the historical as well as contemporary and continuing consequences of slavery and the transatlantic slave trade.

Conclusion

Justice is a jealous master. Justice was never be meant to be sacrificed and compromised in order to serve the expedient ends of lawmakers. It must be the law which remains fluid, flexible and adaptable enough to find new ways and means of ensuring that justice prevails, even for (and some might say especially for) historical atrocities committed against vast numbers of people. Justice is the first virtue of social institutions (Rawls 1972: 4).

The invasion of Africa, the mass capture of Africans, the trauma of the middle passage, the chattelisation and dehumanisation of Africans in the New World and the decimation of the communities, families, way of life and culture of Africans, for over five hundred years, constitute sustained crimes against humanity. That justice demands that there be an atonement and reparations for slavery and the transatlantic slave trade is unquestionable. Any law therefore which purports to deny justice for the victims of slavery and the slave trade is unjust and must be reformed or abolished.[7]

Far from just being a 'Black people issue', without earnest international efforts to reconcile and heal the deep inner wounds of slavery and the transatlantic slave trade, there will never be human equality and world peace. The world can ill-afford to address and repair what lies at the root of racism and discrimination against Black people – the prevalent policy and perception of the superiority of the White man.

As it was the law and its institutions which played and continue to play such a important role in the dehumanisation and disenfranchisement of Africans, so too must the law mature and evolve mechanisms that are to deliver effective remedies for the same: 'The law must seek to decolonise society . . . by a conscious propulsion of new law, and indeed, if warranted, new legal systems, to promote a more egalitarian social, economic and political system' (Antoine 1999: 18).

Reparations must be adequate and effective (Lenzerini 2008: 13–16). Special measures are one way, legally and diplomatically, in which to achieve greater recognition and reparations for slavery and the transatlantic slave trade. This will never be non-contentious, but may be less contentious and will possibly bear more fruit and be less expensive than litigation. It will take many years, as did the UNDRIP, to be negotiated. However it requires an organised movement instead of the existing 'relatively isolated advocates' to mobilise the sentiment pools and 'frame align' the individual activists, organisations and informal networks with more formal organisations into a cohesive representative advocacy body (Howard-Hassmann and Lombardo 2007: 44).

In its 'Programme of Action', the UN-sponsored WCAR NGO Forum recommended the establishment and resourcing of (a) a Working Group on Africans and African-descendants throughout the world; (b) a world institute based in Africa that would be dedicated to research, fact finding and resource networking for Africans and Africans in the diaspora; and (c) an international tribunal to measure the extent of the damages resulting from the slave trade, slavery and colonialism on Africans and African-descendants.

The claim should be assessed by experts in each aspect of life and in each region of Africa and the diaspora affected by the institution of slavery. Each affected country should be studied, under various categories of damage. This should not just include monetary compensation but also other forms of reparations like an apology, restitution, rehabilitation, and the granting of educational and skills training scholarships to Africa and Africans in the diaspora, as well as physical and psychological healthcare that will redress the intergenerational trauma of slavery.

There should also be a database of all the organisations, cities, institutions and companies whose capital and equity can be traced to the slavery, so that diplomatic claims for reparations may also be vitally directed at those entities, many of which and/or their successors still exist today and which may very well prove more vulnerable to public moral shame than states.

The European nations and corporations which are liable should be approached diplomatically in the first instance to seek an amicable settlement if possible, it being recognised that litigation is inherently protracted and uncertain. If that process bears no reasonable reparations settlement, then a suitable forum must be sought to bring the guilty to justice for their abominable crimes against Africa and Africans.

We need to learn and strategise from the abolitionist/anti-slavery movement, the Jewish reparations movement, and the movement for debt relief for Africa. In this regard, the momentum and political capital gained leading up to and during the WCAR 2001 and WCAR 2009 can and must be harnessed and built upon. In fact, all relevant and available national and regional organisations which represent African and African-descendant peoples should organise and make a multilateral legal and diplomatic representation on the issues surrounding slave trade reparations in all the relevant international, UN and other human rights, indigenous rights, minority rights, international trade, intellectual property and cultural heritage organisations. This process could be administered under the auspices of the African Union, which has proposed a 6th Region Diaspora constituency to integrate the Africans in the diaspora politically.

Internal organisation must be supported by powerful partners within the international community. Through a reinvigorated and reintegrated African Union, supported by the United Nations, the community of developing and diaspora nations, non-governmental organisations, experts, policy advisers and academics, the global reparations for slavery lobby can be brought to bear tangible fruit.

There is also a fundamental necessity to lobby concertedly for reparations for and resistance against any further erosion and misappropriation of the indigenous knowledge, cultural heritage and intellectual property rights of African and Afro-descendant countries and communities by the countries of the North. This is an area of international trade which possesses great economic potential for the survival of developing countries and which, in light of the history of the slavery-based denial of human rights to the fruits of creative and cultural labour, should also be prosecuted with due diligence and alacrity as a component of reparations.

This perspective and proposed objective to press diplomatically for special measures for Africans and African-descendants is not intended to detract from existing legal national litigation and political strategies. On the contrary, despite the formidable legal hurdles existing in national jurisprudence, the examples of domestic court decisions such as *Mabo* show that, where the force of legal argument and moral authority has gained substantial acceptance internationally, there is every likelihood that more domestic courts will take cognisance and will apply progressive interpretations to otherwise seemingly insurmountable laws like the inter-temporal law, as well as offer justice to the millions of underdeveloped Africans in their families, communities and nations for the damage wrought by slavery and the transatlantic slave trade.

We have seen at the commemoration of the two hundredth anniversary of the abolition of the slave trade a flurry of apologies. The last twenty years have witnessed an increased acceptance of guilt by nations and resultant restitution negotiations as an atonement for historical injustices (Barkan 2000: 307, 318–322). No doubt, as time and human consciences and consciousness evolve, we shall see more. But we cannot afford to be self-defeating reactionaries or apathetic spectators of this evolving global debate. It is only by our continuous commitment to the cause of lobbying, awareness-raising, researching and organising, that justice will ever be realised for the victims of slavery and the transatlantic slave trade. As the tenth anniversary of the WCAR and having been declared by the UN as the International Year for People of African Descent, 2011 is an important opportunity to revisit, restate and advocate for the justice that is centuries overdue for peoples of African descent. Even if it takes another two hundred years, *a luta continua*!

Notes

1 du Plessis 2007: 148 states that at least 13 million were illegally transported from West Africa from 1440–1870, of which 11,328,000 were delivered to the New World, and approximately 1,672,000 died en route.
2 Constitutional Court of South Africa in *Alexkor Ltd v Richtersveld Community* [2003] ZACC 18.
3 In *Sesana and Others v Attorney General* (2006) BWHC 1, the Botswana High Court recognised the aboriginal title of the San people.
4 Chief Justice Conteh interpreted the Constitution of Belize to recognise the right to property of the Maya communities of Conejo and Santa Cruz, citing a similar judgment of the Inter-American Court of Human Rights on the same facts decided in relation to the American Declaration of Human Rights.
5 For an interesting discussion on the prevailing arguments and strategies used to justify the lack of protection for Afro-descendant communities, see Torres 2007: 123–125 and 141.
6 The Ras Tafari community has consistently advocated for repatriation to Africa. See Jamaica National Bicentenary Committee 2007: 83–5.
7 I am not however advocating for financial reparations for individuals but for African and African-descendant communities and nations.

Bibliography

Anghie, A. (2005) *Imperialism, Sovereignty and the Making of International Law.* Cambridge: Cambridge University Press.
Antoine, R. (1999) *Commonwealth Caribbean Law and Legal Systems.* London: Cavendish.
Barkan, E. (2000) *The Guilt of Nations: Restitution and Negotiating Historical Injustices.* Baltimore: Johns Hopkins University Press.
Beckles, H. (2008) 'Reparations for Slavery: Representing the Caribbean's Case to Britain', Conference Presentation at University of Birmingham, June.

Brooks, R. (1999) *When Sorry Isn't Enough: The Controversy over Apologies and Reparations for Human Injustice*, R. Brooks (ed.). New York: New York University Press.

Brooks, R. (2004) 'Toward a Perpetrator-Focussed Model of Slave Redress', 6 *Afr.-Amer. L. & Pol'y Rep.*, 50: 49–69.

Brooks, R. (2007) 'Redress for Slavery – The African American Struggle', in M. du Plessis, M. and S. Pete (eds), *Repairing the Past? International Perspectives on Reparations for Gross Human Rights Abuses*. Oxford: Intersentia. pp. 297–313.

Castellino, J. and Allen, S. (2003) *Title to Territory in International Law: A Temporal Analysis*. New York: Ashgate.

Collins English Dictionary (2009) Complete Unabridged 10th Edition. London: Harper Collins. Available at: <http://dictionary.reference.com> (accessed 14 November 2010).

Curtin, P. (1998) *The Rise and Fall of the Plantation Complex: Essays in Atlantic History*. Cambridge: Cambridge University Press.

Davis, D. (1975) *The Problem of Slavery in the Age of Revolution, 1770–1823*. New York: Cornell University Press.

Dommann, M. (2008) 'Lost in Tradition? Reconsidering the history of folklore and its legal protection since 1800', in C. Beat Graber and M. Burri-Nenova, M. (eds), *Intellectual Property and Traditional Cultural Expressions in a Digital Environment*. Cheltenham: Edward Elgar. pp. 3–16.

du Plessis, M. (2007) 'Reparations and International Law: How are Reparations to be Determined (Past Wrong or Current Effects), against whom, and what form should they take?', in M. du Plessis and S. Pete (eds), *Repairing the Past? International Perspectives on Reparations for Gross Human Rights Abuses*. Oxford: Intersentia. pp. 147–177.

Eltis, D. (2000) *The Rise of African Slavery in the Americas*. Cambridge: Cambridge University Press.

Fortson, R. (2004) 'Correcting the Harms of Slavery: Collective Liability, the Limited Prospects of Success for a Class Action Suit for Slavery Reparations, and the Reconceptualization of White Racial Identity', 6 *Afr.-Am. L. & Pol'y Rep.*, 71–127.

Francioni, F. (2008) 'Reparations for Indigenous Peoples: Is International Law Ready to Ensure Redress for Historical Injustices?' in F. Lenzerini, F. (ed.), *Reparations for Indigenous Peoples: International and Comparative Perspectives*. Oxford: Oxford University Press. pp. 27–46.

Ghanea, N. (2005) 'Repressing Minorities and Getting Away with it? A Consideration of Economic, Social and Cultural Rights', in N. Ghanea and A. Xanthaki (eds), *Minorities, Peoples and Self-Determination: Essays in Honour of Patrick Thornberry*. The Netherlands: Martinus Nijhoff. pp. 193–209.

Gowok, S.M. (2007) *How Slavery Underdeveloped Africa: The Human Rights Aspect and the Need for Reparation*. New York: Routledge.

Green, L. and Dickason, O. (1993) *The Law of Nations and the New World*. Alberta: University of Alberta Press.

Greene, K.J. (1999) 'Copyright, Culture & Black Music: A Legacy of Unequal Protection', *21 Hastings Comm. & Ent. L.J.*, 339–390.

Greene, K.J. (2008) '"Copynorms," Black Cultural Production, and The Debate Over African-American Reparations', *25 Cardozo Arts & Ent.L.J.*, 1179–1227.

Howard-Hassman, R.E. and Lombardo, A.P. (2007) 'Framing Reparations Claims: Differences between the African and Jewish Social Movements for Reparations', *African Studies Review*, 50(1): 27–48.

Inikori, J.E. (2002) *Africans and the Industrial Revolution in England: A Study in International Trade and Development*. Cambridge: Cambridge University Press.

Irvine, K. (1970) *The Rise of the Colored Races*. New York: Norton.

Jamaica National Bicentenary Committee (2007) Jamaica and the Debate over Reparation for Slavery: A Discussion Paper.

Jenkins, C. (2007) 'Taking Apology Seriously', in M. du Plessis and S. Pete (eds), *Repairing the Past? International Perspectives on Reparations for Gross Human Rights Abuses*. Oxford: Intersentia. pp. 53–81.

Lenzerini, F. (2008) 'Reparations for Indigenous Peoples in International and Comparative Law: An Introduction', in F. Lenzerini (ed.), *Reparations for Indigenous Peoples: International and Comparative Perspectives*. Oxford: Oxford University Press. pp. 3–26.

Maloka, E. (2007) *Engaging the Diaspora as a force for a better Africa*. Available at <http://www.anc.org.za/284> (accessed 29 November 2010).

Marrus, M. (2007) 'Official Apologies and the Quest for Historical Justice', *Journal of Human Rights*, 6(1): 75–105.

Mengisteab, K. and Logan, B.I. (1995) 'Introduction', in K. Mengisteab and B.I. Logan (eds), *Beyond Economic Liberalization in Africa: Structural Adjustment and the Alternatives*, Southern Africa Political Economy Series (SAPES). London: Zed. pp. 1–14.

Menski, W. (2006) *Comparative Law in a Global Context: The Legal Systems of Asia and Africa* (2nd edn). Cambridge: Cambridge University Press.

Ogletree Jr, C. (2002) 'Litigating the Legacy of Slavery', *The New York Times*. Available at <http://query.nytimes.com/gst/fullpage.html?res=9905EFDD163 AF932A05750C0A9649C8B63> (accessed 28 September 2010).

Okupa, E. (1998) *International Bibliography of African Customary Law*. Hamburg: LIT and International African Institute.

Pete, S. and du Plessis, M. (2007) 'Reparations for Gross Violations of Human Rights in Context', in M. du Plessis and S. Pete (eds), *Repairing the Past? International Perspectives on Reparations for Gross Human Rights Abuses*. Oxford: Intersentia. pp. 3–28.

Rawls, J. (1972) *A Theory of Justice*. Oxford: Oxford University Press.

Rodney, W. (1972) *How Europe Underdeveloped Africa*. Kenya: East African Educational.

Sandbrook, R. and Barker, J. (1985) *The Politics of Africa's Economic Stagnation*. Cambridge: Cambridge University Press.

Schiebinger, L. (2004) *Plants and Empire: Colonial Bioprospecting in the Atlantic World*. Massachusetts: Harvard University Press.

Torpey, J. (2004) 'Paying for the Past? The Movement for Reparations for African-Americans', *Journal of Human Rights*, 3(2) (June): 171–187.

Torres, G. (2007) 'Indigenous Peoples, Afro-Indigenous Peoples and Reparations', in F. Lenzerini (ed.), *Reparations for Indigenous Peoples: International and Comparative Perspectives*. Oxford: Oxford University Press. pp. 117–141.

United Nations (2010) 'Basic Principles and Guidelines on the Right to a Remedy and Reparation for Victims of Gross Violations of International Human Rights Law and Serious Violations of International Humanitarian Law'. Available at <http://www2.ohchr.org/english/law/remedy.htm> (accessed 20 November 2010).

Williams, E. (1944) *Capitalism and Slavery*. North Carolina: University of North Carolina Press.

Index

Gambia 14, 197
Garvey, Marcus 85
General History of Africa (UNESCO)
   14
genocide *see* Holocaust
German Foundation, The 213, 214
Germany
   Nazi 80, 81, 82, 90
   post-WWII 212–13, 214
   see also Holocaust
Ghana 10–11, 31, 79, 86
Gifford, Anthony (Lord) 77–80, 85–6,
   88–90, 157, 196
Gifford, (3rd) Lord 79
Gold Coast 31, 128
Golding, Bruce 95
Goldman, Nahum 212
Gomes, Diogo 196–7
Gorée Island (Senegal) 78
Grant, Bernie 77–8, 88
Granville, Lord 138
Green, D. 202–3
Gregson v Gilbert (*The Zong* case) 134,
   137, 181–3, 184, 186, 197
Grenada 136
Grotius, Hugo 7
Group of Eminent Persons on
   Reparations to Africa and
   Africans in the Diaspora 78–9
Guinea 13–14, 33
Guyana 33

Habeas Corpus Act 1679 172
Hagenbach, Peter von 16–17
Hain, Peter 152
Haiti compensation 96
Hamilton, C.V. 200
Hardwicke, Lord 171–2, 188
Hargrave, Francis 177, 178, 180
Hart, Richard 88, 89
Hattusili II 5, 6
Hausa tradition 9–10
Havana 29
Hawaii 107
Hawkins, Sir John 126, 235
Helsinki Agreements 214
Henry, Mike 95
Heward, E. 178
Hippisley, John 128–9
Hittites 5
Hochschild, J. 161
Holocaust

litigation 103, 146
   Swiss banks 148, 161–2
victims/survivors 209
see also Germany; Jews; post-World
   War II settlements
Horne, G. 28, 34
Horowitz, David 147, 202, 205
House of Lords debate *see under* case
   formulation
How Europe Underdeveloped Africa
   (Rodney) 91
Howden, Lord 26
Human Rights Council 69
Hungarian Jews 217

Immediate not gradual Abolition
   (pamphlet) 32
indentured labourers 30
India, British 30
indigenous peoples 82
   comparison 231–2
   cultural heritage 237
   land claims 106–7
   special measures 232–3
   terra nullius principle 230–1
Inikori, J.E. 9
institutional racism
   conferences 197–9
   as legacy 195–6, 199, 206
   link with reparations 203–6
   meaning 200–3
   slave-trade background 196–7
International Association of Democratic
   Lawyers 93
international law
   compensation for injury, principle 6
   European national laws 15–17
   jus cogens 18
   justice and humanity, principles
      18–19
   no limitation period 82–3
   non-retroactivity 3–4, 106
   recognition of reparation 81–2
   responsibility 17–18
   trafficking *see* trafficking in persons,
      international legal framework
   see also case formulation; special
      measures, case for
International Law Commission (ILC),
   Draft Articles on Responsibility
   of States for International
   Wrongful Acts (Articles) 3